Credit and Consumer Society

The language of credit and debt is almost ubiquitous in daily life. In advanced modern societies, financial institutions and other organizations have become increasingly active in lending money to consumers, and consumers apparently more than willing to take advantage. This ground-breaking new book offers an analysis of this important phenomenon, arguing that we have entered an era in which credit and debt are sanctioned, delivered and collected through new cultural and economic mechanisms.

Written in an accessible and straightforward style, the book takes a multi-disciplinary approach, examining consumer credit and debt in both societal and economic contexts. It explores key topics such as:

- the historical context of credit and debt
- current theories of a consumer-centred society
- the credit industry
- attempts at government regulation.

Credit and Consumer Society establishes the wider analysis of consumer credit and debt as a discipline in its own right. It is important reading for students and researchers in business and management, finance, public policy and sociology, as well as for policymakers and consumer groups working directly in this field.

Dawn Burton has taught sociology and marketing at leading British universities. She has held numerous research grants and has acted in a consultancy capacity for mainstream and sub-prime financial institutions. She is the Founding Editor of the journal *Marketing Theory*. Her work has been published in leading journals within the fields of marketing, management, sociology and geography.

Credit and Consumer Society

Dawn Burton

Routledge
Taylor & Francis Group

LONDON AND NEW YORK

First published 2008
by Routledge
2 Park Square, Milton Park, Abingdon, Oxon, OX14 4RN

Simultaneously published in the USA and Canada
by Routledge
270 Madison Avenue, New York, NY 10016

Routledge is an imprint of the Taylor & Francis Group, an informa business

© 2008 Dawn Burton

Typeset in Times New Roman by
Keystroke, 28 High Street, Tettenhall, Wolverhampton
Printed and bound in Great Britain by
Antony Rowe Ltd, Chippenham, Wiltshire

British Library Cataloguing in Publication Data
A catalogue record for this book is available from the British Library

Library of Congress Cataloging in Publication Data
A catalog record for this book has been requested

ISBN10: 0–415–40521–1 (hbk)
ISBN10: 0–415–40522–X (pbk)
ISBN10: 0–203–93598–5 (ebk)

ISBN13: 978–0–415–40521–8 (hbk)
ISBN13: 978–0–415–40522–5 (pbk)
ISBN13: 978–0–203–93598–9 (ebk)

This book is dedicated to my father, Edward Raines, who died of cancer at the age of 66 in October 2003. His death taught me more about life than I could have possibly imagined. Life will never be the same.

Contents

Tables

Introduction

One of the major changes in consumer financial behaviour in recent years is the trend for larger numbers of consumers to use credit to fund their consumption. The more extensive use of consumer credit is particularly apparent in advanced Western societies, although similar developments are also well established in Japan and emergent in Latin America. The widespread use of credit has contributed to what Martin (2002) has termed 'the financialization of everyday life' and has extended debates about consumers and their relationship with financial institutions (Burton 1994). Once the domain of economists and accountants, debates about consumer credit and its contribution to national economies have entered popular discourse. Rarely a day goes by when some story does not make media headlines. Moreover, as consumer credit has become a distinctive aspect of consumption, it has become the subject of investigation across a wide range of academic disciplines and sub-disciplines, including social and economic history, law, psychology, sociology, social anthropology, social policy and politics. Much of this literature is of recent origin and has emerged over the past decade. The purpose of this text is to synthesize and consolidate some of the most recent scholarship in consumer credit and debt across a range of disciplines and to help establish this domain of academic inquiry and promote it as an important area of teaching and research in its own right.

Given the contemporary high profile of consumer credit in advanced societies, one might be forgiven for believing it to be a recent phenomenon. In fact, consumer credit has a very long history; however, there have been important trends in the acquisition and use of credit and levels of indebtedness over time. The purpose of Chapter 1 is to provide an overview of some of the main features associated with the history of consumer credit. A number of themes will be discussed, including some of the historical origins of consumer credit and the methodological debates about sources of data in tracing consumer behaviour. Religion has played an important role in determining the acceptance or rejection of consumer credit in society. Some of the main debates surrounding the contribution of the Protestant work ethic will be considered in the context of framing attitudes to credit and debt. There have also been significant differences in the availability of credit to individuals within different social classes, and this trend has continued to the present day. Some of the social divisions involved in credit acquisition and its use will be discussed, as will the fate of consumers who have found themselves in debt. Furthermore, recent research has identified that the acquisition and use of credit have traditionally been highly gendered. While women were excluded from obtaining credit in their own right in many societies until the twentieth century, this viewpoint undermines the contribution of women in managing credit within households that has existed for centuries. The chapter will therefore provide a basis upon which continuities and variations in credit portrayal, acquisition and use have occurred over time.

Chapter 2 will raise the issue of whether some of the recent developments in consumer credit are explained by contemporary theories of consumer society. Some of the contemporary debates about the history of consumption and consumer behaviour will be addressed, along with characteristics that are associated with consumer society. From this discussion it will become clear that consumer credit has been persistently neglected as a topic of investigation. Some of the potential reasons for this neglect will be addressed. The emergence of consumer credit as a powerful force in society in the 1920s will be discussed in the context of a wider range of suppliers and a changing ideology in society that sanctioned the use of consumer credit as an acceptable method of purchasing goods and services. An important aspect of investigating credit and consumer society is to reveal some of its dysfunctional effects. In this chapter, compulsive consumption, compensatory consumption and gambling will be used as examples of dysfunctional effects of consumer society and their implications for credit and debt.

The theme of Chapter 3 is to explore how the widespread use of credit has been dependent on institutionalizing particular models of consumer trust and control. A distinction is made between personal trust as a basis for sanctioning credit, and a move to institutional trust that has allowed the widespread sanctioning of credit through credit scoring. The history of credit scoring will be addressed, alongside some of the new developments. Contemporary systems have become more sophisticated and can discriminate between credit, behavioural scoring and profit scoring. Probably the most controversial development in the credit scoring debate is the widespread use of risk-based pricing. The theory and practice of risk-based pricing will be discussed, particularly in the context of reflecting and exacerbating social inequality. The chapter will conclude by discussing the spatial aspects of trust and control where credit is concerned. A controversial issue in recent years has been the process whereby mainstream financial institutions have deserted areas that they viewed as unprofitable. In their wake, new institutions have emerged that have become known as the alternative credit market, and certain suppliers have been called predatory lenders because of some of their practices, which exploit vulnerable consumers.

Chapter 4 will focus on contemporary developments in the organization of credit markets. As the credit industry has matured, new suppliers have entered the market, each focusing on their particular segment of consumers. It is argued that these changes reveal a transition from an 'old' to a 'new' economy of credit. There are a number of features that account for this new economy, and they will be discussed in this chapter. Some of the new entrants and the products they market are not without controversy. Often there are concerns about the high cost of credit for those who have a tarnished credit history, and the ethics of targeting groups that might be regarded as vulnerable. The provision of credit for individuals who would previously have been excluded because they presented too much of a risk is an issue that has come to the attention of the banking regulators since it exposes financial institutions to potentially higher levels of default. Under the new regulatory framework that has become known as Basel II, financial institutions are required to provide information about the degree of risk within their lending portfolios. Some of the implications of this new regulatory framework will be assessed.

The marketing of credit will be the focus of Chapter 5. Marketing is an activity that is central to most accounts of the development of consumer society. This chapter will provide an explanation of the development of marketing as an organization function in advanced societies. Theories of consumer society have also played a significant role in our understanding of consumer behaviour. How the consumer behaviour literature has developed and incorporated different theoretical and methodological approaches will be discussed, including their contribution to our understanding of consumer financial behaviour. While the marketing of financial services as a specialism in its own right can be traced back to the 1980s, the marketing of credit by financial institutions is of more recent origin. Moreover, it has become a highly controversial activity in some quarters. For example, consumer groups and some consumers themselves have blamed the aggressive marketing tactics of lenders for contributing to the much higher levels of credit and debt in many advanced societies. This chapter will chart some of the unique properties of marketing financial services as opposed to other goods and services, and credit as a sub-set of financial services marketing. Some of the arguments levelled at lenders for employing unethical and undesirable marketing practices will be considered.

The theme of Chapter 6 will be consumer misbehaviour. One of the issues that lenders always have to face is that borrowers hold the power of knowledge as to whether they are willing or able to repay their debts. This chapter will explore the relationship between consumer misbehaviour and consumer society in its historical context. Various types of consumer misbehaviour will be considered, including bankruptcy. Contemporary techniques used by lenders for recouping debt will be assessed. There will be a discussion of the emergence of a debt sale market in personal finance as a new feature of the credit landscape, as lenders who are unable to extract debts from consumers sell on their default accounts to debt collectors for a fraction of their value.

Chapter 7 will address some of the social and public policies that have arisen from increasing levels of credit and debt in society. There are a very significant range of features that are relevant in this respect. The relationship between credit and sustainable consumption is a very important issue. Approaches to sustainability will be discussed alongside the development of alternative lifestyles that are less dependent on the use of credit. Debt, credit and consumer well-being has been an under-researched issue, but the significant increase in credit has led to more research in this emergent field. The available research does demonstrate a link between credit, debt and well-being that could have significant social and public policy issues in the future. The commodification of debt counselling is a practice that has emerged within the past decade. The shift from free, publicly available debt advice to debt advice that is commercially available has caused concern about the nature of the advice that is being provided and the charges that are being requested for the service. The selling of consumer debt is generating considerable amounts of consumer resistance. The debt sale process will be examined, alongside some of the methods of resistance that consumers are adopting. Affordability in credit assessment models is a new area of research that has been given a high profile, owing to the larger numbers of consumers who are finding themselves unable to service their credit commitments. However, the process of operationalizing affordability is fraught with difficulties. Some of the issues that are being encountered and the problems that still remain to be overcome will be discussed. The final section will concern privacy and secrecy issues relating to consumer credit.

1 Consumer credit

Historical approaches

Consumer credit has a long history, as old as civilization itself. However, the nature of consumer credit has changed over time and space. Strasser (2003: 376) maintains that incorporating historical perspectives in discussions of consumer culture has a range of advantages:

> Historical accounts illuminate the abundance of our choices, help us understand that to be human is not necessarily to be like us, it provides insights into other cultures that facilitate a process of self-reflection and an awareness of alternative futures. History is often relegated to the 'background' – a static stage set, in front of which the 'real' action takes place. Such representations of historical experience trivialize the past. They justify the world as we know it now.

The reading and re-reading of history in the way described by Strasser is especially valuable in our understanding of credit and consumer society. So endemic has credit become that one could be forgiven for believing that credit and debt were always part of society in much the same way as they are today. However, an understanding of historical scholarship enables us to understand continuities and changes in the role of credit and debt in society.

Traditionally, access to credit has been deeply fractured along the lines of social class, gender and, more recently, ethnicity. Large numbers of working-class consumers have been denied, or had limited access to, mainstream credit and instead have been forced to deal with an alternative range of suppliers. The relationship between women and credit is particularly complex. Women were forbidden to enter into economic transactions in their own right, yet

> long before Thorstein Veblen had pronounced his now classic formation of the central role of leisured ladies in capitalist consumption, successive generations of English observers had condemned women's increasingly visible and voluminous acquisitive activities as prime catalyst of financial ruin.
>
> (Finn 1996: 703)

An overarching issue that has informed attitudes to credit for centuries, and in fact still does, is the role of religion.

This chapter will provide a broad overview of some of the contemporary historical scholarship in the field of consumer credit and debt. It is not the intention to provide a history of credit since time began, since other scholars have covered aspects of this material with respect to credit (Gelpi and Julien-Labruyere 1999; Thomas, Edelman and Crook 2002; Vukowich 2002; Peterson 2004) and money (Davies 1996). The purpose of this chapter is to provide an important touchstone for the subsequent discussion of credit in contemporary society by illustrating some salient themes in the debate. Historians have not paid a great deal of attention to consumption, but the recent heightened profile of credit and debt has prompted many more historical studies that have served to enrich the field. The sub-specialism can be best described as work in progress. Nevertheless, some fascinating historical insights have already been uncovered.

The chapter will begin with a discussion of methodological issues that have informed scholarship in this area. The second theme is the role of religion on developments in credit and debt in different countries. The third part of the chapter will discuss the complex relationship between social class and consumer credit. The final section will explore the relationship between gender and consumer credit and debt.

Credit, historical sources and research methodology

Historical scholarship presents some interesting methodological issues in connection to our study of credit. The relative merits of a variety of different sources are at the heart of the debate, especially concerning what they tell us and what they leave out. Lewis (1992) speculates that the earliest formal record of credit dates from around 2000 BC and is inscribed into a stone tablet bearing the following promise: 'Two shekels of silver have been borrowed by Mas-Schamach, the son of Adadrimeni, from the Sun Priestess Amat-Schamach, the daughter of Warad-Enlil. He will pay the Sun-God's interest. At the time of the harvest he will pay back the sum and the interest upon it.' Opposition to usury in the Roman Republic was enshrined in laws in which those guilty of theft were fined double the amount taken, whereas for usury the figure was fourfold (Brunt 1971).

Postan (1924) provides a valuable framework of historical sources pertaining to the nature of credit transactions that includes registers of debt held by official institutions, pleas, and a non-specific/miscellaneous category that included private archives, inventories and accounts. Rents and leases recorded credit agreements, with arrears serving as *de facto* credit agreements. Of equal relevance were records of purchases that remained unpaid until the consumer's death. Wills and probates were valuable for just this reason, especially from the fifteenth century onwards, since they provide information on the size of outstanding debts and the names of creditors and debtors. However, even this range of documentary evidence could grossly underestimate the amount of credit that was used. Muldrew (1998) maintains that because of literacy problems some credit agreements were verbal affairs in which the two parties would agree to the transaction in front of witnesses.

Latterly, analytical insights of credit and debt through the reading of fictional writing have provided new avenues of inquiry. Literary texts offer an important way of making private credit relations visible and therefore provide a vehicle for challenging economic theory since they provide examples of the day-to-day experiences of consumers (Finn 2003; Livesey 2004). Business failures were a major theme in many nineteenth-century novels and plays (Weiss 1986; Scheuermann 1993; Posner 1998). Victorians viewed debt as a national economic problem, and not just for creditors, since ultimately merchants had to pass losses from bad debt on to customers in the form of higher prices. Literature of the time that highlights debt includes Thackeray's *Vanity Fair* and *The Newcomes*. Charlotte Brontë's *Shirley* and Trollope's *The Way We Live Now* are other examples. Charles Dickens' father was imprisoned for debt, and Dickens chose debt as themes in some of his novels, such as *Little Dorrit* and *Dombey and Son*. Lawyers and failed lawyers were prolific writers of fiction, thus highlighting legal themes within novels for a wide audience (Brooks and Gewirtz 1996).

Other literary sources have included diaries and autobiographies that report on the 'mundane practices and affective meanings of the market' and the 'interpenetration of social relations and economic exchange' (Finn 2003: 64). Diaries often reflected themes that the writers had read about in novels and helped them construct their sense of self. Because diaries were written by individuals from all social backgrounds, they provide a rich data source of patterns of credit and debt. Copeland (1995) provides revealing insights about credit and debt by examining correspondence sent to the Royal Literary fund, a charity that was established during the 1890s to provide financial assistance to destitute authors. The inability to pay corner shops or pay the rent, and tales of those who had gone into hiding to avoid prison, were recurrent themes raised by female authors.

The language of credit and debt were also incorporated in drama, an obvious example being the work of Shakespeare (Woodbridge 2003). The most famous play on the theme is *The Merchant of Venice*, whose central character is Shylock the moneylender, but there were many others. Nugent (2003) explores depictions of usury and counterfeiting in Robert Wilson's *The Three Ladies of London* and *The Three Lords and Three Ladies of London*, and in Shakespeare's *Measure for Measure*. She notes that although some of the early modern dramas depicted usurers as 'malevolent parasites on society', there was also evidence to suggest that moneylending 'created constructive communal bonds within an emerging culture of credit' (2003: 202). Jowett (2003) analyses *Timon of Athens*, a collaborative effort by William Shakespeare and Thomas Middleton, which portrays social relations built on greed and self-interest and credit networks that were in a state of collapse. Others plays include Philip Massinger's comedy about miserliness, *A New Way to Pay Old Debts*, and Webster's tragedy about uncharitable litigation, *The Devil's Law Case* (Muldrew 1998). Art history provides another, although much more marginalized, area of data on attitudes to credit and debt. The painter William Hogarth highlighted the plight of debtors who were tortured in prison by depicting a debtor showing the prison committee the manacles and shackles that he has been forced to wear by Bambridge, the jailer at Fleet jail (Aris 1985).

Researching the history of credit behaviour among consumers within various social classes is fraught with difficulties. The wealthiest groups in society have left far more documentary evidence than those lower down the social scale. For example, Owens *et al.* (2006) use probate valuations of the estates of aristocratic families in England to provide some insights into the credit–debt relationship. Equivalent records were not applicable for working-class people since they did not leave personal accounts, and historians have had to rely on other sources, including court records on small debtors, insolvents and bankrupts (Jones 1989; McIntosh 2005). Using this data presents a methodological problem since these sources provide data about people who have run into trouble and as a consequence are the exception rather than the rule. Another source of information about the credit habits of the poor comes from the accounts of charitable institutions that helped those in need, as demonstrated by Galvin's (2002) account of parochial charity in fifteenth-century Brugge (Bruges), Briggs' (2004) examination of the operation of manorial law in later thirteenth- and fourteenth-century rural England, and Livesey's (2004) account of case notes about people applying for relief from the Charity Organisation Society in late Victorian and Edwardian London.

Credit, debt and religion

Some of the earliest accounts of the role of credit in society are biblical references that focus on the religious prohibition of usury. The debate over usury has a long pedigree dating back to the book of Exodus (22:25), in which it was condemned by God. This view was reinforced in Deuteronomy (23:20–1), in which the Hebrews were told not to lend to their brethren at interest, while Ezekiel (18:7–8, 13) took a stronger line and argued for the execution of individuals who engaged in usury. In Leviticus (25:35–36) the concern for one's brother was reinforced by urging believers not to revert to usury. Psalms (15:5) states that the godly will aid their neighbours and not lend at interest. The case for usury being ungodly was strengthened in Luke (6:35), which urges that individuals who lend to others should do so without any hope of return. Christian theologians built on the teachings of the Old and New Testaments to create a Christian view which denounced all lending with the intent to secure a return over the principal sum loaned. The conclusion was clear: God does not permit usury.

This view of moneylending existed until the middle of the sixteenth century. Up until this period, economics remained a branch of theology which regarded human activities within one central schema determined by the spiritual destiny of humankind. Tawney (1926: 272) maintains that economic transactions were judged by the way they conformed to 'the moral standards derived from the traditional teaching of the Christian Church' and not the movements of markets. The strict biblical interpretation of moneylending began to be reassessed by European reformers in the light of their education and experience. At the crux of the debate was clarifying how usury was defined, and how and when it occurred. The biblical passages make clear that God does not permit usury, but an alternative reading would be that you should not lend at interest to your brother or the needy, but charging interest to everyone else is permitted.

Jones (1989) uses the English Act against Usury of 1571 to demonstrate the shift away from a theologically dominated interpretation of usury to one that focused on individual conscience. The supporters of the original Act were at pains to 'place secular law in proper relationship to God's law without serious regard for the economic effects of the law' (Jones 1989: 197). By 1624 a widely held view was that the state had a right to, and should, regulate usury, but for secular and economic reasons rather than because it was forbidden by God. The reasons for this change in attitude, which spanned three-quarters of a century, were a complex interaction of economics, law and theology. In part it was due to a more widespread awareness of the uses and abuses of money.

In Elizabethan society the view that only the needy borrowed and the borrower always oppressed the lender began to be questioned by large sections of the population, for whom this position was not part of their life experience. The terms of the 1571 Act allowed usury interest rates of up to 10 per cent to be charged. Anyone found guilty of lending at a higher rate was faced with a triple forfeiture of the principal. The statute was enforced by informers who were willing to accuse usurers. In this respect the market 'was shaped within and by the legal structure: not just by the statute law, but by techniques of enforcement, contracts, and judicial decisions' (Jones 1989: 4) As a consequence, usury became defined more narrowly as lending at rates over 10 per cent, and there was a prevalent view that not all usury was against God's law. Interest rates at 10 per cent came to be considered legal and normal. The widely held view was that lending at interest could have positive and negative effects and it need not be forbidden unless it was clearly causing harm to the community. This opened up the space for an emphasis on the concept of freedom of conscience and ethics relating to individual agency.

Jones maintains that the Act on Usury provides an important link between the Reformation and the rise of capitalism in England. In this respect his work supports the main tenets of Max Weber's work on the relationship between religion and the rise of capitalism set out in *The Protestant Ethic and the Spirit of Capitalism* (1999). Weber's thesis advocates that the economic doctrines of the Catholic Church delayed the advent of modern capitalism, owing to their strict adherence to the biblical views on usury. In contrast to the high-minded and controlling Catholic approach, Calvinism morally embraced the accumulation of wealth in the context of promoting the merits of an industrious career, work as an end in itself, thrift and self-discipline. Wealth was condemned only when it was associated with a life of idle luxury or self-indulgence. According to Weber, Calvinism furnished the moral energy and drive of the capitalist entrepreneur. Moreover, although Weber uses Calvinism to illustrate the relationship between religion and capitalism, his interpretation extends to other Puritan sects.

There have been a number of criticisms of Weber's work (see Tawney 1926; Gilchrist 1969). Of particular relevance to our theme of consumer credit is the work of medievalists, who have long questioned the reported intransigence on the part of the Catholic Church with respect to usury, arguing that the Church had adapted to meet the needs of changing economic circumstances in which usury became established at every level of society (Nightingale 2002). Gilchrist (1969) provides evidence that the Catholic Church did in fact make exceptions to the biblical interpretation on usury on thirteen different counts. These included the lender's sharing of the risk, the loss of profit on the capital, and a new emphasis on the intention of lenders. Gelpi and Julien-Labruyere (1999) have recently provided an analysis of six centuries' worth of the Catholic Church's rhetoric on the issue of usury, and conclude that the Church was hypocritical. It condemned usury but was simultaneously participating in the activity.

The role of the English parochial clergy as investors and creditors in the first half of the fourteenth century provides some important insights into the attitudes towards usury within the Church and community (Nightingale 2002). If the clergy were to seek out usurers within the community because this activity was condemned by God, they would be highly unlikely to engage in the practice themselves. The parochial clergy were well placed to become moneylenders within their own communities. While there were variations in their income, most had a standard of living in excess of that of the richer peasants, and many received additional revenues which gave them a surplus to invest. Furthermore, there was a long medieval tradition of the clergy providing safe deposit services and acting as executors of wills, and therefore they may have had access to money to invest on behalf of others. Celibacy also had financial advantages. In theory, the clergy had no wives or children to provide for, and thus were under no pressure to invest in property or land to meet their dependants' needs. Their main interest was to provide for themselves in retirement, so they had every incentive to make investments for the future.

Certificates exist that indicate that parochial clergy (rectors, parsons, vicars, chaplains) from all over England lent money, the average loan being £20, which was substantial (1,600 days' wages for a skilled craftsman). The loans tended to be over relatively short timescales of four to five months, and the clergy took action to chase their defaulting debtors in much the same way as other lenders. However, there were geographical variations in lending behaviour. Areas that were poverty-stricken, remote or small in size tended to have few loans provided by the clergy. The same was true of large towns where there was a wealthy merchant class. Nightingale (2002: 101) concludes: 'thus economic interests, rather than the moral influence or local needs of the community seem to have motivated the parochial clergy as creditors and investors in the first half of the fourteenth century'.

Despite the controversy over the precise relationship between religion and capitalism established by Weber, what is not at issue is Protestantism's influence on attitudes to credit and debt. Calder (1999) maintains that at the close of nineteenth century in America, moralistic ways of thinking about finance were reasonably well established. The underlying theme was that the power of money could be mastered by adhering to moral laws of money management. Positive aspects of money were that it was the basis for careers and businesses, and could be used to help the poor obtain medical treatment. Language of the day emphasized the view that people did not *borrow*; they were *trusted*. Credit was character, credit was trust, credit was good. But debt, the necessary analogue to credit, was an entirely different matter. According to Victorian moralists, debt was 'a calamity', 'an oppressive and degrading incubus', 'an inexhaustible fountain of dishonesty'. Protestant moralists counselled against 'wasteful expenditures' and 'present gratification' (Calder 1999: 93).

A common way of talking about money had been established by the political, literary and religious elite and was disseminated through the popular media. The literature appeared in a variety of forms, including sermons, pamphlets, textbooks on political economy, gift books for young men and women, didactic short stories, financial advice books, and guides to domestic economy. Similar messages were propagated to children via Sunday schools, since these were some of the main distributors of children's literature. In the United States, *McGuffey Readers* were first published between 1836 and 1838 and comprised a primer, a speller and four readers. They proved to be very popular, and during the period 1836–1920, 122 million copies were sold (Spring 2003).

Consumer credit and social class

Social class divisions in credit and debtor relationships are an important part of social and economic history. In the absence of a formal financial services infrastructure that met the needs of various groups in society, the credit available to various social groups was highly differentiated. The sources of credit and the prices charged were highly variable and there was a high reliance on social networks. Parker (1990) captures the essence of this state of affairs in her observation that while the gentry ran up bills, the pauper pawned her wedding ring. Roberts (1973) maintains that those who were extremely poor did not find themselves in debt, since nobody would be willing to give them credit. Inequality in the context of accessing credit, especially within the lower socio-economic groups, remains an important debate.

Schofield (2002) provides an interesting account of credit and debt among the early fourteenth-century English peasantry. He notes that it used to be taken for granted in medieval scholarship that peasants produced a cash crop that paid for their rent and what was left over supported the family. However, this viewpoint has been disproved in some cases since a significant number of peasants produced enough surpluses to sell in local, semi-urban and urban markets for profit. The work of Kowaleski on medieval Exeter demonstrates that peasants from the hinterlands went to Exeter to buy more than they sold. They also viewed Exeter as a place to secure cash loans and appeared in the Exeter borough courts records as defendants and debtors (see Schofield 2002).

The earliest surviving records of a county court in England relate to the Bedfordshire court session in 1332–1333. Schofield (2002) discovered that nearly half of the pleas issued during that period were for debt. Furthermore, while the creditors came from relatively large towns in the county, the debtors were much more widely geographically dispersed. Some of the debtors were relatively poor villagers, but other defendant debtors included a chaplain, an attorney at law and the Sheriff of Bedfordshire and Buckinghamshire. Thus, some credit relationships were negotiated between men of elevated socio-economic standing. However, most small-scale borrowing occurred at the manorial level, and villagers would not have needed to move beyond where they were living to obtain credit. Any disputes would have been settled by the manorial courts and would never have reached the county courts.

Approaching 50 per cent of borrowing at manorial level was for credit sales, the deferred payment of goods (cereals or animals), followed by leases involving land and animals, and finally cash loans, although it needs to be acknowledged that these proportions could vary across different geographical areas. Lending and borrowing at manorial level was localized, as one would have expected, and the credit relationships were vertical, with the wealthiest landowners lending the most, along with local gentry and clergy. Some of the wealthiest peasants also lent money, grain and livestock to the poorer families. Schofield maintains that these vertical lending relationships are significant and illustrate the economic investment that creditors were making as opposed to small-scale horizontal lending that was undertaken by family and close acquaintances, which largely remained invisible. There is also evidence of considerable inter-peasant litigation in manorial records, which suggests that significant numbers of debtors did not repay what was owed.

Some interesting insights into peasant access to credit in France between 1680 and 1780 have been provided by Fontaine (2001), who focuses on the trust–credit nexus. He maintains that the relationship between the creditors and the debtors was organized within a number of pre-existing circles. First one would ask family members. If that request was unsuccessful, those who provided one with work would be the next port of call. Dependent on the region, the next group of people to approach might be the 'aristocracy, religious institutions, or the village elite' (Fontaine 2001: 49). The next group of potential creditors were the regional elite, and if that approach failed, foreigners (Jews, Italians or Savoyards) were the lenders of last resort. A hierarchy of creditors comprising family members and nobility were obliged to help, despite the fact that only a fraction of debts were paid in the allotted time. Outstanding debt owed on death that could take a long time (20–25 years) to recover was not uncommon.

Systems for recording peasant debt varied widely, and some peasants took advantage of the secrecy surrounding credit and debt by using a multiplicity of creditors to meet their needs. Over-indebtedness became a way of life for some, but, as Fontaine (2001: 41) explains, the poor also used the courts to prompt payment of debts owing to them:

> The poor also benefited from credit activities: in trials for debt, they were as likely to be on the plaintiff's bench (appealing against unpaid salaries) as they were to be defendants; even patients in the hospice were part of the chain of debt. These connections, far from indicating a compartmentalization of society, cut through it vertically, binding social groups, institutions, and regions together in dependent relationships where each participant was simultaneously creditor and debtor. Thus, different groups in the creditor–debtor network interconnected, although their geographical and social positions were infinitely variable.

At the other end of the social spectrum, Owens *et al.*'s (2006) study of wealthy English families from the beginning to the middle of the nineteenth century indicates that few men or women died without owing money. But in their sample of affluent families, the dead rarely left executors and descendants to grapple with estates overburdened with debt. Probate records demonstrate that personal loans and consumer credit were part of everyday life. The amount of credit offered and the length of time allowed for repayment were indicative of a person's social standing. If a large sum had been loaned over a long time-frame, then one could conclude that the borrower was indeed highly trustworthy. The social spectrum to whose members credit was extended was very large, spanning professionals, farmers, skilled craftsmen and peasants. Interestingly, an analysis of the money owed by peasants shows that peasants' debts turn out to be the debts that were most successfully recovered. Some of the largest loans were made to family and friends, carrying little or no interest. Some of the smaller loans were never repaid.

Finn's (1998) analysis of the Victorian county courts in England and Wales that were established in 1846 provides some valuable insights into consumer markets and working-class credit. The purpose of the courts was to deal efficiently and effectively with small claims. Judges had the authority to order payments for debts of £50 or less and commit petty debtors to prison for periods of six weeks at a time should they default on their payments. The courts proved a popular method of resolving disputes, and between 1847 and 1872, creditors lodged 18 million plaints, to recover debts in excess of £48 million. In 1873 the annual number of plaints entered was 863,300, and by 1901 it had risen to 1,193,895. Although the courts have not been the subject of a great deal of investigation, they provide a valuable dataset to aid our understanding of consumption and credit among the working classes.

Finn maintains that county courts operated as a site for the reproduction of social class relations. The occupation of the debtor was provided in court records, and these demonstrated a preponderance of manual occupations (Finn 2003). However, some professional people also found themselves on the wrong side of the law. On 26 May 1827 the *Lancet* reported that a surgeon was fined and put in a debtor's prison cell pending payment of a fine for removing a dead body from a churchyard (*Lancet* editorial, 1997). The norm was for upper-class judges to condemn the activities of the dissolute working classes, and reinforced Victorian views that imprisonment was the action of last resort in disciplining individuals for unruly behaviour such as drunkenness and gambling. In the eighteenth century, debtors were the largest single category of prisoner in English jails. In 1709 Daniel Defoe put the number conservatively at 5,000, dividing them into three classes: the very poor (2,000), gentry and clergy down on their luck (2,000), and 'tradesmen and other' (Aris 1985). The maximum sentence for petty debtors during the latter part of the eighteenth century was one, two or three months. One proviso was that prison-keepers were allowed to retain debtors indefinitely if they were unable to pay their jail fees on release. Finn (2003) cites prison records which indicate that an 80-year-old man had been in prison for twenty years for petty debt. There were wide variations in the proportion of debtors who went to prison in different districts, which demonstrates that judges had considerable discretion as regards sentencing.

Some judges believed the majority of the working class were respectable people and that credit was a necessary evil to make ends meet and pay for necessities. Few could afford to save out of existing income, and the vagaries of the labour market meant that credit was an accepted way of life. As a consequence of the large number of debtors who were sent to prison by the late 1850s, and an awareness of the circumstances that had caused the difficulties, some judges began to question whether the working classes were the source of the problem. The debate shifted to examining the marketing and sales practices of unscrupulous travelling packmen or hawkers who seduced and harassed consumers with their goods.

The courts took on a different role: policing petty commercial transactions in order to protect working-class people from unjust commercial practices. For example, some judges disallowed suits from tradesmen who they believed had intentionally caused women to spend beyond their means. The practice of subcontracting out debt-collection practices to agents and solicitors was also condemned by some judges, and they refused to award costs to retailers that sent debt collectors to represent them in court. The reporting of judges' pronouncements in the local newspapers in addition to the commercial and legal press ensured that the moral meanings of retail practices reached a wider public audience than might otherwise have been the case. Between 1869 and 1890 the numbers of debtors sent to prison dramatically decreased.

The previous discussion of social class and consumer credit and debt has not been product-specific but rather has discussed the issue at an aggregate level. By contrast, the role of credit in providing for funerals had a much more deeply symbolic function since it was a reflection on how one had lived one's life. There were few things that stigmatized an individual and close kin more than the pauper's grave, since it signified abject poverty and carried associations of the workhouse. A good funeral reflected the competence of the male breadwinner and the thriftiness of the wife; it was a very public display of the private grief of the bereaved but also signified the family's respectability within the community. The ultimate disgrace for a Victorian worker's family was a pauper burial; it pauperized the entire family. Public graves contained as many as ten bodies, and cemetery by-laws often prohibited the use of a headstone. In this respect the pauper grave condemned the deceased to 'eternal anonymity' (Strange 2003: 175). Pauper's coffins were made in cheap, flimsy wood and were of a standard size, which meant that larger corpses were crammed into them. This poor construction meant that sometimes the coffins cracked, revealing the corpse inside.

Strange's (2003) account of the pauper grave between 1880 and 1914 provides some insights about individuals who had to suffer the disgrace of the pauper funeral and sources of credit that were available for families that wished to obtain funding to save their reputation. The importance of a decent burial was reflected in the widespread investment in burial insurance (Knights and Vurdubakis 1993). Indeed, saving for one's funeral remains a part of contemporary working-class culture in some localities. Home collection organizations including the Prudential and Co-operative Insurance that go from door to door collecting premiums have sustained this practice among their consumers (Burton *et al.* 2004). Strange (2003: 153) maintains that '[f]or those without the buffer of a burial policy, the pawnbroker and/or sympathetic friends might provide the necessary finance to purchase a grave'.

In some cases, burial boards initiated schemes whereby a grave could be obtained on hire purchase on condition that 50 per cent of the costs were secured as a down payment in advance. An alternative arrangement was for graves to be leased for a period of fourteen years, after which they reverted to the trustees of the cemetery to be used as public graves. This arrangement enabled families to avoid the shame of a pauper burial without going to the expense of a private grave. A more unorthodox arrangement was to have the corpse placed in a common grave while the family raised the necessary finances in order that the body could be exhumed and placed in a private grave. This arrangement was a protracted business and it was also a more expensive option, yet burial boards accepted this practice as normal. The initial interment in a common grave served to advertise to the community that the family did not have the financial resources for a proper burial. The reburial served as a damage-limitation exercise.

In the remainder of this section the focus of attention will turn to sources of credit available within working-class communities. A raft of non-bank lenders targeted different segments of the market, and various products were developed to meet the needs of specific groups. However, despite the fact that millions of customers used the alternative credit market that these organizations developed, they are infrequently discussed in historical research (O'Connell and Reid 2005). Pawnbrokers were traditionally known as the poor man's banker. Some upmarket brokers did exist, but they were not numerous and they tended to deal in jewellery and silverware (Johnson 1985). Within Britain it has been a regulated trade since the thirteenth century, with most pawnbrokers being located in large towns and cities. In New York, pawnbrokers were first legalized in 1803. Jews were the earliest pawnbrokers in Britain, but the community was expelled in 1290. Their place was taken by Italian Lombards. The pawnbroker's sign of three gilt balls is believed to have originated with the three gold coins which, when painted on a flat board, indicated that the Lombards had called (Tebbutt 1984).

Many pawnbrokers in the United Kingdom and the United States were family firms that were passed down from one generation to the next. Pawnbrokers as privately run organizations were a different concept from the system in Catholic Europe, where public pawnshops controlled by official bodies were established to meet the short-term borrowing needs of poor people (Tebbutt 1984; Gelpi and Julien-Labruyere 1999). Calder (1999) argues that positioning the pawner as male was a misnomer, since the typical pawner was female. In working-class households it was traditionally the wife's task to manage the household budget and make one pay packet last from one week to the next. Pawning was a regular practice for many, an integral part of the family budget. It has been estimated that every working-class family in Britain at the end of the nineteenth century placed at least one pledge a fortnight, amounting to around thirty each year. The practice was not welcome in all areas of Britain. For example, in Scotland pawnbroking was linked with Irish immigration and it did not fit neatly with indigenous people's view of thriftiness, Calvinism and temperance. The opposition in Glasgow was particularly pronounced, and the local newspaper ran a series of articles setting out its undesirable traits (Tebbutt 1984).

Pawnbrokers advanced small loans against goods or chattels provided as security. Legislative restrictions determined what goods pawnbrokers could accept. Perishable goods were not accepted, and fashionable items were also excluded since they could be out of date after twelve months and become less valuable. The articles most frequently pawned were those that were easily portable, and included 'clothing, bedding, watches, jewellery, and ornaments' (Johnson 1985: 167). If the goods were not redeemed within twelve months, they became the property of the pawnbroker. Most pawnshops were divided into two areas: the sales counter situated at the front for the disposal of unsold goods; and a pledge counter, often reached by a separate entrance, where the pledging and redeeming occurred. Pawnbrokers were legally obliged to keep records of all their transactions, including goods that were sold at auction. Pawning was an expensive business to conduct and there was always the risk that unredeemed goods could not be sold for the amount loaned on their security. Furthermore, during periods of economic difficulties due to unemployment, strikes or illness, the number of forfeits increased, redemptions declined and the pawnbroker's profits declined. The practice of pawnbroking suffered a steady decline in the years between the world wars as a result of competition from other suppliers.

Moneylenders have been a persistent feature of credit provision in working-class communities. Moneylenders have long been criticized for their high interest rates and dubious business methods (Rowlingson 1994). With reference to the interwar period, Taylor (2002) makes the distinction between street moneylenders and loan sharks operating in working-class neighbourhoods in Britain. Most of the street moneylenders were women who would provide the service from their own homes for the benefit of other women living in the street in need of cash to meet their living expenses. To some extent this form of moneylending was an extension of neighbourliness. Male moneylenders invariably came from outside the area, and more often than not their customers were men. A significant amount of business was transacted in public houses so that men could afford to buy beer and cigarettes. Often debtors would buy moneylenders a pint of beer in lieu of interest. In the post-war period, many street lenders were replaced by what became known as loan sharks, who were by definition from outside the community. They used terror to ensure payment, and since 1960 most loan sharks have been part of the criminal fraternity. Moneylending continues to exist in working-class communities as an important method of fast cash (Rowlingson 1994; Leyshon *et al.* 2004).

Check trading made its first appearance in Britain in the 1880s with the launch of the Provident Clothing and Supply Company Limited in Bradford in

Yorkshire. The company was founded by Joshua K. Waddlilove, an active Methodist and employee of an industrial insurance company. Checks were initially valued at sums of 10 shillings, £1.30, £2 and upwards. By the early 1960s the upper value for the checks had increased to £30. The largest check trading companies had long lists of retailers from whom consumers could buy goods, including clothing, electrical goods, furniture, coal and even false teeth. Food, drink and luxuries could not be bought using checks. The checks allowed customers to shop at different stores and buy goods at the same price as if they were using cash. The checks were divisible, so that retailers could document on the back of the check how much had been spent and the customer could take it to another shop or shops to spend the remainder. By the 1930s, Provident had agreements with approximately 14,000 retailers and in excess of 616,000 customers.

Another source of credit in working-class communities was the corner shop (Taylor 2002). Small shops occupied locations on many street corners and were at the hub of the community. Women tended to run small shops and provide a second income while their husbands were engaged in paid employment outside the home. Tick books were the main form of credit, and the creditors were predominantly women. Under this arrangement, customers would take goods from the shop, the amount would be noted and the account would be settled at the end of the week. The payment of the tick account was a mark of integrity in those communities and was the basis of trust and mutual understanding. Indeed, some customers referred to getting goods not on tick but on trust (Wolvendge 1976). Keeping up with the payments was also a guarantee against being hungry in hard times, but only for those who could guarantee future earnings. Consumers who could not keep up with the payments were publicly blacklisted on local shop windows (Johnson 1985). In many instances, tick credit died out in the post-war period when redevelopment schemes disrupted and destroyed local communities. Tick credit still exists in some inner-city and rural areas and is most frequently used by older people who grew up with the system.

A final source of credit was attached to catalogue shopping in order that households could afford to purchase items for the home and clothes for the family (Ford 1990; Rowlingson 1994). Catalogues were a popular method of shopping in urban, working-class areas, where an agent would have the responsibility for securing sales from groups of women and collecting the credit payments on a weekly basis. The cash price was shown in the catalogue alongside the credit price, which was divided into weekly instalments. The weekly instalments appealed to individuals on lower incomes even though the prices of goods were generally higher than those on offer on the high street. The weekly visit of the agent reinforced financial self-discipline to ensure that customers kept up with their credit agreements. The visits also provided a marketing research opportunity for the agents, who could prompt the consumer into buying goods that might need replacing, or simply draw attention to current offers.

Women and credit

The trend away from product-oriented analysis to consumer-oriented approaches in the social sciences has had a positive effect in opening spaces to discuss the relationship between women and credit in its historical context. Focusing on individuals whose working lives were outside the formal economy and whose economic activities were closely involved in the reproduction of families has opened up spaces to discuss the ways in which households were provisioned and centred the role of women, as distinct from supply-side accounts that favoured men. To what extent consumption has historically been sustained by credit and the gender relations in which credit was embedded has been a neglected area of research inquiry, but has recently attracted more attention from scholars interested in developing women's history (Finn 1998, 2001). The main sources available to scholars in their attempts to construct accounts of credit and debt have been debt records, and few women appear in them, but despite these difficulties some vivid accounts are emerging within this sub-specialism.

Women throughout history have traditionally been thought to play a subordinate role within families. This viewpoint was reinforced in later medieval and early modern England. Literature, plays and sermons stressed that daughters should be obedient to their parents, and wives to their husbands. The sources of this inequality were biblical and medical texts in which male authors argued that 'women were physically, intellectually, and emotionally incapable of equality with men, either in the household or in the public world' (McIntosh 2005: 143; Mate 1998; Aughterson 1995). However, recent studies have begun to shed light on the ways in which women challenged these stereotypes in England (Briggs 2004; Mate 1999; Mendelson and Crawford 1998), in sixteenth-century Paris (Crowston 2002) and in the rural United States in the nineteenth century (Heller and Houdek 2004).

McIntosh's (2005) work is instructive in exploring how women of lower and middle rank became involved in credit dealings, often involving legal action, as a result of family relationships in the period between 1300 and 1620. During this period, credit had a variety of meanings that included both *social* and *economic* components. An individual had their own credit standing in the eyes of others, but that often reflected trustworthiness – whether the person's word could be accepted. Households or families would have collective credit, or a shared social or economic standing. The other aspect was financial: unfulfilled debt to another person, or credit relationship. Delayed obligations assumed many different forms: borrowed clothing, tools, animals; or late payment of servants' wages. Nearly everyone was involved in complex networks of obligations at some level, involving family, friends and neighbours. By the latter part of the sixteenth century, a more formal system of credit emerged that made it difficult for women to compete with men.

Women became involved with credit interactions that related to their family roles at different stages in the life cycle. During her younger years, and in preparation for marriage, a woman might inherit land or goods from a relative and then find it difficult to realize the inheritance and have to resort to legal proceedings. This was particularly the case in instances where the relationship was irregular or involved concubinage or illegitimacy. A woman who received a bequest while she was under age could leave it in someone else's hands to be stored as credit until a later date. For female servants, unwanted pregnancies, either from masters or from other servants, opened another area of credit by way of making those responsible pay for maintenance. Furthermore, it was common for couples thinking of marrying to give or loan goods or money to each other. This arrangement caused problems if the marriage failed to materialize.

Once married, the woman did not have a separate identity from her husband in the eyes of the law. A woman could not access credit without her husband's permission, and should a legal or financial matter arise, she had to sue or be sued in her husband's name. However, women were involved in credit transactions in numerous instances. For example, a woman's husband might be away abroad or incapacitated, and in these circumstances her own reputation or credit (trustworthiness) came to the fore. These transactions could involve the running of the house or business dealings. Widows were involved in several types of credit transactions. For example, a widow who inherited property or land could become involved with unpaid obligations owed by tenants. Conversely, she had to find her late husband's creditors and settle the sums he owed. If she failed to do so, she could be sued, with the possibility of considerable economic loss and, perhaps, imprisonment.

Women's dealings with credit arising from children and other relatives took a number of forms. Mothers, especially widows, acquired credit and debts as a result of having children. For example, one instance might be the obligation to increase the value of any inheritance for minors. A widow who wished to remarry might have wanted to safeguard the legacies of children from a previous marriage from misuse by her future husband. Arranging for the apprenticeship of a child might again mean entering into a credit relationship, since the parents would have to pay for their offspring's training. However, not all arrangements were amicable, especially if the apprenticeship were withdrawn without financial recompense. Likewise, putting children through higher education led some women into debt. Widows might give or receive credit as part of the financial arrangements that went along with the marriage of their children. Economic commitments that went along with stepchildren could be particularly problematic, especially in instances where any inheritance of the husband would be given to the children of a former marriage rather than the widow.

Another interesting insight into the relationship between women and credit is provided by Finn (1996) in her account of women's consumption and coverture in England between 1760 and 1860. Coverture prevented wives from entering into economic relationships in their own right, and a married woman's legal identity was subsumed under that of her husband. According to William Blackstone (1765) 'by marriage the very being or legal existence of a woman is suspended' (quoted in Finn 1996: 703). Nineteenth- and twentieth-century feminist critics emphasized the common law practice of coverture as one way in which women were excluded from public life, and helped to establish the ideology of separate spheres. Under coverture, 'married women had no right to make economic contracts or to purchase goods on credit, no ability to represent themselves or their spouses in court, indeed no economic or legal existence separate from their husbands' (Finn 1996: 708). Lester (1999: 118–119) provides an account by a magistrate for the City of Leeds in 1906 in which he describes the circumstances in which a husband was imprisoned as a result of his wife's behaviour:

> Under an expanding system of credit, articles of adornment are palmed off upon the wife by unscrupulous traders, and purchased by her without the husband's knowledge or, perchance, wages handed over for rent and necessaries are wasted by her gaming or drinking, or misapplied to the cash purchase of trinkets, leaving the butcher and baker to sue for their bills. Soon afterwards comes the County Court summons, served on the wife who destroys it or conceals it from her husband. The plaintiff gets judgment after giving little or no proof of the wife's agency, or, perhaps she appears and admits the debt. Next comes the judgment order under which a few instalments may possibly be paid – then, when default occurs, there arrives the judgment summons, followed by commitment and arrest.

Finn maintains that feminist critics have played an important role in drawing attention to the legal status or legal nonentity of women under coverture. However, more recent work using probate accounts demonstrate that women enjoyed considerably more economic authority than is generally acknowledged. Finn's (1996) account of married women as consumer debtors in the century before the Divorce Act of 1857 demonstrates that three practices undermined the norms of coverture. The first was the *law of necessity*, which recognized that married women were responsible for the smooth running of households and were allowed to enter into credit relationships for necessities in their own right, acting as agents for their husband. The legal precedent for the law of necessities preceded the reign of Henry VI and provided for the wife to obtain funding for necessities whether she lived with her husband or was separated from him under justifiable circumstances.

The law of necessities was intimately related to fidelity, since the law only provided for wives who were chaste. Women who were forced from their homes because of their own adultery lost the right under the law to obtain credit in their husband's name. But wives who were compelled to leave the marital home for reasons of cruelty remained entitled to obtain credit, as did those who were adulterous but remained within the family home. In some instances, what constituted a necessity was open to considerable interpretation. One often-reported example in the eighteenth century is that of an estranged wife of a former judge who purchased lace and silver fringes for her side-saddle from an unwary tradesman. Valued at the considerable sum of £94, these articles were considered necessities for someone of her social status, and her husband had to pay the bill.

The second way coverture was undermined was through the *strategic use of the law of necessity* as an instrument of credit by women who were determined to separate from their husbands. Informal separations were more widely practised among a range of social groups than has hitherto been believed to be the case, and provided an escape route from an unsuitable marriage. Wealthy women turned into voracious spenders, charging large sums in their name in an attempt to force advantageous divorce settlements. Charlotte Calvert reportedly spent £3,000 in her husband's name between 1705 and 1707. Her husband responded by confiscating the goods in 1709, at which point she implored the retailers to take her husband to court for non-payment of debts. In other cases some husbands were imprisoned owing to the actions of vindictive wives. In instances where a man and woman lived with each other without being married, the man was responsible for honouring the woman's debts. In one instance cited by Finn, a man attempted to relinquish his obligation to pay his bereaved partner's debts, but the judge ruled that if a man lived with a woman, then he was liable for her debts.

The third was through the use of the county court system, which dealt with debts of £20 or less. During their first ten years of operation the county courts were an important forum, and they settled 4,600,000 suits to a value of £14,500,000. Women who remained within the marital home exerted a degree of autonomy in county courts that was denied them in common law. For example, the Commissioner's description of the operation of the Birmingham court indicated that women's appearances were 'very frequent, and very loud, and . . . their fondness for speaking is a stagnation to business' (Hutton 1785, quoted in Finn 1996). The appearance of women in the county courts had the advantage that all parties were able to listen to the account of a woman who had been intimately involved in the transaction in question rather than the husband, who was merely liable for its payment. Creditors who attempted to present wives as individuals who could obtain credit in their own right were unsuccessful, since the presence of women in court representing their husbands did not change the fact that they could only legally enter into debts as their husband's agent. This led to claims by some traders that husbands and wives were conspiring together to defraud traders (Rappaport 1996). The strategic importance of women occurred in the negotiation of small debt claims. In some courts, 25 per cent of husbands were represented by their wives, and the percentage was even higher in some occupational groups. For example, among the working classes wives would be more frequent attenders in order that their husband would not lose a day's pay.

Under the county court system the plight of women who were unmarried was quite different from that of their married contemporaries protected by coverture. Imprisonment for non-payment of debts was confined to young single women, women who had borne illegitimate children, spinsters and widows. Finn (1998) has provided statistics for women debtors committed to prison in the Bedford county court between 1855 and 1858. In 1855, women comprised 5 per cent of debtors imprisoned; in 1856 that figure had increased to 10 per cent, in 1857 to 16 per cent and in 1858 to 25 per cent. The moral character of these women also came under close scrutiny, given the pervasive beliefs in the close relationship between female consumer activity and female sexual transgression that were found in Victorian society, whether there was evidence of a relationship or not. A particularly disturbing development was that some women were imprisoned with their children. The plight of a deserted wife was particularly severe, since when husbands deserted their wives they rarely took the children, and the wife of a man who was not creditworthy could rarely obtain credit herself (Perkin 1989).

The scholarship pertaining to women and credit has provided some valuable insights about the operation of credit markets and consumer markets, gender relations, and the operation of the courts in the recovery of debt. Historians have also shed light on the credit relationships that women entrepreneurs entered into during the course of their business activities and their role in providing credit to their customers. Credit enabled women merchants to develop relationships with other men and women based on business activities as opposed to familial or sexual ties. A particularly high-profile case is provided by Crowston (2002) in her account of Rose Berlin, who rose from humble beginnings to become a famous fashion merchant in Paris. This case is interesting because of the publicity Berlin attracted when she allegedly filed for bankruptcy in January 1787 with debts of 2–3 million livres. What was astonishing about this case was the amount of money that was involved, which testified to the importance of women in mercantile credit networks. Berlin was famous for her notoriously high prices and rich clients, including Marie-Antoinette and the royal families and wealthy individuals in Europe. As with many other merchants, Berlin's business functioned almost entirely on credit, and many of the accounts were sent to women to be settled, demonstrating that they had a measure of economic independence from their husbands. Wealthy clients did not pay cash for goods and services but paid in instalments, and their tardiness in paying bills was legendary. Berlin's accounts provide an insight into bad payers. An entry in May 1791 indicated that a baron owed the sum of 3,699 livres, but only one payment of 12 livres had been paid in a period spanning thirteen years and the account remained unpaid. Some Parisian aristocrats used innovative goods that they had acquired to pay tradesmen, and this is how the semi-luxury market developed among the less affluent (Coquery 2004). After her death, Berlin's heirs enlisted the help of lawyers to recover outstanding accounts. The exercise generated 7,000 pages of accounts across several hundred clients.

Conclusion

The work of historians has been particularly valuable in widening our frame of reference for understanding contemporary developments in credit and debt. To some extent our understanding is constrained by the limited sources available, and we tend to know more about the behaviour of affluent sections of society. Religion has played a pivotal role in the acceptance of credit and debt in society, and is an issue that has been commented upon by a significant number of scholars. The ways in which religious discourse was used to suppress credit acquisition in the United States in the 1920s is a theme that will be discussed in more detail in the next chapter. The relationship between credit and social class is particularly complex. Because of literacy difficulties, many credit transactions between those in lower socio-economic groups are not formally documented, so we have limited knowledge of day-to-day credit exchanges. We tend to know more about relationships that ended up in the courts, but these were probably atypical. It is interesting to note that many of the sources of working-class credit that were established centuries ago are still a feature of the contemporary credit landscape. One example is working-class people saving up to pay for their own funeral by paying small amounts of money to a door-to-door collector. The relationship between women and credit is a fascinating and emergent area of scholarship. Analysing that relationship provides a way of questioning many of the assumptions about women playing a subordinate role within households.

Questions

1   How have developments in literary theory assisted our understanding of developments in attitudes of credit and debt?
2   What does the English Act against Usury of 1571 demonstrate about the relationship between credit and religion?

3   What are the strengths and limitations of court records in assessing social class differences in attitudes towards credit and debt?
4   Explain what you understand by the concept of coverture.

Further reading

Briggs, C. (2004) 'Empowered or marginalized? Rural women and credit in later thirteenth- and fourteenth-century England', *Continuity and Change*, 19, 1: 13–43.

Finn, M. (1996) 'Women, consumption and coverture in England, c.1760–1860', *The Historical Journal*, 39, 3: 703–722.

Finn, M. (1998) 'Working-class women and the contest for consumer control in Victorian county courts', *Past and Present*, 161, November: 116–154.

Fontaine, L. (2001) 'Antonio and Shylock: credit and trust in France, c.1680–c.1780', *Economic History Review*, 54, 1: 39–57.

McIntosh, M.K. (2005) 'Women, credit, and family relationships in England, 1300–1620', *Journal of Family History*, 30, 2: 143–163.

Muldrew, C. (1998) *The Economy of Obligation: The Culture of Credit and Social Relations in Early Modern England*, Basingstoke, UK: Palgrave Macmillan.

O'Connell, S. and Reid, C. (2005) 'Working-class consumer credit in the UK, 1925–60: the role of the check trader', *Economic History Review*, 58, 2: 378–405.

Owens, A., Green, D.R., Bailey, C. and Kay, A.C. (2006) 'A measure of worth: probate valuations, personal wealth and indebtedness in England, 1810–1840', *Historical Research*, 79, 205: 383–403.

Schofield, P.R. and Mayhew, N.J. (2002) *Credit and Debt in Medieval England c.1180–c.1350*, Oxford: Oxbow Books.

Strange, J. (2003) 'Only a pauper whom nobody owns: reassessing the pauper grave c. 1880–1914', *Past and Present*, 178, February: 148–175.

2 Consumption, credit and consumer society

This chapter will explore the complex relationship between credit, consumption and consumer society. There is a considerable literature charting the development of consumer society and a significant range of theoretical approaches to consumption. Yet despite this unparalleled attention, the relationship between credit, consumption and consumer society has rarely been addressed. The first part of the chapter will assess the historical development of consumer society. The second theme of the chapter will be to explain why there has been a lack of attention to credit in the consumption literature. The third part of the chapter will examine the relationship between credit and consumption in a period of rapid transformation in the late nineteenth and early twentieth centuries. The final part of the chapter will focus on some of the dysfunctional aspects of the credit–consumption relationship through a discussion of compulsive and compensatory consumption and gambling.

Consumer society: theoretical approaches

A starting point in discussing consumer society is to come to some definition of what the term means. Fine (2002: 156) argues that this is a difficult thing to do, for two reasons. First, the concept is used so extensively that it would be an endless task in itself to devise an all-encompassing definition. Second, where the term is used, its meaning is often taken for granted; there is an assumption that everyone knows what the term means and that it is at all times being used in the same way. However, within the literature there is a consensus around the central role that consumption plays in consumer societies.

A recurrent issue in debates about the nature of consumer society is when it began, when was 'take-off'. Agnew (1993) presents an informative assessment of some of the key debates in the area, and McCracken (1987) provides a valuable survey of the history of consumption. But one of the most influential texts to directly address how consumer society developed as a distinctly different system of capitalist modernity is McKendrick, Brewer and Plumb's (1982) account of consumption in eighteenth-century Britain, *The Birth of a*

Consumer Society. These authors argued that it was eighteenth-century England that witnessed the first 'consumer revolution'. At that time it was England that presented the right mix of attributes to enable a new consumer society to emerge. Some of the key factors included a fluid social structure, rising wages, an emulative bourgeoisie and a showcase capital city. They explored the ways entrepreneurs could create markets for new products and services and how the pressures and problems of commercial society helped the development of a new middle class politics. The text was influential since it opened up space for a thorough investigation of the relationship between consumption and consumer society in its historical perspective. Since its publication there have been many other major works that focus on consumption in its historical context (Brewer and Porter 1993; Williams 1982; Mukerji 1983).

It is probably true to say that far more attention has been given to the role of consumption in everyday life than to historical debates about the emergence of consumer society. Perhaps the most prominent account of the role of consumption in social life is Thornstein Veblen's (1912) *Theory of the Leisure Class*. Miller (1987) maintains that Veblen could almost be credited with initiating the study of consumption as a social phenomenon. Veblen argued that in affluent societies consumption is a social signifier through which individuals establish their social position. Conspicuous displays of wealth and leisure marked a person's worth for the outside world. Through their conspicuous consumption the rich advertised themselves in order to secure a place in the social hierarchy. Those located further down the social hierarchy aspired to the consumption patterns of the better off, giving patterns of consumption a trickle-down effect. The patterns that Veblen identified were apparent in other societies. For example, Italian nobles in the seventeenth and eighteenth centuries built opulent palaces with beautiful façades that incorporated tiles engraved with the words 'Pro Invidia' (To Be Envied). For centuries, wealthy aristocrats passed laws that forbade the aspiring nouveaux riche from copying their style in fashion. At the turn of the eighteenth century, the wealthy published in newspapers menus that they were serving at dinner parties.

To some extent, Bourdieu (1984) builds on work by Veblen in his work *Distinction: A Social Critique of Taste*, first published in France in 1979 and available in English in 1984. Bourdieu's emphasis is on understanding social relationships of domination and submission being based not on people's possessions but on their tastes, which constitute symbolic or cultural capital. For Bourdieu (1984), practices of consumption are the sources of group-based social distinction generated through shared socio-economic constraints. The view that social position matters is a sentiment that has found some support (Savage *et al.* 1992; Warde 1997; Skeggs 2003). Other scholars maintain that consumer freedom through making symbolic consumption decisions that form the basis of an individual's lifestyle and identity is undermining readily identifiable social divisions (Gabriel and Lang 1995; Featherstone 1991; Bauman 1992; Beck 1992; Giddens 1991; Baudrillard 1998).

Lury (1996: 29–36) highlights a number of features that she believes characterize modern consumption: a larger and wide range of goods; the commodification and marketization of a wider range of goods and services; the expansion of shopping as a leisure pursuit; the emergence of different forms of shopping; political organization by and of consumers; a heightened visibility of sport and leisure practices; wider acceptance of credit and debt; an increase in the sites for consumption, including shopping malls and theme parks; the growing importance of packaging and promotion and style, design and appearance; the emergence of consumer crimes; illnesses associated with consumer society such as compulsive shopping; and an interest in collecting, including the collecting of art, antiques and so forth. Lash and Urry (1994) focus on the celebration of the creative and empowering possibilities of material consumption, the pursuit of hedonism, and the heightened importance of style in the quest for personalized meaning and identity.

In his extensive review of the consumer culture literature, Featherstone (1990) identified three main approaches to consumption. The first theme was 'the production of consumption'. The expansion of scientific management and Fordism at the turn of the twentieth century necessitated the construction of new markets and the education of the public to become consumers through advertising and other media (Ewen 1976). This process was intensified in post-Fordism as leisure time pursuits, the arts and culture were filtered through the culture industry (Lash and Urry 1994). The second theme concerned 'modes of consumption', focusing on the ways that different groups engaged in consumption practice, emphasizing various lifestyles which demarcated social relationships. Within this context, knowledge becomes important: knowledge of new goods, their social and cultural value, and how to use them appropriately. The third category comprised a compilation of themes concerned with 'consuming dreams, images and pleasure'. Some of these included issues of excess and waste, the creative potential of mass culture, the aestheticization of everyday life, and the collapse of boundaries between high and popular culture.

The focus on consumption in defining one's identity has led to a plethora of research that has focused on the cultural significance of shopping and shopping sites (Douglas 1997; Falk 1997; Campbell 1997; Miller 1997). The idea that consumers use consumption as a means of constructing their identities has significant implications for retailing. Shopping malls facilitate consumer fantasies; they are public spaces that become appropriated for forms of social interaction that are in no way a result of the efforts of retailing institutions themselves. The need to be sympathetic to aspects of hedonic consumption has led some retailers to place more emphasis on the entertainment aspects of retailing, or 'entertailing', as a competitive strategy. The range of activities is endless, from face painting for children in shopping malls, to singles' nights in grocery stores, to off-road test tracks in Land Rover dealerships (Arnold and Reynolds 2003). However, the meaning that consumers give to the shopping experience may have less to do with the activities of retailers than with the perceptions and meanings that individuals give to a specific time and space. In some instances shopping could be incidental to the whole experience. For example, Brown (1998) discovered that shopping among students on a Saturday afternoon could be more about shopping for a date that Saturday night than about shopping for a pair of shoes.

Credit and consumption: addressing the missing link

There is a considerable body of literature that charts the development of consumer culture and the centrality of consumption in everyday life. Yet curiously, the cultural independence and power of money remains largely unquestioned (Zelizer 1994). This observation is particularly significant with respect to consumer credit and its role in underpinning consumption. Daniel Bell (1976) describes consumer society as resting on the pillars of three social interventions – mass production, mass marketing and mass finance, or consumer credit – but he does not provide an assessment of the role of credit, merely maintains that it is important. George Ritzer (2001) goes further by suggesting that consumer credit is the linchpin that holds consumer society together. Calder maintains (1999) that no single linchpin can account for the vitality of modern consumer culture, but the importance of credit should not be underestimated.

One of the first commentators on the culture of money was Simmel in his major work *The Philosophy of Money* (1978). Simmel's interest in money and the development of the money economy was driven not by an urge to understand the economics of money, but by a desire to address the issue of money as a sign and symbol of modern culture. He demonstrated how money was symptomatic of modern forms of interaction and embedded in life in contexts other than the economic. The meaning of money is intimately connected to how we use it, to our propensity to spend, invest, save or hoard the money we have. Credit is of particular interest within money cultures since it enables people to hold on to some view of reality about a future date or possibly another location in which the transaction will be completed.

Taking Simmel's analysis of money culture further, Allen and Pryke (1999) make the distinction between money cultures and cultured monies. At the level of cultural practices there are many ways in which money has been defined. Following Zelizer (1994), it is possible to identify how money is transformed from one social context to the next. Within the household the use of money may comprise very different sets of social relations, such as those involved in gift-giving, or social welfare payments. Moral practices may serve to regulate monetary relationships in one context while utilitarian logic may suffice in another. Thus, people improvise and personalize and differentiate monies, which reflects what money symbolizes in societies at particular moments in their development. Increasingly there is a willingness on the part of enterprising individuals to 'financialize' the future, taking risks and reading their lifestyles in a monetized way.

The financialization of daily life is a theme taken up by Martin, who argues that it becomes the means through which people are measurably different. Martin (2002: 17) maintains that

> when personal finance becomes the way in which ordinary people are invited to participate in that larger abstraction called the economy, a new set of signals are introduced as to how life is to be lived and what it is for.

He makes the distinction between consumption and credit in Fordism and post-Fordism. The Fordist dream for Americans was a clear separation between the present and the future. To be a dreamscape, the future had to be different from the present in describable terms that could be saved for. The elimination of savings that increase consumer debt loads is akin to post-Fordist just-in-time production that reduces levels of inventory but also means that we live in a perpetual present without a buffer for the future.

A similar sentiment is articulated by Ritzer (1995), who argues that the implosion of monies earned in the past, present and future constitutes a market-driven manipulation of time that increases expenditure at the expense of mounting disorientation. Consumer reliance on credit has become an accepted part of everyday life and directly linked with the desire for goods in a competitive society. Individuals must decide between accepting the immediate benefits of consumer credit or the limiting choices when credit is not available. It would seem that many consumers are choosing the former option, since the market for credit has rapidly expanded in most advanced societies.

So endemic has consumer credit become that, as far as the financial services industry is concerned, individuals not accepting credit are viewed as atypical (Klein 1999) and those denied access, inferior (Burton *et al.* 2004). Access to credit has therefore become a central feature in a system of economic status recognition, an accepted passage point to being a fully fledged member of the consumer society. Detailed credit histories can be stigmatizing or enabling; they legitimate consumers. An individual's credit report provides an 'objective' measure of citizenship and personal financial responsibility; it is also a means of reproducing inequality. The role of financial institutions is central to understanding the development and maintenance of consumer credit, but to date its influence has been largely defined quite narrowly in the context of credit card providers (Klein 1999; Ritzer 1995).

The apparent lack of attention to consumer credit within the consumption literature has occurred for several reasons. First, consumer credit has long been the province of economists. In this respect it is not too dissimilar from other areas of finance and financial services. Until the mid-1980s, research in these fields was dominated by economic theory, economic models and quantitative research techniques. One only needs to take a cursory glance through textbooks on credit scoring and the relationship between credit and risk (Thomas, Edelman and Crook 2004) to identify that this bias remains. The focus on economics in discussions of credit is even apparent in historical works (Calder 1999), although some studies, such as Martha Olney's (1991) account of the rise of consumer credit in the United States during the 1920s, entitled *Buy Now, Pay Later*, are written in a more accessible style. Delving into uncharted and unfamiliar literature that uses different theoretical approaches and research techniques can be off-putting, especially to scholars who are interested in broader social trends.

A second reason for the lack of attention could be the lack of glamour, fun and frivolity of credit compared to other areas of consumption. Gronow and Warde (2001: 4) maintain that 'ordinary consumption', typically activities that 'are neither highly visible nor in any way special and which often stand in a subsidiary relation to some other primary or more conscious activity', have been marginalized within the consumption literature. The sanctioning of credit as a business process often lacks the appeal of other developments that emphasize the extraordinary rather than the ordinary and the conspicuous rather than the inconspicuous aspects of consumption. The granting of credit is a serious business compared to researching hedonistic consumption. Consumers often find dealing with their finances a rather dull business (Burton 1994), and researchers may feel likewise.

A third contributory factor in the lack of attention to credit relates to invisibility. Calder (1999) argues that credit has few material artefacts that can be 'read' as text and be studied and researched over time. Historically, relatively few advertisements have exclusively focused on credit or have given credit a high profile (Olney 1991). Studying the ledgers of large retailers has been one strategy employed by business historians, alongside the study of trade journals, annual reports and public relations pamphlets (Jeacle and Walsh 2002). However, in some instances the trail is thin. It is understandable that some credit institutions would not keep and preserve meticulous records, and loan sharks and pawnbrokers had little interest in doing so, let alone in making any records public. However, the lack of records is also a prohibiting factor in studying the giants of the consumer credit industry of the twentieth century (Calder 1999).

Credit's invisibility is also significant in another respect: the issue of confidentiality governing its acquisition and use by consumers. Money is deemed a private affair often not spoken about in public – or private, for that matter. Even between spouses it is a confidential affair, which perhaps is a testament to its importance. This level of secrecy does make it a difficult area to research (Pahl 1989). Miller (2001) argues that within industrial societies what tends to matter most to people is occurring behind the closed doors of the private sphere. It is for this reason that marketers want to penetrate the home as a site for research to obtain a more accurate reading of the nature of social relations. This issue applies as much to budgeting as it does to other areas of material culture. Secrecy as a barrier to studying credit is as pertinent today as it was over a hundred years ago. In advanced societies awash with credit there remains a degree of reluctance to speak about one's financial affairs. In this respect, secrecy almost takes the form of a consumption ritual where credit and debt are concerned (see Otnes and Lowrey 2004 on consumption rituals). This characteristic is neatly summed up by Williams (2004: 55) when she notes:

> I know a lot more about my friends' sex lives than I do about their finances. . . . The one thing they will never permit to be known about them, to any friend, the only thing that cannot be discussed, is how much money they have in the bank. . . . Therefore, we have no joint knowledge of how we are dealing with the money issues in our lives; each of us faces the problem alone.

The acquisition and use of credit is an activity that remains a social stigma in some quarters and interpreted as evidence of lack of restraint, an inability to plan and budget.

A final reason why credit has gone unstudied could be due to its lack of interesting or strong leadership. As Calder (1999: 13) explains, the consumer credit industry was not

> built through the vision and energy of a Henry Ford. . . . It was built up mostly by shopkeepers, credit managers, reformed loan sharks and unsung reformers, people who shared the values, as well as the anonymity, of the middle classes. The absence of notable personages, not to mention the documentary evidence they tend to produce, is another reason credit has gone unstudied.

It is also noteworthy that stereotypes of the accountancy profession have not always enjoyed a positive image in popular culture, which may have deterred some scholars from studying it. However, a recent project that assessed images of accountants portrayed in films since the mid-1930s indicated that the perception of the profession is not as dull and boring as one might suspect (Dimnik and Felton 2006). It is a combination of the factors noted above that has contributed to the dearth of accounts of credit and society.

Credit and consumer society

Chapter 1 demonstrated that credit has a very long history in most societies. Credit's form and characteristics have changed over time, and the acquisition and use of credit has been embedded in existing social class, gender and ethnic relations. The purpose of this section of the chapter is to address the relationship between the growth of credit and the emergence of consumer society. The availability of credit has been intimately related to the development of consumer society and specifically the ability to consume, and this practice has a longer tradition in the United States than in other countries. In the early nineteenth century, buying durable goods with cash was the norm, and financial guides of the Victorian era counselled against running up accounts and getting into debt. In the late nineteenth century several of the largest department stores and mail order agencies actively promoted cash-only policies, which they claimed saved customers 25–50 per cent as compared with goods from credit-granting stores. Sears supported cash purchases particularly strongly and used its catalogue to warn consumers of 'the evil of the credit system' (quoted in Calder 1999: 71). However, it was an ideal difficult to live up to when cash was in short supply. Trade journals and account books of retailers revealed discounts of between 10 per cent and 30 per cent for payment in cash. Often these favourable terms were a result of retailers overextending their own credit and creating problems with cash flow.

By the end of the first decade of the twentieth century, consumer purchases had become increasingly based on credit. Evidence that US households used credit to fund the purchase of durable goods has been described as 'scattered but uniform'. Calder (1999) maintains that in the United States credit for consumers was invented twice over. The first occasion was between 1910 and 1925, when licensed lenders and retailers made financing available to credit-hungry consumers. In the United States, total consumer debt outstanding doubled in each of the first two decades of the twentieth century. It doubled again in the 1920s, increasing from $3.3 billion in 1920 to over $7.6 billion in 1929. Household debt nearly tripled between 1900 and 1918, and nearly doubled during the 1920s.

Similar trends in using credit to underpin consumption were evident in Britain and Japan. Johnson (1985) notes that there was an enormous growth of goods bought on hire purchase agreements in Britain after World War I. In 1921 there were 16 million hire purchase agreements in force, and 4 million new agreements were being entered into annually. By 1935 the corresponding figures had risen to 24 million and 7 million respectively. The goods that were predominantly purchased on credit were major items and closely resembled the categories of goods purchased in the United States, namely cars, sewing machines, furniture, pianos, wireless sets and gramophones. Approximately 80 per cent of cars, 90 per cent of sewing machines, 75 per cent of furniture and 95 per cent of pianos, wireless sets and gramophones were purchased on instalment plans.

In Japan, consumer financing took longer to become established. Gordon (2006) notes that around 1900 there were a number of foreign companies providing instalment finance in Japan, but by far the largest supplier was the Singer Sewing Machine Company. By the mid-1920s, credit was being used to purchase household goods including furniture, ceramic or lacquer products, and clothing. In the last category, men's expensive Western suits were the items bought most frequently on credit. Another credit provider is the company now known as Yamaha, which began selling pianos and organs in 1924. By the mid-1930s a third of all car sales were on credit, but most of these were taxis, not cars purchased by individual consumers. By 1934 an estimated 8 per cent of goods were paid for by credit.

In the United States, consumers reduced their debt loads during the Great Depression, and by 1933 only two-thirds as much debt was outstanding. Explanations for the reduction in debt during the Depression are not self-evident. In *Time and Money: The Making of Consumer Culture*, Cross (1993) argues that economic hardship during the Depression was unevenly distributed. The price of goods and services dropped faster than hourly wages, so that those who remained in employment were better off and could possibly afford to pay off debts and live off existing income. Those who were impoverished would have had difficulties in accessing credit, since they could not be trusted to repay what they owed without a steady income.

After the US Depression the growth of goods bought on credit was even stronger than during the 1920s. Purchases of 'furniture, household appliances, pianos and other musical instruments, radios and phonographs, house furnishings, jewelry and watches, books and maps' all witnessed significant increases (Olney 1991: 82). The purchase of a car was a major instalment credit purchase for many American households. In 1919, 5 per cent of households purchased a car on credit, but by 1929, 15 per cent did so. Approximately 70 per cent of new and 65 per cent of used cars were purchased on instalments in the 1920s. Without credit financing, households would not have been able to support this level of consumption (Olney 1991).

Retailers came to learn that credit was a powerful selling force. Marshall Fields, a Chicago department store, had generated 180,000 charge accounts by the late 1920s. Sears, Roebuck & Co. introduced credit facilities for the first time in 1919, and seven years later credit was being extended liberally with limited investigation in what became known as the 'No Money Down' era. In the United Kingdom, Harrods had a cash-only trading policy prior to 1885, but by 1926 the store was conducting 80 per cent of its business on credit (Jeacle and Walsh 2002). New lenders played a central role in the expansion of consumer credit. Prior to World War I, the options open to households that wished to borrow money included banks, small loan institutes, pawnbrokers and instalment buying. Instalment buying tended to be extended by the sellers or manufacturers of consumer goods. For example, furniture and pianos were purchased on instalment credit extended by the seller. The Singer Sewing Machine Company had offered instalment plans since 1856. Banks rarely lent money to customers for the purchase of durable goods. Only three banks provided small loans for customers in 1925. Personal credit was still frowned upon and factory workers were not considered a lucrative market (Germain 1996). Furthermore, furniture stores took an active role in serving as their own collection agents and frequently had a service desk for this purpose at the back of the store. The regular monthly payment involved contact with consumers and presented an opportunity to cross-sell. It was standard practice for retailers to display a cash price and an instalment credit price.

By the 1920s, most instalment credit extended to households was financed not by sellers or manufacturers but by sales finance companies, which were separate corporate entities that bought the buyer's promise to repay. Olney (1991) notes that in 1929, 40 per cent of consumer instalment credit was provided by finance companies and a little over 5 per cent by commercial banks. Their numbers had increased from less than 100 in 1920 to well over 1,000 in 1928. Two of the most successful US consumer finance companies prior to 1930 were Household Finance Corporation and Beneficial Industrial Loan Corporation. Beneficial was launched in 1914 in New Jersey, and by 1932 operated 303 offices and had around $40 million in loans. Household Finance Corporation was established in 1881, and in 1882 the first advertisements for the business appeared in local newspapers: 'Money loaned on furniture, pianos, horses, wagons and personal property at low rates without removal and all other articles of value' (Germain 1996: 160). However, once the banks realized that it was an expanding, lucrative market, they made their presence felt, and by 1939 25 per cent of instalment lending was written by commercial banks compared with 30 per cent by finance companies. However, it is worth putting instalment credit in its context of credit provision *per se*. In *Financing the Consumer* (1931), Clark noted that the greater part of the market share of the small loan market in 1930 was held by unlicensed lenders (28.9 per cent) and pawnbrokers (23.2 per cent), with personal finance companies having less than 20 per cent of the market (19.3 per cent).

Despite the development and success in bringing into effect a new credit system, the old moral strictures about the evils of credit remained. The more successful the credit system became, the more it began to lose its legitimacy. Rising debt levels caused concern about what was disparagingly termed *'consumptive' credit*. Consumption was a colloquial term for tuberculosis, a serious disease of the time that sometimes led to death. There was an undercurrent of support for the view that credit was a threat to the morals of society and could bring economic catastrophe. For example, Henry Ford's personal stand against credit was reflected in the company's policy that consumers should pay cash or take out a plan to save for a vehicle, which persisted long after it became apparent that the policy was inflicting damage on the company's sales. The famous department store Macy's ran an advertising campaign throughout the 1920s with the slogan 'No one is in debt to Macy's'.

Its campaign was repealed only in 1939 when it become too unprofitable to sustain.

There was concern among prominent credit providers that a counter-revolution could be in store, with a customer backlash against credit that would threaten their businesses or generate legislative restrictions. Furthermore, there was embarrassment among some consumers who had bought goods on instalment plans. General Motors Automobile Company (GMAC) was one of the biggest providers of consumer credit, and, fearful that it would lose significant amounts of business as a result of a potential counter-revolution, it took the proactive step of commissioning a Harvard academic, Professor Seligman, to undertake what was at the time the largest study of consumer credit yet carried out. His findings were published in 1927 in his book *Economics of Installment Buying; A Study in Consumer's Credit*. The research design included five strands, including a consumer study that analysed data on consumers' purchasing patterns in clothing, furniture, jewellery and hardware. A second element was a merchandise study that provided information about selling in key industries. A third part was a dealers study that included a survey of car dealers who used GMAC financing to determine the percentage of cars bought on credit. The fourth strand was a repossession study that examined cases of consumer delinquency and potential strategies of prevention. The final aspect was the depression study, which sought to examine the fate of debtors in adverse economic conditions. The culmination of the report supported the view that credit had many positive features. Rather than being the frittering away of money, it could be put to productive use, as in the case of purchasing durable goods to make something new, such as purchasing a sewing machine to make clothes and household furnishings. Although the report was not widely read, it was authoritative and had a substantial impact upon policymakers with respect to changing views about credit.

In the late 1920s, credit was reinvented for a second time as *consumer credit*. The linguistic different between *consumptive* and *consumer credit* was not purely one of semantics but heralded a victory over Victorian attitudes towards consumptive debt. The remarketing of credit as consumer credit gave moral support to its legal and institutional basis. This is not to suggest that credit's critics went away, but rather that their power to dominate the public debate was reduced. The perceived legitimacy of consumer credit used by the middle classes to fund the purchase of durable consumer goods marked a decisive development in the maturation of American consumer culture (Baritz 1982; Cochran 1985; Galbraith 1969; Lasch 1978; Bell 1976). Prior to this landmark, consumers had not been perceived as worthy of credit. As a consequence, consumers received access to their future earnings and were publicly legitimized as being consumers (Calder 1999). This period was a major turning point, a new era in which a culture of thrift and rugged individualism gave way to consumerism and personal debt.

Paul Nystrom, a pioneering marketing scholar of the period, observed, 'not a few people in western nations have departed from old-time standards of religion and philosophy' (1928: 68). Likewise, Professor Leach, another marketing guru, noted that the old order of 'abstinence, self-denial, practical utilitarianism, renunciation, and saving were being increasingly undermined and discredited as the pre-industrial environment which helped to sustain them disappeared' (quoted in Fullerton and Punj 1998: 396–397). This change is illustrated by a young person's experiences of credit growing up in a Midwest town in the 1920s:

> First, when my mother bought her sewing machine; second, when my father bought his reaper, third, when the family purchased a piano; fourth, when I bought my first good suit . . .; and fifth, when I purchased my *Encyclopaedia Britannica* in place of the college education that was beyond my reach.
>
> (Hanch 1927: 660)

By the 1930s the availability of credit financing was being used as a tool to actively market products in advertising (Olney 1991).

It is also noteworthy that, from its outset, consumer credit was a highly feminized activity, which reflected important social and cultural changes. One English visitor to New York commented upon the fact that everybody seemed to be living beyond their means, and women were some of the worst offenders (Steevens 1897). The ideology of the male breadwinner and female carer and homemaker was one that assigned women as the buyers and spenders within households. This feature was reinforced by the concept of Mrs Consumer (Rutherford 2003) – a theme that has persisted (Scott 1976; Bartos 1989; Cunningham and Roberts 2006). In this context, credit from the very beginning was women's credit that relied on their husband's earning power. It was estimated that at least 80 per cent of personal credit was extended to women (Kniffen 1914). Women's dominance in the use of credit marked a significant shift in gender relationships within households, in which women traditionally were given a small cash allowance for the weekly budget, or money to meet a special need. For some women, access to credit was a liberating experience, but it was for this reason that women were criticized and stigmatized for being spendthrifts and unable to manage debt. However, records of retail store credit contradict this view, since there were low levels of default and retail store credit was a highly feminized activity. Indeed, the view that women cannot manage money, find it difficult to resist temptation, do not understand the value of money, buy now and worry how it will be paid for later remains a contemporary debate in some circles.

A third major change was the arrival of the credit card in the 1950s. Americans remain the most avid users of credit cards, with 1.5 billion cards held by nearly 158 million cardholders. A typical US adult has four retail cards, three bank cards, one phone card, one gasoline card and one travel, entertainment or miscellaneous corporate credit card (Manning 2000). In the United States it was the consumer-citizen who was a supporter of the American way of life as opposed to Soviet communism, and was seen as a responsible consumer taking advantage of free choice. In contrast to the nineteenth-century puritan ethic, with the emphasis on saving, avoiding debts and simple living, shopping became something of a 'patriotic act' that promoted the American way of life as one that was superior to other economic and political systems (Spring 2003: 4).

Dysfunctional effects of credit in consumer society

Credit has underpinned many aspects of consumption and has been instrumental in the development of what has become known as consumer society. Though the benefits of being an active participant in consumer society are considerable, the cultural significance of consumption in defining one's identity has led to some unintended and disastrous consequences where credit is concerned. In this section we will focus on three aspects of dysfunctional effects of credit and consumer culture, namely addictive shopping, compensatory consumption and gambling.

Initially, these three different activities may appear very distinct from each other. But there is growing evidence to suggest that similar processes lie behind all addictions, whether they have a behavioural or a chemical element. According to this interpretation, addictions to gambling, shopping, exercise or sex have more in common than they have differences. There are a number of common features associated with most types of addiction. Addiction dominates the addict's life, leading to cravings and a complete preoccupation with the habit. Addicts do not participate in the activity because they like it but because they are compelled to do so; they believe they have little choice in the matter. Another integral feature is what is referred to as tolerance. As time goes by, the addict needs more of the activity or substance to get the same high. Withdrawal can be problematic for all addictions but changing shopping or gambling behaviour can result in excessive moodiness, irritability, nausea, headaches and sweats (Phillips 2006).

The belief that individuals may have a predisposition to certain types of addictive behaviour such as shopping and gambling has raised the issue of the role of genetics in consumer behaviour. This has led to a rethinking of our notions of free will (Hirschman and Stern 2001). For example, should consumers be excused from behaviour that would normally be considered unacceptable on the basis that they have a particular gene that makes them behave in a certain way? What are some of the implications for consumer policy?

Compulsive and compensatory consumption

Buying addiction has a long history. In the early nineteenth century the psychiatric literature provides evidence of lack of control in respect of buying behaviour. Yet it was not until the 1980s that research in the field began to increase momentum, and contributions from other academic disciplines (sociology, psychology, social anthropology, medicine) appeared. Compulsive shopping, compulsive consumption (Faber, O'Guinn and Krych 1987), compulsive buying (O'Guinn and Faber 1989; Benson 2000), addictive shopping (Elliott 1994), compensatory consumption (Gould 1997; Woodruffe 1996; Rindfleisch, Burroughs and Denton 1997), impulsive buying (Wood 1998; Rook 1987; Beatty and Ferrell 1998; Bellenger, Robertson and Hirschman 1978) and excessive shopping (Dittmar and Drury 2000) have all been used to describe the dysfunctional processes whereby consumers are compelled to purchase regardless of the negative social consequences of doing so (Baudrillard 1998; Dodd 1994; Elliot, Eccles and Gournay 1996). Additional sub-types of addictive shopping have also emerged, including collecting and compulsive gift-giving (including self-gifts) (Benson 2000; Friese 2000). Compulsive consumption has been investigated over a number of domains in addition to shopping, including drug abuse (Hirschman 1992), alcoholism (Blum and Noble 1994) and kleptomania (Marlatt *et al.* 1988).

Most research on compulsive consumption focuses on advanced industrial societies, including the United States (O'Guinn and Faber 1989), United Kingdom (Elliott 1994), Canada (Valence, d'Astous and Fortier 1988), Germany (Scherhorn *et al.* 1990) and Belgium (Dittmar and Drury 2000). However, Park and Burns (2005) maintain that compulsive buying among the fashion-conscious is also being spurred on by credit card spending in the Far East. The numbers of consumers who engage in compulsive consumption or impulsive buying are not widely documented, so the scale of the problem is not fully understood. Estimates suggest that compulsive shopping affects 2–5 per cent of the population in developed Western economies. If these estimates are correct, more than 10 million adults in the United States and around two million in the United Kingdom are affected (Dittmar and Drury 2000).

The compulsive aspects of consumption have been reflected in the phrase 'I Shop Therefore I Am' (Benson 2000), reflecting the need to shop to reinforce a sense of identity. Shopping provides people with a means to discover who they are, giving form to parts of the self that might otherwise have remained hidden. In this sense, shopping can be viewed as a process through which individuals solve the problem of personal identity (Campbell 2004). Giddens (1991: 198) maintains, 'The consumption of ever-novel goods becomes in some part a substitute for the genuine development of self; appearance replaces essence.'

Compulsive consumption tends to be gendered, since the shopping experi-ence has emerged as a major leisure activity for women and a form of self-expression facilitating the construction and maintenance of their identities (Elliott 1994; Dittmar and Drury 2000). However, it needs to be acknowledged that shopping has not always been feminized. For example, until the late nineteenth century contemporary accounts of shopping portrayed the shop-keeper as a woman and the shopper as a man (Jones 1996). Dittmar, Beattie and Friese (1995) demonstrate that there are gender divisions in the goods that male and female compulsive shoppers purchase. Men tend to purchase instrumental and leisure items projecting a sense of independence and activity, whereas women tend to purchase symbolic and self-expressive goods concerned with appearance and emotional aspects of their identity. With respect to the socio-demographic profile of addicted individuals, factors such as education, social class, marital status, or urban or rural origin appear to have little relevance. The frequency and duration of compulsory consumption are extremely variable, but it tends to occur at specific times of the year and on specific days of the week, and at particular retail outlets (Wood 1998; Benson 2000; Friese 2000).

Compulsive shoppers give various reasons for their addiction, including improving their self-esteem and confidence; improving their self-image, for example by purchasing clothes that make them feel better; and improving their mood, including preventing suicidal tendencies (Elliott 1994). A sense of regret is a sentiment that many compulsive consumers exhibit. Dittmar and Drury (2000) maintain that regret is a multifaceted phenomenon that includes regret over the low quality of goods purchased, the value for money they offer and their unsuitability for the intended purpose. Compulsive shoppers also mention that they did not benefit as much psychologically as they thought they would, and rue the financial implications of their actions.

The financial implications of compulsive consumption, especially its relationship to money and credit, is an issue that is raised by most compulsive shoppers (Faber and O'Guinn 1988). Hanley and Wilhelm (1992: 16) have demonstrated that compulsive shoppers, more than 'normal' shoppers, indicate that 'the self can be reflected through money attitudes, beliefs, and behaviours as well as through ownership of specific goods'.

Compulsive spenders reported a greater likelihood than 'normal' consumers to be preoccupied with the importance of money as a solution to problems and to use money as a means of comparison. Additionally, compulsive spenders were more likely to report the need to spend money in a manner that was reflective of status and power. In contrast, the compulsive spenders were less likely than 'normal' consumers to take a traditional, more conservative approach to money. Compulsive spenders were more likely to report that they did not have enough money for their needs, especially in comparison to friends. Finally, compulsive spenders reported a greater tendency than did 'normal' consumers to feel a sense of conflict over the spending of money (Hanley and Wilhelm 1992: 16–17).

Reports of spending money set aside to pay the mortgage, council tax and utility bills to a point where homes are under threat of repossession are not unusual among addictive shoppers (Elliott 1994). The availability of credit cards and other readily accessible forms of revolving credit facilitates compulsive buying. Lenders increasing credit card limits when the existing limit is reached proved too much of a temptation for many individuals. The ability to remortgage property to generate additional funds, along with consolidation loans whereby credit card debt could be bundled into a personal loan to reduce monthly payments and reduce credit card balances to zero, are strategies used to keep the true amount of debt hidden. Lying to partners and family members about financial matters is also a persistent feature of the addict's behaviour. Yet the compulsion to purchase often overshadows the severe financial consequences of doing so (Dittmar and Drury 2000). Dealing with the severe financial consequences of compulsive consumption is often incorporated as part of the treatment of the addiction, whether that takes the form of mutual self-help (Debtors Anonymous), economic recovery (financial recovery counselling) or the adoption of alternative lifestyles that rely less on materialism.

Compensatory consumption is different from compulsive consumption, although compensatory consumption can also be addictive. Compensatory consumption refers to individuals who shop to compensate for something that is lacking in their life, so the motive for shopping can differ from person to person. Compensatory shoppers may use shopping as an escape from the mundane aspects of everyday life, as a form of mood repair to alleviate depression, or as a way of coping with marital problems. Friese (2000) maintains that the perceived discrepancy of the addict between the actual self and the ideal self is an excellent predictor of buying addiction tendencies. Back in the 1960s, Miller (1968) observed, 'Because you see the main thing today is – shopping. Years ago a person, if he was unhappy, didn't know what to do with himself – he'd go to church, start a revolution – something. Today you're unhappy? Can't figure it out? What is the salvation? Go shopping' However, Zukin (2005: 7) argues that while shopping is consuming our lives, it can ultimately bring less satisfaction. A huge variety of goods are for sale but we find difficulties in finding exactly what we want. 'Each store promises happiness, every label guarantees high quality – but we're still dreaming of the virtuous ideal: Truth. Beauty. Value.'

In the late 1980s Richard Elliott estimated that there were upwards of 700,000 shopaholics in the United Kingdom, who were mostly women and otherwise living mundane, unfulfilled lives. The financial consequences of their consumption were considerable, with many individuals owing amounts equal to the then national average yearly wage. Elliott, Eccles and Gournay (1996) found that compensatory consumption was used to take revenge on a partner. For example, a wife might spent huge amounts on her husband's credit card if she feels betrayed or hard done by. In this respect, Zelizer's (1994) analysis of the social meaning of money can be extended to include revenge that replaces personal bonds with calculative, instrumental, materialist concerns. Revenge money can be squandered – wasted on non-essential items, including going out or buying clothes – without any feelings of guilt.

Both compulsive and compensatory consumption are contemporary aspects of consumer behaviour in advanced societies that have developed as a result of increasing shopping opportunities and the central role of consumption and shopping in everyday life. What effects remote shopping that can be undertaken 24 hours a day, 365 days of the year has on both these aspects of consumer behaviour is not clear. Burton (2002b) has highlighted the importance of a plethora of methods of remote shopping and the social interaction involved in each when consumers are not required to leave their own home. Koran *et al.* (2006) maintain that ease of access is exacerbating levels of compulsive buying in the United States, while Clarke (1998) provides a detailed account of consumers shopping using a catalogue and a localized classified paper within the home by social groups precluded from expensive high street shopping. Zukin (2005: 238) notes the effects that stores opening in Sundays have had on the propensity to shop:

> Sundays lost their quiet, restful – even sleepy– quality. Instead of going to church, having big family lunches, playing outdoors, or just lying around, we began a new routine of having brunch, piling into the car, and going to the mall. The Internet drives these habits to farther extreme. When we can shop anytime and anywhere, we wind up shopping more.

One would suspect that remote shopping would be more of a temptation for addictive and compensatory shopping because of the relatively easy access it affords. Furthermore, online shopping necessitates the use of paying with plastic, and while that may not necessarily mean credit, from studies that have been undertaken in conventional shopping settings we know that it often does.

Gambling

Gambling has a very long history in many societies. McMillen (1996: 6) maintains that it has occurred in nearly all cultures and in every period of time. Gambling in China can be traced back more than 4,000 years. 'Excavations at Ur (2000 BC), Crete (1800 BC), Egypt (1600 BC), and India (1000 BC) have unearthed dice and gaming boards; betting on horse-racing was common among the Hittites (4000 BC).' In many societies, gambling involves an economic transaction whereby participants make bets with money, making a calculated assessment of winning or losing. However, McMillen argues that this is not always the case. In some pre-capitalist societies, including Bali, China, parts of Africa, and Australian Aboriginal communities, gambling is an activity that has often been organized around religious or communal activities that have little direct economic significance. Despite gambling's existence in most societies, its function as a form of consumption and its relationship to consumer credit are often neglected in contemporary studies of consumer society. Kingma (1997: 174) maintains that reasons for this neglect concern the oppositional characteristics of gambling with the predominant ideology of consumption. While consumption focuses on 'the glamorous, the exciting and the happy-go-lucky aspects, addiction emphasises the negative sides, that is stress, debt, filth, disease and crime'.

In capitalist societies, gambling is an activity that has increasingly been undertaken to maximize profit from the transaction. It is a leisure pursuit that has been practised in one form or another across all social classes (Clapson 1992; Reith 1999). The risk taking and the potentially destructive effects of gambling for the individual, their family and society have attracted considerable attention. At the end of the eighteenth century and during the first quarter of the nineteenth, anti-gambling literature in the United States and Britain highlighted numerous instances of despair resulting in financial ruin and, at worst, suicide as a result of gambling losses. Duelling over gambling debts was common, and a regular cause of death and injury to either or both parties (Miers 2004).

Contemporary discussions of gambling draw on insights from a variety of disciplinary traditions, much of which can be broadly grouped under the term 'gambling studies', which emerged in the second half of the twentieth century. This diverse body of work 'includes behavioural studies of gamblers, the investigation of "problem" gambling, mathematical analysis of different forms of wagering, economic analysis of gambling patterns and studies of gambling policy and the law' (McMillen 1996: 7). The medicalization of gambling as an addiction, with the gambler being described as someone who is sick and has an illness, remains a point of controversy (M. Walker 1996; Reith 1999). However, the phrase 'compulsive gambling' is one that is widely understood and used in the same way that 'compulsive shopping' has been a term used to refer to a facet of human nature. A survey conducted by the British National Centre for Social Research in 2000 found that around 1 per cent of the population had a pathological gambling problem, and trends are upwards, especially among women. In the United States it has been estimated that 10 per cent of the population have a gambling problem (Hugel and Kelly 2002).

The view that gambling can result in significant problems of indebtedness is unequivocal. Rather less attention has been given to the relationship between credit and gambling, yet it is an important area of investigation (Smith 2004). Clapson (1992) maintains that legal credit bookmakers emerged in Britain in the 1860s and were an early example of credit being advertised in the sporting press. Their clientele were mainly middle-class consumers who could afford to keep a cheque account with a bookmaker. Since gambling debts could not be legally recovered, a 'sizeable regular wage and an address in a respectable suburban or artisan district would have been required for a bookmaker to extend trust and credit' (Clapson 1992: 27). A rather different aspect of contemporary gambling has been provided by Mark Griffiths's (1995) study of adolescents with a slot machine gambling habit. The group of adolescents used informal methods of obtaining credit, including borrowing and stealing money from friends and family, to fund their fruit machine gambling.

In the earlier discussion of addictive and compensatory consumption, online shopping was raised as a potential vehicle for enticing more people into debt. The same arguments might also be relevant to online gambling. Record numbers of consumers are signing up to online gambling sites, which were estimated to number 2,000 in 2005. Many operate offshore and in what have been described as countries with questionable legal environments (Hugel and Kelly 2002). In 2005 there were an estimated 23 million online gamblers, of whom 8 million live in the United States and 4 million in the United Kingdom. The industry is estimated to be worth $12 billion a year. As with most other purchases on the internet, credit cards are the preferred way to play. Online gambling therefore provides a direct and systematic link between gambling and credit that has hitherto largely remained hidden. The exact number of gaming transactions paid for by credit cards has not been made public by MasterCard International and Visa International, despite the fact that they require online casinos to include a unique code in their transactions. However, information from independent sources suggests that credit cards are used in about 90 per cent of online gaming transactions (Simpson 2001). In the United States there has been discussion of prohibiting banks and credit card companies from processing payments for online bets, although there is some concern at the level of monitoring that would be required to enforce this policy (Wolfe 2006).

Casinos are also tempting targets for credit card fraud because they are twenty-four-hour operations and criminals are aware that personnel may not be as alert to fraud in the middle of the night. Furthermore, fraudsters are less likely to attract suspicion by making large bets (Mitchell 2004). There are also concerns about the use of internet sites for money-laundering purposes. As a money-laundering protection measure there are recommendations that punters should be paid their winnings in the same way that the money was deposited (Hugel and Kelly 2002).

Conclusion

Theories of consumption and consumer society have proved instructive in helping us understand how society has changed and the role of consumption in constructing a sense of identity. Most accounts of consumption neglect to take into account the role of credit in underpinning current levels of purchasing power. In this respect, credit has much in common with other areas of ordinary consumption that have also been marginalized. It is clearly evident that at the end of the nineteenth and the beginning of the twentieth century credit was an important factor underpinning consumption in the United States and Britain. It was also an era when a range of new lenders came on the scene. While credit has enabled consumers to fulfil more of their consumption requirements, it has also facilitated a range of dysfunctional consumer behaviour, including compulsive consumption and gambling.

Questions

1   Explain why the consumption of credit has been marginalized within the consumption literature.
2   What were the ideological differences been the terms 'consumptive credit' and 'consumer credit'?
3   What were the drivers and inhibitors of credit adoption in the United States in the 1920s?
4   Explain the relationship between compulsive consumption and consumer society.

Further reading

Bell, D. (1976) *The Cultural Contradictions of Capitalism*, New York: Basic Books.

Calder, L. (1999) *Financing the American Dream: A Cultural History of Consumer Credit*, Princeton, NJ: Princeton University Press.

Dittmar, H. and Drury, J. (2000) 'Self-image: is it in the bag? A qualitative comparison between "ordinary" and "excessive" consumers', *Journal of Economic Psychology*, 21: 109–142.

Elliott, R. (1994) 'Addictive consumption: function and fragmentation in postmodernity', *Journal of Consumer Policy*, 17: 159–179.

Hanley, A. and Wilhelm, M.S. (1992) 'Compulsive buying: an exploration into self-esteem and money attitudes', *Journal of Economic Psychology*, 13: 5–18.

Jeacle, I. and Walsh, E.J. (2002) 'From moral evaluation to rationalization: accounting and the shifting technologies of credit', *Accounting, Organizations and Society*, 27: 737–761.

McKendrick, N., Brewer, J. and Plumb, J.H. (1982) *The Birth of a Consumer Society: The Commercialization of Eighteenth-Century England*, London: Europa.

Manning, R.D. (2000) *Credit Card Nation: The Consequences of America's Addiction to Credit*, New York: Basic Books.

Olney, M.L. (1991) *Buy Now, Pay Later*, Chapel Hill: University of North Carolina Press.

Ritzer, G. (1995) *Expressing America: A Critique of the Global Credit Card Society*, Thousand Oaks, CA: Pine Forge Press.

Ritzer, G. (2001) *Explorations in the Sociology of Consumption*, London: Sage.

3 Credit and the production of trust

The previous chapter focused on unravelling the complex relationship between credit and consumer society. This chapter will assess the relationship between lenders and borrowers and how this relationship has been transformed as credit has become more deeply embedded in the fabric of consumer society. As more consumers have been willing and able to access credit, new systems have been developed to handle larger volumes of decisions. Central to the lending relationship are discussions of trust and risk and the ways that both have been institutionalized. The first section of the chapter will address the concept of trust in lending relationships and how this has been operationalized in lending decisions. The shift from personal trust to institutional trust is central to this debate. The subsequent sections will address the ways in which lenders have used increasingly sophisticated levels of technology in their lending decisions. The history of credit scoring is discussed, alongside some of its limitations. Behavioural scoring and profit scoring are more recent developments that are concerned with charting the behaviour of existing consumers over time.

Discussions of risk in lending relationships have tended to focus on mainstream institutions and consumers. Far less attention has been paid to alternative credit providers that lend to consumers outside the prime market but do not have access to sophisticated levels of information technology on which to make lending decisions. This parallel market will be addressed as a counter to the contemporary literature. The last section of the chapter will address the spatial aspects of credit relationships.

Trust, credit and consumer society

The lack of academic attention paid to the role of credit in society is paralleled by a dearth of in-depth accounts of the role of trust in credit relationships. Two aspects of trust have attracted attention in financial services. One approach has focused on theoretical and empirical research concerned with the dependence of financial services organizations on the establishment and sustenance of a climate of public trust (Knights *et al.* 2001; Morgan and Knights

1997; Dodd 1994). A second use has been in the context of the construction of the trustworthy consumer through practices including credit rating (Leyshon, Thrift and Pratt 1998), demographic analysis or direct marketing (Knights and Odih 1999).

There is a burgeoning literature on trust in the social sciences, but, despite the vast amount of attention, there is a 'good deal of conceptual confusion regarding the meaning of trust and its place in social life' (Lewis and Weigert 1985: 975). A number of interconnected themes that run through most discussions of trust are particularly relevant to our analysis of credit. By viewing trust as a means of coping with the indeterminacy of other agents, much of the contemporary debate on trust tends to evoke the 'Hobbesian problem' of order (Knights *et al.* 2001). This is the paradox of orderliness in a society of otherwise free and self-interested subjects. Drucker (1990: 89) argues that organization depends on trust, and 'trust is mutual understanding. Not mutual love, not even mutual respect. [But] Predictability'.

Luhmann (1979) suggests that trust and distrust are functionally equivalent strategies for dealing with what he terms the problem of double contingency; that is, where trust has to be granted or withheld in advance of its being confirmed. In essence, trust and distrust constitute relevant responses to 'situations where one must enter into risks one cannot control in advance – or [be] forced to refuse participation' (Luhmann 1979: 129). The attempt to control events in advance through the exercise of power (where the use of power is an option) is an alternative means of influencing 'the selection of actions in the face of other possibilities' (Luhmann, 1979: 112). In this sense, 'trust' – which signals a vulnerability on the part of the truster to the actions of the other, the trustee – and 'power' – which attempts to control the actions of the other – are alternative social mechanisms for resolving problems of order and organization.

Trust is fundamental to human nature; it is the way in which people deal with the unpredictable freedom of others. By making agreements with each other, individuals attempt to make future actions predictable so that they can depend on them. This aspect of trust is as true today as it was many centuries ago. However, Luhmann (1979) makes the distinction between trust in what he describes as small, face-to-face, 'simple' societies that depend on emotional responses in making a judgement on whether or not to trust, and systems trust, which only exists in modern complex organizations. Underpinning Luhmann's view of systems trust is that in an increasingly complex world society must develop more systematic ways of dealing with trust. In complex social societies, emotional trust can exist between people who know each other well, but in situations where strangers need to deal with each other, the unpredictable variability of responses and other factors at work when emotions become involved need to be reduced to achieve social stability. Modern systems of trust are used in complex political organizations such as banks, government and media organizations, and these organizations need to be trusted by citizens. In addition, these organizations are justified in terms of their role as expert systems of knowledge whose 'truth' requires a degree of trust in society. Without this trust there is a problem of legitimation, and political protests could ensue. Zucker (1986) makes a similar observation to Luhmann in his distinction of a shift from *(inter)personal* trust to *institutional-based* trust, where trust has been increasingly abstracted and lifted out of the local.

Some support for Luhmann's view of the importance of emotional responses in granting trust comes from Muldrew's work on credit in the sixteenth century. Muldrew (1998: 2) argues that in the sixteenth century, credit was governed by personal obligation. He advocates the concept of a '*culture* of credit, because more than anything credit was a public means of social communication and circulating judgment about the value of other members of communities', which he refers to as the currency of reputation. He maintains that although most accounts of credit before the sixteenth century concentrate on moneylending, by far the greater part of credit was extended as a normative part of tens of thousands of daily market sales and services. In part, this was necessitated by the lack of currency, with demand always tending to outstrip supply. However, this situation led to long and complex chains of credit and caused an explosion in disputes and litigation over unpaid debts. Furthermore, it contributed to a significant amount of downward social mobility as debt loads became larger. Although money was the measure of all economic transactions, it was a small element in a much larger system of credit. 'What existed was a credit economy in which everything was measured by monetary prices, but where money was not the primary means of exchange' (Muldrew 1998: 101). Money was never used on a large enough scale to alienate economic exchange from social exchange.

There are few areas of contemporary social and economic life where the problems of trust are more formalized than in the production, distribution and consumption of financial credit. This is not surprising, since trust is a basic feature of the existence of most financial services. Indeed, financial institutions can be said to be in the business of trust (Knights *et al.* 2001) – not least because the medium in which financial organizations deal – money – is a fiduciary object. It is a socially constructed object in which we have faith and trust that it will deliver what it promises (Ingham 1996). In relation to credit, there is an even more intimate relationship to trust, because etymologically the word derives from the Latin term *credito* or *credere*, which is 'to put trust in'. Thus, credit is associated with belief, faith, confidence and trust.

The concept of trust is central to lending relationships where financial institutions loan money to consumers on the basis of their trustworthiness to repay. The difficulty for financial institutions is overcoming the chronic information asymmetries that they confront in their dealings with potential customers (Dymski 1994; Stiglitz 1985, 2000). Borrowers are always likely to hold the 'balance of knowledge' as to whether they are indeed able or in fact willing to service the debt. Lenders are unable to rely upon a straightforward expression of capability by the potential borrower since their interests could be diametrically opposed (Leyshon and Thrift 1999). Each time the lender provides credit there is a possibility that the money will not be returned and ultimately will be lost. The problem of information asymmetries is usually manifest in the necessity to make an a priori decision about the suitability of customers. In order to minimize the risk of default, lenders have sought to determine the extent to which consumers are capable of servicing their debt. Traditionally this has been achieved through co-presence: by meeting potential borrowers and assessing their creditworthiness and trustworthiness through face-to-face dialogue and evaluation.

This particular solution to the problems of information asymmetries helps to explain the formation and persistence of financial centres and the way in which retail financial service organizations expanded their network of branches and agents. Branches and agents played an important distribution function, but equally they acted as a point of surveillance through gathering information about customers and monitoring their performance in the servicing of their accounts. In the not too distant past, customers had to go to the bank in person and have an interview with the bank manager if they wanted a loan. If consumers found difficulty in repaying the sum owed, they would also be required to present themselves at the bank and provide an explanation for their behaviour, and the lender could advise on the most appropriate form of action and issue any warnings. Field agents used to be employed in significant numbers by insurance companies and other non-bank moneylending organizations to act as a commission-driven sales force (Leidner 1993). But equally, their role was to visit households and remind them to pay their debts.

In the previous chapter it was noted that the expansion of credit was an important feature in generating sales of consumer durables and other goods in the 1920s. Similar credit-related trust was evident in store-based credit. Jeacle and Walsh (2002: 740) note that credit was advanced only to retail customers who were well known to the store:

> [L]ocal knowledge [of customers] appears to have been a precondition for credit. In the absence of local knowledge, larger stores generally insisted upon cash with the exception of the affluent customer and the use of in-store banking facilities. Smaller stores continued to be a part of a local nexus of credit and . . . it was the ability to offer credit which ensured the survival of smaller stores in the United Kingdom.

The recent development of technologies that allow lenders to tackle information asymmetries at a distance negated the importance of face-to-face contact and the physical infrastructure that accompanied it. Branch networks began to be reduced in the 1980s, and some offices were downgraded (Burton

1990). Expensive agents out in the field were removed or replaced by less skilled staff in favour of other means of direct marketing (telesales, mailshots) and automated payments via direct debits.

Credit scoring and the production of trust

The risk-averse nature of contemporary financial institutions has led to the development of screening processes that reflect subjective assessments of the risk ('perceived risk') attached to prospective borrowers. The 'double contingency' referred to above, wherein we find it necessary to trust people in advance of having that trust confirmed or denied, is in effect reversed when it come to credit. Instead of trusting people, institutions develop technologies that seek to remove the uncertainties of human behaviour by calculating the risks to the point of almost complete control.

Lending practices in financial institutions have therefore been constructed as socially and historically constituted moral practices within projects directed towards the construction of socially responsible subjects via attributes of prudence, forethought and personal responsibility (Burton 1994). Subjective assessments are subsequently converted into an 'objective' measure of risk through the 'scientific' process of credit scoring whereby statistical analysis facilitates prediction and control of uncertainty. In this respect, calculations of risk become

> a way of managing the tension between the vision of stability and pre-
> dictability and a precarious and uncertain world. Constituting something
> as statistically describable, risk makes possible the ordering of the future
> through the use of mathematical probability and calculus.
>
> (Knights and Vurdubakis 1993: 730)

Credit scoring is a fairly recent development in the sanctioning of credit. Some of the earliest related work in the field was concerned with developing 'a way to identify different groups in a population when one cannot see the characteristic that defines the groups but only related ones' (Thomas, Edelman and Crook 2002: 3). The earliest work was undertaken by Fisher (1936), who was interested in differentiating between two different varieties of iris by using measurements of the physical size of the plant and in differentiating the origins of skulls by using their physical measurement. David Durand (1941) was one of the first scholars to recognize that the same techniques could be used to make the distinction between good and bad loans. He wrote a report entitled *Risk Elements in Consumer Installment Financing*, published in the United States by the National Bureau of Economic Research, which was based on data from 7,200 reports on good and bad instalment loans sanctioned across thirty-seven firms. By 1946 he had developed a 'credit guide score' for assessing new loan applications.

There were some parallel developments in addition to the application of statistical theory to credit decision making. During the 1930s a number of mail order companies had developed numerical scoring systems in order to provide a systematic basis for their lending decisions (Smalley and Sturdivant 1973). At the onset of World War II the finance houses and mail order companies began to experience difficulties in managing their credit portfolios. Significant numbers of experienced credit managers were drafted into military service and there was a severe shortage of people with the requisite skills to replace them. In order for businesses to continue to manage their credit relationships with customers, experienced people were asked to document the rules of thumb, the tacit knowledge, that they had acquired during their career. These written records comprised some of the numerical systems that had already been introduced in addition to conditions that had to be satisfied before a loan was granted. These instructions could then be used by non-experts to undertake the job of credit managers and thus marked the beginning of expert systems design. After the war the benefits of using an automated process to assess lending decisions based on newly emergent statistical developments became obvious, and the first consultancy was formed in San Francisco in the 1950s by Bill Fair and Earl Isaac (Thomas, Edelman and Crook 2002). Fair Isaac scores are still used today in many areas of consumer lending.

Credit-scoring systems used in the 1950s and early 1960s were based on score cards that had been developed by analysing accounts that had terminated. The selection of variables and scores assigned to them were essentially judgemental, but the systems did bring a degree of predictability and uniformity to the credit-granting process. Despite these advances, the adoption of credit scoring was not universal or widespread, and was subject to rearguard attempts by lending officers who were wedded to judgemental decision-making despite appeals from statistical and operations research experts (Marron 2007). It was not until the late 1960s and 1970s that credit scoring systems based on empirical valuation methods really came of age, aided by advances in computing technology (Johnson 2004). These developments enabled the huge and very rapid expansion of the credit card industry.

It is currently estimated that adults in the United Kingdom or the United States are credit-scored or behaviour-scored on average at least once a week (Thomas 2000). Credit scoring and associated data-mining techniques are rapidly expanding as lenders look to statistical models to simultaneously reduce risk and increase profitability. There is a flourishing industry in developing new textbooks to support this new specialism, ranging from introductory texts including *An Introduction to Credit Scoring* (Lewis 1992) to more advanced approaches in *Credit Scoring and its Applications* (Thomas, Edelman and Crook 2002). Retail credit scoring is also an expanding area of academic research, as a special issue of the *Journal of the Operational Research Society* testifies (see Crook, Edelman and Thomas 2001).

Credit scoring can be viewed as a modern version of what Foucault (1979) described as a dividing practice whereby the 'bad' are separated from the 'good', the criminal from the law-abiding citizen, the mentally ill from the normal. If an individual passes the credit threshold, then as far as a credit-granting organization is concerned, that individual is a person of moral substance, someone to be trusted. To fail such a test means that the individual is judged as falling short of normative financial expectations. In short, the method for organizing or ordering consumers within the sphere of credit relies far more on power than trust. Neither side really trusts the other, to the extent that mutual exploitation often results, wherein providers impose charges and interest that can be non-transparent and consumers take advantage of discounted competitive offers, operating as 'rate chasers' continually shifting between providers on the basis of the lowest rates of interest (Leyshon, Thrift and Pratt 1998).

Trust is derived from the ability of organizations to track credit records by using comprehensive credit-scoring data. In this respect, credit scoring is deemed to be transparent, uniform, consistent and unbiased. Risk in this sense is not merely confined to making a calculation about the ability of the consumer to repay but is also a safeguard, minimizing the legal threat to the lender of not doing so (Marron 2007). Credit-scoring systems have largely taken the place of tacit, local knowledge embodied in people in the granting of credit decisions (Leyshon and Thrift 1999). The use of credit scoring has provided significant cost benefits for organizations in addition to providing a high level of managerial control over lending decisions, albeit at considerable social cost (Marron 2007). Ritzer (1995: 21) maintains that rationalization in the way that consumer loans are made has had a negative effect on social relations and contributed to the 'dehumanization' of society.

Credit-scoring systems have become increasingly sophisticated, and inextricably linked to the emergence of powerful specialist credit-scoring bureaux. Credit-reporting agencies were first developed in the United States in the first quarter of the twentieth century. In 1918 there were 300 credit-reporting bureaux in that country, a number that had increased to 1,400 by 1925 (Truesdale 1927). These organizations provided information about the credit histories of approximately 10,000 consumers and offered a debt collection service. For the first time, customers could not dupe merchants by providing only good references and thus covering up their poor credit histories. Some stores established their own credit offices, which had the function of sanctioning credit, monitoring its repayment and, sometimes, the responsibility for bringing in new business. The establishment of retail credit management as a specific area of expertise led to the development of a professional association linked to the scientific and skilled training that the job entailed (Jeacle and Walsh 2002).

An important distinguishing feature in contemporary society is the highly concentrated nature of the credit-scoring industry, which is dominated by a small number of bureaux. In the United States, three major credit-reporting agencies dominate the industry: Equifax, TransUnion and Experian. A similar pattern is evident in the United Kingdom: Experian accounts for 75 per cent of credit searches, Equifax 23 per cent, while Call Credit accounts for most of the remainder (see also Gelpi and Julien-Labruyere 1999 on similar trends in France). For many years the bureaux fought to keep credit-scoring information confidential within the industry. However, consumers can now access their credit history via the internet for a small charge. Fair, Isaacson & Co. in collaboration with Informa Research has also begun to release comparative credit information for free. This development in the United States will allow consumers to compare average interest rates in any state for various types of loans, correlated with the Fair Isaac Corporation's credit score ratings (Peterson 2004).

The function of contemporary scoring bureaux is the same as for those that existed a century ago. In most advanced societies, credit-scoring bureaux are central 'nodes' in a sophisticated network within the credit knowledge industry. In this respect, bureaux operate as a contemporary version of the panopticon (Foucault 1979) or super-panopticon (Poster 1995) in their role of observing and recording the behaviour of individuals, albeit through electronic means and the use of text. However, the panopticon is not merely a simple device for observing and recording the behaviour of subjects. Its disciplinary effects lie in the ability to make 'individuals . . . reflect upon the minutiae of their own behaviour in subtle and ongoing ways' (Haggerty and Ericson 2000: 607). The credit panopticon results in consumers having to pay a premium for previous misdemeanours. Based on these data, sophisticated methods of risk-based pricing are developed with respect to what credit limit to provide, what interest rate should be charged, whether and when to market new products, and how to manage the recovery of debt (Thomas 2000; Neri 2001).

The sale and marketing of credit are constructed around the concept of the 'normal' consumer that is held within specific organizations at historical periods of time and within different geographical spaces (Knights, Sturdy and Morgan 1994; Burton 1994). These normative expectations become embedded within organizational cultures, and this knowledge, including informal knowledges, is developed about normality and deviance, and ultimately comprises discourses of the consumer (Gabriel and Lang 1995). For example, consumers can be 'read' off from the organizations with which they have dealings and the goods and services they consume (Knights, Sturdy and Morgan 1994). Traditionally, financial institutions have focused their attention on the prime section of the market comprising the affluent middle and upper classes of society and have marginalized or excluded riskier segments of the market. The preferred financial services consumer has been constructed by financial institutions according to a particular profile (Knights, Sturdy and Morgan 1994). Positive features include full-time, permanent employment, preferably with large employers, home ownership and married status (Leyshon and Thrift 1999). As many as 8 million people in the United Kingdom, or 23 per cent of the population between the ages of 18 and 65, are considered 'non-standard' by the retail financial services industry and are routinely refused credit by conventional lenders (Kempson and Whyley 1996).

Credit-scoring systems provide credit-granting institutions with a relatively low-cost yet efficient filtering system, yet the systems themselves are subject to numerous risks that stop them providing accurate measures of default risk. Marron (2007) classifies these into *methodological risks*, *procedural risks* and *temporal risks*. *Methodological risks* concern the specific techniques used in the construction of credit-scoring models. For example, discriminate analysis suffers from the assumption of equal co-variance and normal distribution within the population, while accuracy of logistic regression can be limited if sample sizes are insufficient. Furthermore, some aspects of statistical development in credit-scoring models are in their infancy and are still evolving. The instance of incorporating affordability measures in credit-scoring systems is a case in point and will be discussed in Chapter 7. Furthermore, there is also a trend towards identifying not just individual risk for consumers but portfolio risk, which adds another dimension to the methodological debate. Some of the implications of the new regulatory environment and portfolio scoring will be discussed in Chapter 4.

Procedural risks relate to the construction of the model and some of the underlying assumptions that underpin its development. For example, Avery, Calam and Canner (2004) maintain that credit-scoring systems are ill-equipped to discriminate according to situational and contextual factors. A linear conception of the individual financial subject, who is assumed to have a stable or continuously improving employment and life chances, is not applicable for many individuals, owing to events such as divorce, unemployment and bankruptcy (Burton *et al.* 2004). For example, an individual who has experienced credit problems for transitory reasons, including unemployment or divorce, would be assigned a credit rating comparable to that of an individual whose credit problems reflect chronic excessive spending or an unwillingness to repay debts. Yet the outlook for these two individuals may be quite different. Many consumers in this category have highly impaired credit histories and represent too much of a risk even for sub-prime companies. But others who have remained outside the banking system and have never constructed a credit history for themselves are also included in this category (Kempson and Whyley 1996). Often individuals never apply for credit for fear of being refused, even though they are no more likely to default than mainstream consumers (Crook 1999).

Credit scoring divides individuals into acceptances and rejects, but data on the rejects are not followed up to determine their creditworthiness, if in fact they were a bad risk. While statisticians maintain that reliable reject inference is impossible (Hand and Henley 2004), this is little consolation for consumers who may have been incorrectly labelled as bad risks. This is an important point to make, since by the time they are implemented, scorecards are using data that can be up to three years old (Lucas 2004). Three years is a long time lag in a rapidly changing credit climate, and since scorecards operate on the basis that the past will repeat itself, some individuals could be severely disadvantaged.

Temporal risks can interfere with the prediction of default risk by threatening the integrity of the model's risk determination. The problem of what is commonly referred to as 'population drift', the correlations between variables to make risk predictions, are fixed within the model, but in the real world, changes are occurring on a continuous basis. There is little certainty that a specific model will work equally well over time, and the challenge for systems designers is to ensure that changes are incorporated as soon as they become evident.

A recurrent theme within the credit-scoring process is whether some groups are discriminated against more than others. Credit scoring by its very nature is a discriminatory process. What is at issue is whether it breaks the law. A very useful summary of the anti-discriminatory laws on credit scoring in the United States and Europe is provided by Andreeva, Ansell and Crook (2004). In the United States, legislation has been specifically directed at discrimination in credit markets, whereas in the European Union general anti-discrimination law exists that covers other areas in addition to credit. In the United States the Equal Credit Opportunity Act prohibits discrimination on the basis of race, colour, national origin, age, gender, marital status, religion, receipt of public assistance, or exercise of rights granted by consumer protection statutes. In US regulation the distinction is made between *overt discrimination, disparate treatment* and *disparate impact. Overt discrimination* involves the use of forbidden variables in scoring models. *Disparate treatment* includes judgemental or subjective discrimination when the score derived from the statistical model is adjusted at the discretion of the lender. *Disparate impact* occurs when the model does not include prohibited variables but, all the same, results in the excessive rejection of borrowers with particular characteristics, such as those of a particular race or gender.

It was assumed that to avoid discrimination all that was required was the elimination of variables that indicated membership of specific groups. Unfortunately, the process is not that straightforward. Andreeva, Ansell and Crook (2004) review a significant amount of research from the United States in which variables associated with race were both included and removed but there remained a bias against some racial groups. Research has also demonstrated that women and older borrowers are less risky than other borrowers, so some protected classes can turn out to be more creditworthy. Equality of opportunity in scoring models can also lead to higher costs for some trustworthy groups. For example, in some models male and female applicants with full-time jobs are constituted as better credit risks, but part-time status appears to be associated with more creditworthy behaviour if no distinction between the sexes is made. Yet although women are better credit risks than men, they are not rewarded for this characteristic in the 'sexless' scorecard. In conclusion, Andreeva, Ansell and Crook (2004: 29) note:

> It appears that the anti-discriminatory legislation works against at least some protected groups. It fails to ensure greater access to credit for disadvantaged groups, but at the same time it leads to a deterioration of the predictive power of scoring models, which in turn results in an increased number of bad risks that were granted credit, when good risks were denied it, making credit more expensive.

Behaviourial scoring and the forecasting of financial risk

Credit scoring refers to the process that organizations undertake to decide whether credit should be awarded to new applicants. Behavioural scoring relates to lending decisions for existing customers. For example, if a customer wants to increase their credit limit, should the organization agree? When should marketing be undertaken to generate new business? If a customer falls behind in repayments, what action should be taken? Behavioural scoring systems allow lenders to make better decisions in managing existing consumers by forecasting their future behaviour. An important distinguishing feature of behavioural scoring is the ability to draw on extra information relating to repayment and ordering history of the customer. Behavioural models can be divided into two approaches: those that use credit-scoring methods with the two extra variables added, and those that build probability models of the consumer. Probability models can also be classified in two ways, either by estimating parameters obtained from a previous sample of customers, or by Bayesian models that update the firm's assessments in the light of the consumer's behaviour (Thomas 2000).

The choice of time horizon is frequently more critical for behavioural scoring than for credit-scoring systems. Behavioural scoring is designed to provide a longitudinal forecasting system by using cross-sectional data of behaviour at particular intervals. Organizations vary in their use of time periods, and this will ultimately depend on the nature of the data available. In many instances, time intervals of twelve to eighteen months are sufficient. However, some lenders use shorter periods of six months. Probability models classify various states of the consumer, including using variables from the application form and those denoting recent and current behaviour. Some of these variables may include the outstanding balance, the number of periods since a payment was made, the average balance, and so forth.

Incorporating economic conditions into credit and behavioural scoring is important since different conditions could affect default rates. The effect of economic conditions is potentially more important in behavioural scoring than credit scoring since the emphasis is on patterns of change over time. Rapid changes in economic conditions are particularly problematic since there can be a time lag before scorecards can be updated, and changes in consumer behaviour can occur in advance of amendments. Furthermore, this time lag can expose lenders to significant risk of default. Crook, Hamilton and Thomas (1992) developed two scorecards on a sample of customers for the same lending product. One of them was built on customers joining the organization in 1988 using their credit history in 1989, when economic conditions were relatively buoyant. The other scorecard was developed using customers who joined the organization in 1989, using their history in 1990 when conditions were worse. Adjusting for the cut-offs to accept the same percentage in each year, they found that 25 per cent of the group who would be rejected in one year would be accepted in the other and vice versa. These findings should not be interpreted as meaning that economic conditions are the only changes in risk behaviour. The causes can be multifaceted, including the actions of lenders reducing their cut-off levels in the face of increased competition. However, this example does demonstrate the importance of changes over time.

Profitability scoring and risk

A relatively new development among lenders in recent years is an emphasis on maximizing the profit a customer brings to the organization rather than minimizing the risk of default. The distinction between the two different strategies is succinctly summarized by Thomas (2000: 165): 'Whereas default rates are acceptance decisions, credit limit decisions and default recovery decisions, profits are affected by many more decisions including marketing, service levels and operation decisions as well as pricing decisions.' It has become clear that some of the most profitable consumers are the ones that have a high risk attached to them. Credit cards are a case in point. It has long been recognized that the most profitable customers are those who pay the minimum monthly payment each month and continue to pay high interest rates on outstanding balances. Customers who pay off their balances each month are not profitable – in fact, quite the reverse, since credit card operators have traditionally provided incentives to keep these consumers via air miles and free insurance on purchases. The derogatory term used for customers who pay off their balances each month is 'deadbeats', which some consumers find offensive (Manning 2000: 294). The move towards profitability scoring is also generating developments in risk-based pricing and the emergence of sub-prime markets as lenders seek to build profitable niches among new groups of consumers. These developments will be discussed in greater depth in the next chapter.

Moving to profit-scoring systems is a complex undertaking, and organizations wishing to move in that direction face a number of difficulties. First, there are problems related to data warehousing to ensure that all the information that relates to the different elements of customer profitability are accessible. For example, credit card organizations obtain a percentage of each purchase made on the card back from the retailer in the form of a merchant service charge. The amount of the fee varies substantially according to the purchases made, and the credit card companies have had to change their systems in order that this information might be captured. Another instance may be where the lender writes off all or a fixed percentage of debt and never checks how much is recovered by the debt collection department. Where debt is sold on to another company the level of recovery will never be known (see Chapter 6 on the debt sale market).

Data-mining techniques that are being developed will deal with some of these issues, but there are other difficulties: for example, determining what constitutes an appropriate time-frame in which to measure profitability, and whether it is justifiable to charge high prices at the start of a relationship, only to alienate consumers in the future. Second, profit includes economic conditions in addition to consumer characteristics such as interest rates. Profit is also a function of how long a customer stays with a lender and whether they default or move their business elsewhere. Attrition rates are an important part of profit scoring. A final issue concerns which methodology to choose. Should a lender assess profit on each product in isolation or calculate the total profit over all possible products? For example, a lender may refuse a customer a new credit card because they do not use it enough, at the expense of the customer then moving their mortgage because they were offended.

A number of approaches to profit scoring are being tried (see Thomas 2000), but all appear to be more complex than originally thought. However, being able to identify profitability accurately would bring considerable financial benefit. Furthermore, it is a technique that could make good use of all the data obtained via loyalty cards.

Alternative credit providers and the production of trust

Most of the existing literature on credit and trust focuses on what might be termed the formal or mainstream market for credit and the techniques used in credit and behavioural scoring. Though it is not stated explicitly, from the overview provided in this chapter it is clear that there are assumptions within the existing research about the nature of lending decisions and the tools that lenders use in reaching those decisions. What are rarely considered are what might be termed alternative credit providers, and markets that do not conform to the model outlined above. As we noted in Chapters 1 and 2, mainstream lenders are a large section, but only a section, of organizations in the market. Moneylenders, for example, are another, very different form of credit provider, and they have different ways of assessing the trustworthiness of consumers.

Within the existing literature, the credit choices available to low-income con-sumers who are most vulnerable to extortionate interest rates, high charges and dubious terms and conditions have rarely been addressed in academic research (Karpatkin 1999; Bazerman 2001). In emphasizing affluent, mainstream consumers, research on credit is replicating a pattern found elsewhere in retailing and marketing more generally, in which the more prosperous members of society are over-represented in research samples (Hirschman 1992; Clarke 1998; Burton 2002c).

The use of credit scoring in this section of the market is extremely limited, with only one or two of the largest moneylenders using it as a screening process. Moneylenders still rely on the local knowledge of agents to be able to identify good and bad areas and customers to limit the risk of default (Rowlingson 1994; Leyshon *et al*. 2004). There is a low-trust relationship in this sector because of the high risk of default, and the weekly visits of the agents to enforce financial discipline are an important method of control. Kempson and Whyley (1999: 6) provide an assessment of the monetary costs of the lack of trust with respect to moneylending:

> Interest rates vary according to the size and the length of loans and range from 105% for a 104 week loan of £800 to 481% on a 20 week loan of £60 (Rowlingson, 1994, p29). It should be noted, however, that these charges include the costs of home collection as well as the costs of late payment. Indeed, the Consumer Credit Association (the trade association representing the majority of such companies) has calculated that the cost of home collection is around 15% of the total sum collected by their agents. Of this 8% is paid back as commission to agents and a further 7% covers management of the agents and back office loan and repayment administration of small weekly payments. So, for example, a £100 loan repayable over 26 weeks would incur total charges of £40. Of this £21 would cover the costs of collection (ie 15% of the £200 plus £40). It is also claimed that the majority of loans are not paid on time, and for example, a 26 week loan is typically repaid over 30 weeks. Taking both these factors into consideration would reduce the APR on a £100 loan from 292.4% to 82.8%.

There is often a presumption that customers purchasing sub-prime products have impaired credit histories and present a higher degree of risk. However, research in the United States has demonstrated that consumers presenting different levels of risk are in fact paying similar costs. Between 30 and 50 per cent of consumers classified as low-risk creditors are paying high-risk rates for mortgages, vehicle finance and credit cards (Getter 2006). These findings suggest that many customers are not sourcing the best deal and are being sold inappropriate high-cost products. To some extent the mis-selling of loans is understandable in companies that have no conforming products. When sub-prime products are the only ones available, the salesperson has a choice between making a sale or not. Research has demonstrated that Citigroup is one of the worst offenders, which is particularly troublesome given that it has a full portfolio of products. For example, regulators have investigated the fact that in North Carolina, Citigroup's sub-prime lender Citifinancial had more than 100 outlets selling sub-prime loans and not one single Citibank outlet marketing conforming loans. The numbers of sub-prime mortgages sold exceeded 20,000 a year, while conforming loans totalled 500. It was calculated that one-quarter of the sub-prime loans sold were to creditworthy customers (Lord 2005).

Furthermore, there appears to be an ethnic or racial bias in the provision of some credit products. For example, Getter (2006) found that minorities in the United States do not pay a premium for mortgages and used cars but do for new car loans and credit cards that have an outstanding balance. However, there could be a spatial element to the ethnic bias, since the investigations into Citifinancial's mortgage lending referred to above found that African-Americans were particularly disadvantaged in North Carolina. Just 10 per cent of conforming borrowers were members of minorities, compared to 22 per cent of sub-prime borrowers. Nationally, Citigroup's prime lenders were twice as likely to be reported as white as was a customer of its sub-prime subsidiaries. Lord (2005) maintains that there were two reasons for sub-prime lenders attracting a disproportionate amount of African-American business. First, this segment of the market did not trust banks after 100 years of segregation and redlining. Second, sub-prime lenders advertised heavily in African-American communities. The ethnic bias of some sub-prime products is not confined to the United States. In Ireland the Professional Insurance Brokers Association claims that non-European nationals are being forced to purchase expensive sub-prime mortgages because conventional lenders will not give them mortgages. Many foreign nationals earn less than Irish nationals because of the nature of their jobs, but are nonetheless very creditworthy. They often come from countries that have a strong savings culture; they work hard and spend less money on day-to-day expenses than Irish nationals (Weston 2007).

Credit, space and trust

So far in this chapter the role of trust in credit relationships within a variety of institutional contexts has been discussed. In this section the implications of these credit–trust relationships for the configuration of different types of lenders in specific localities will be addressed. Over the past twenty years the spatial location of financial institutions has become a political issue. Access to financial services has become an integral part of being included in contemporary consumer society, and there is recognition that those who are excluded are severely disadvantaged. Mainstream lenders have traditionally located themselves in affluent areas. The first banks in Britain in the eighteenth century were private banks, and many felt that overcrowded cities comprising working-class people (miners, factory hands, or the unemployed) could never be as lucrative as customers in quiet little country towns. Furthermore, the banks' upmarket image could be tarnished by moving into cities. Urban areas tended to be the province of the savings banks (Booker 1991). The development of joint-stock banking in the mid-nineteenth century saw the expansion of banks into more working-class areas in an attempt to increase profitability.

This expansion continued until the early 1980s, when the combined effects of increased competition from new entrants, including retailers and manufacturers, direct suppliers, including telephone and internet banking, and high overheads associated with branch networks led to banks retreating from many deprived areas. The trend to move out of poor neighbourhoods is in part a reflection of the lack of profitability and the quality of the business on offer, and is a pattern that is evident in many advanced countries. Andrew Leyshon and Nigel Thrift (1997) have described these processes as geographies of financial exclusion. The practice of identifying geographical areas that were off limits as far as lending was concerned was called redlining, and is now illegal in many countries, although its effects remain on the urban landscape. A study conducted by the World Bank across a range of societies concluded:

> In the presence of dysfunctional state institutions, poor people turn for help to institutions of the private sector or civil society. In the private sector, local shops and moneylenders emerge as the unlikely heroes because, although they may sometimes be 'bloodsuckers', they are present when needed and quick to respond.
>
> (Narayan *et al.* 2000: 197)

The departure of mainstream lenders from inner cities was followed by several new signifiers of urban poverty and has been referred to as reverse redlining (Graves 2003). New types of credit providers to emerge in these vacated spaces have included deferred deposit lenders (popularly known as payday lenders), rent-to-own appliance stores and pawnbrokers. These transformations have opened up spaces for discussion about what have become known as predatory lenders and lending practices. The issue of predatory lending is highly controversial and will be discussed in Chapter 4 in more detail. However, lenders tend to charge high fees and high interest rates, and provide relatively low levels of service quality. In some quarters their business practices are regarded as abusive, since they exploit the limited resources and lack of choice of low-income consumers.

Once mainstream financial institutions began to observe that alternative lenders were transacting profitable business in their once-deserted spaces, they began to reconsider the potential of consumers whom they had once marginalized and excluded. The Union Bank of San Francisco in the United States was hailed as a pioneer in providing services for consumers in low-income neighbourhoods. Yolanda Brown, the bank's vice-president, explains the basis of their strategy:

> Traditional thinking determines that low-income households represent low profit potential due to a small revenue base, high risk, and high cost of service. But if you shift the paradigm you find that financial services can be re-engineered, reinvented, repriced, and repackaged to meet legitimate demand at a significant profit.
>
> (quoted in Williams 2004: 99)

Put simply, the bank was servicing a once-neglected market by charging higher fees and interest rates to compensate for the higher levels of risk. In effect, risk-based pricing was applied to the range of business activities in urban spaces where this strategy could be accommodated.

Despite the shame, expense and tedium of having to deal with predatory alternative lenders, millions of people in some of the most advanced countries in the world are forced to do so. In effect, these customers are outside the mainstream banking system, and even if there is a bank in the locality, impoverished residents cannot always afford the minimum balance required to keep the account open, or the fees for writing cheques or charges for returned items such as bounced checks due to insufficient funds. Hudson has sketched what he terms the contours of the 'poverty industry' in the United States. He maintains that the new multi-million-dollar landscape of lenders is not a task for community-based entrepreneurs:

> More and more, the merchants who profit from the disadvantaged are owned or bankrolled by the big names of Wall Street – Ford, Citibank, Nationsbank, Bank America, Bank Express, Western Union. Lesser known Wall Street companies are also grabbing a piece of the action. Add up all the businesses that bottom-feed on the 'fringe economy' and you'll come up with a market of $200 to $300 billion a year.
>
> (1996: 88)

In effect, large global financial companies have become the market makers in these new areas of business.

Leyshon *et al.* (2004, 2006) have argued that contemporary differences in the credit experiences of consumers living in different sorts of areas constitute varying ecologies of knowledge that reflect the different relationships between borrower and lender in different places. They argue that the

> middle-class suburb represents an ecology and network of privilege within the contemporary retail financial services market. . . . It is made up of

subjects and household formations that are associated with the requisite amount of disposable income to constitute residents as the most desirable financial customers.

(2004: 631)

These customers are more likely to be more financially literate and confident, and engage in churning accounts. At the extreme end of this behaviour is the credit card rate chaser who moves their balance on a regular basis from one supplier to another to take advantage of 0% introductory offers for a limited period of time. Another trend is for consumers to move their mortgage on a regular basis for the same reasons. This group of people are able to play the system in this way because most financial institutions have similar credit-scoring procedures that identify this group as desirable customers.

By contrast, poor inner cities and public-sector housing estates have a distinctly different ecology as compared with the middle-class suburbs. Their socio-economic characteristics fare much more poorly on the credit-scoring systems developed by mainstream financial service organizations. For example, 'Lower incomes, a lower instance of homeownership, and a more limited engagement with financial service products in the past mean that such individuals become categorised as risky, potentially problematic, or unprofitable consumers' (Leyshon *et al*. 2004: 633). Other characteristics including unemployment and unstable employment do not live up to the expectations of financial institutions that require a linear employment record and evidence of stability. The source of credit in these areas is rather different from that in the affluent suburbs. Consumers have to rely on expensive forms of credit from moneylenders that are often very small companies having fewer than ten employees.

The knowledge these two sets of consumers have about the availability of credit in their locality, the terms and conditions on offer, the companies concerned and the products on offer is highly differentiated. Furthermore, consumer knowledge of these alternatives is reproduced in these places by being passed on through families, friends and acquaintances. In this way, these distinctive ecologies of knowledge continually reproduce themselves over time. The existence of these parallel systems has been known for some time, and action has been taken to try to alleviate the problem and diversify the existing ecologies. Responses in the United States and the United Kingdom have been quite different (Marshall 2004). In the United States the 1977 Community Reinvestment Act was introduced to curb redlining and ensure that lenders were using non-discriminatory lending practices. In the United Kingdom where there is more emphasis on self-regulation, the financial services sector has been left to its own devices to present some solutions. Unfortunately, they have not always been readily forthcoming. Many of the large financial institutions do have units that deal with community banking initiatives, and it is in this forum that some solutions have been trialled.

To date, most of the financial services literature has addressed the spatial location of financial institutions and their function within the community. Absent from this discourse has been the economic and political relationships that exist between different lenders. Partnerships between credit unions and mainstream lenders are one development that looks promising, since credit unions have an in-depth knowledge of problems consumers face in different localities. Credit unions also tend to be more aware of the existence of other suppliers in the area and the marketing strategies that they use to generate business. Some mainstream financial institutions are underpinning important work in the community being undertaken by credit unions. For example, Leeds City Credit Union in the United Kingdom received funding from Barclays Bank to underwrite the debts of twenty families to enable them to escape from the clutches of moneylenders. The funding was used to pay off the moneylenders, and the customers then took out a loan with the credit union at much lower rates of interest to pay the capital that was owed.

Conclusion

In this chapter the central concept of trust and control in credit relationships has been explored. The shift from personal to institutional trust within mainstream credit markets has been a necessary development in consumer societies, where the demand for credit to fund current consumption has expanded exponentially. Credit scoring has developed into a science of assessing risk in order to provide a low-cost screening facility for lenders and their consumers. Credit-scoring bureaux that pool data from a significant number of lenders and other debt-related information have become extremely powerful organizations in monitoring the financial behaviour of consumers. The extension of statistical modelling to relatively new areas of credit assessment, including behavioural scoring and profit scoring, have provided even higher levels of, and more continuous, consumer surveillance than conventional credit scoring. Together these multiple methods have provided a platform for developments in risk-based pricing whereby consumers are charged different interest rates and fees according to the degree of risk that they are perceived to present to the lender.

It was argued that the current discourse of trust and control in credit relationships is too heavily dependent on mainstream consumers, with there being far less emphasis on alternative credit providers outside the dominant financial institutions. One of the biggest growth areas and one that is the most profitable is what has become known as sub-prime lending. New institutions that have entered this market charge high fees to cover what they perceive to be higher levels of risk. Mainstream suppliers have also entered this market, given its highly profitable nature, using separate subsidiaries to distance the business from the parent brand. Also lacking in much of the current credit literature is an appreciation of the interdependencies of credit, space and trust. Relationships between lenders and borrowers do not exist independently of their spatial location. Attention was drawn to the distinction between inner cities and local authority housing estates on the one hand and the affluent middle-class suburbs on the other with respect to the constitution of risk and consumer knowledge.

To conclude, the relationship between trust and control where credit is concerned is a highly complex one, and much is yet to be unravelled. However, what is becoming increasingly clear is that the dynamics of trust and control have given way to the development of highly segmented credit markets. New organizations have emerged to meet the needs of various segments of consumers. Some of the pertinent issues relating to these trends will be discussed in the following chapter.

Questions

1   Explain the processes that underpin the movement from personal to interpersonal trust.
2   What issues does the highly concentrated nature of power in credit-scoring bureaux raise about consumer sovereignty?
3   Explain the differences between credit scoring, behavioural scoring and profit scoring.
4   What do you understand by the term 'ecologies of financial knowledge'?

Further reading

Andreeva, G., Ansell, J. and Crook, J. (2004) 'Impact of anti-discrimination laws on credit scoring', *Journal of Financial Services Marketing*, 9, 1: 22–33.

Getter, D.E. (2006) 'Consumer credit risk and pricing', *Journal of Consumer Affairs*, 40, 1: 41–64.

Leyshon, A., Burton, D., Knights, D., Alferoff, C. and Signoretta, P. (2004) 'Towards an ecology of retail financial services: understanding the persistence of door-to-door credit and insurance providers', *Environment and Planning A*, 36: 625–645.

Marron, D. (2007) '"Lending by Numbers": credit scoring and the constitution of risk within American consumer credit', *Economy and Society*, 36, 1: 103–133.

Thomas, L.C. (2000) 'A survey of credit and behavioural scoring: forecasting financial risk of lending to consumers', *International Journal of Forecasting*, 16, 2: 149–172.

4 Making credit markets

Developments in the credit industry that were summarized in the previous chapter have important implications for the structuring of different credit markets. Innovations in information technology have facilitated the tracking of customer misdemeanours, sophisticated profiling techniques are used to identify individuals who are at most risk of default, and there has been progress in the development of geographical information systems that have identified more precisely the risks associated with residential neighbourhoods. In this chapter we assess in more detail some of the characteristics of these different markets, emergent trends, and some of the inter-organizational networks that have developed to support the different markets.

The chapter will begin by making a broad distinction between two ideal types of what are described as 'old' and 'new' economies of credit as a way of organizing and understanding changes in the credit environment over time. The main part of the chapter will be concerned with mapping existing credit markets. The distinction is made between the prime, complex prime, sub-prime and non-status market segments. The final part of the chapter will focus on new international regulations governing the management of risk in credit portfolios through an examination of the Basel II Capital Accord.

The 'old' and the 'new' economy of credit

Changes in the retail credit environment can be described as belonging to one of two ideal types: the 'old' and the 'new' economy of credit. Ideal types provide a way of summarizing some of the most important changes in the credit environment and markets. In describing recent transformations in credit markets as belonging to an old or a new economy, it is not being suggested that we are literally witnessing a new economy but rather that the changes are significantly different between what might be described as two distinct eras. The two economies differ according to the following characteristics: the social perceptions of credit and debt, differences in the types of lender, the regulatory framework in which lending occurs, the use of information technology in credit-granting decisions, the pricing and cost of credit, the way that lenders manage debt, the incidence of fraud and default, and the segmentation of credit markets (see Table 4.1).

In previous chapters it was noted that social perceptions of credit and debt have changed in many societies in recent years. Not too long ago the predominant view was that consumers who used credit and ran up debts were to be considered frivolous and morally inadequate. Within the old economy, credit was overshadowed by negative connotations. Within the new economy, credit has become an accepted part of everyday life. This is not to suggest that credit is viewed positively by all groups in society, but rather that it is tolerated and used far more extensively than previously was the case. Indeed, in some instances the tables have turned and consumers are considered victims of a

Table 4.1 The 'old' and the 'new' economies of credit

	'Old'	'New'
Social perceptions of credit and debt	Credit and debt the vice of frivolous and morally inadequate consumers	Consumers as victims of materialistic consumer society and the aggressive marketing practices of lenders
Institutional context	Lending province of financial institutions	All retailers and manufacturers able to provide credit. Credit as a commodity.
Regulatory framework	Constrained by credit controls and cartels	Neo-liberal regulatory framework with respect to institutions, lending criteria and pricing
Information technology in credit granting decisions	Manual systems and rules of thumb, emergent credit departments and systems	Specialist credit departments and institutions, emergence of credit-scoring bureaux
Pricing/cost of credit	Standard, one-price-fits-all pricing policies	Risk-based pricing, variable across products, institutions and consumers
Management of debt	In-house credit teams and legal proceeding through the courts	Secondary credit market, specialized credit management techniques
Incidence of fraud and default	Relatively low levels of consumer fraud and default; can't pay rather than won't pay	Multidimensional and sophisticated fraud and defaulting behaviour, identity fraud, won't pay as an emergent consumer philosophy
Segmentation of the credit market	Prime versus sub-prime segmentation	Prime versus non-prime segmentation, the latter comprising complex prime, sub-prime and non-status

materialistic consumer society and casualties of aggressive marketing practices on the part of lenders.

A second difference between the 'old' and the 'new' economy is that the credit market has become increasingly competitive as a consequence of the deregulation of credit markets, which has allowed different types of lenders to enter the market. For example, manufacturers and retailers have joined mainstream financial institutions and provide their own credit products. In the old economy, credit was more likely to be provided directly from a financial institution, since the regulatory environment separated out different spheres of financial activity, just as building societies were the main providers of mortgages and insurance companies were the main providers of insurance. Providing finance at the point of sale can be very lucrative for manufacturers and retailers since it can maximize the chance of a sale. Retailers use the differences between borrowing and lending rates and the interest on durable goods purchases to influence consumers' choices to purchase by cash or credit as the case may be (Bertola, Hochguertel and Winfred 2005). The use of 0 per cent finance to fund motor vehicle purchases is a very good example of how credit can be used to good effect as an incentive at the point of sale. Indeed, some of the financial service subsidiaries that retailers and manufacturers have established to provide credit are highly profitable entities in their own right, in some instances outperforming the retailing and manufacturing operation.

Another difference between the 'old' and the 'new' economy of credit concerns the internal organization of the credit industry. As was mentioned above, prior to deregulation, credit was highly regulated, rationed and pricing-controlled by cartels. These policies had considerable impact on consumers and affected whether or not they could borrow and how much institutions were willing to lend. For example, in the United Kingdom in the early 1980s, if people wanted to obtain a loan to purchase kitchen appliances such as washing machines and fridges they needed to contribute 20 per cent of the purchase price and borrow the rest. In the case of car loans, the deposit was even greater, accounting for one-third of the purchase price, allowing consumers to borrow two-thirds of the total (Burton 1994). These practices appear restrictive by today's standards, yet this was little more than twenty years ago. In the new economy of credit, often no deposit for credit purchases is required; indeed, in some cases there are interest-free periods of up to a year before the consumer has to start making repayments. The economy is awash with credit for those with good credit histories; there is certainly no rationing. In some cases lenders have also relaxed their lending criteria with respect to who can borrow. So, for example, part-time workers and the self-employed can obtain credit, provided their credit history is satisfactory.

Another difference between the two credit eras is the use of information technology in the credit-granting process. In the old economy the authorization of credit was a labour-intensive process performed by specialist staff. Obtaining credit often meant an interview with the bank manager, who then referred the decision on to a specialist lending department. In an economy where credit was rationed and there were few lenders, financial institutions could be choosy about whom they were willing to lend to, and lent to those who were low risk to minimize the chance of default. In the new economy, credit-scoring bureaux and accessible information systems have meant that virtually anybody with minimal levels of competence can undertake credit searches; indeed, consumers can perform their own credit search on the internet. The same ease of use applies to the programs that interpret credit scores in order to assess risk and provide an overall score upon which lending decisions are made. Activities that were once undertaken by individuals with considerable experience and knowledge, such as underwriters in the case of mortgage lending, have become deskilled as more lending decisions are automated (Braverman 1974).

As has already been noted in the previous chapter, the calculation of risk has become intrinsically related to price in the new economy of credit. In the old economy the lending decision was about whether a particular consumer should or should not be given credit. It was a binary, yes/no decision, and all those who were granted a loan paid the same price. The move to risk-based pricing has meant that the higher the risk a consumer presents, the higher the price of credit becomes. Furthermore, considerable variations exist in pricing strategies across products and institutions. The arrival of specialist sub-prime lenders has meant that consumers who would have been denied credit in the old economy are now able to borrow, though at a higher rate of interest. This scenario is a far cry from the old era, where a one-price-fits-all policy existed for all consumers.

Due to stringent credit controls and the highly selective credit-granting policies that were in place, default was a relatively infrequent occurrence in the old economy of credit by comparison with today's levels. Where default did occur, it tended to be an issue of 'can't pay' rather than 'won't pay'. The contemporary credit environment is very different. The larger volumes of lending, a more highly automated, depersonalized authorization system, and larger numbers of consumers acquiring credit have all contributed to higher levels of default. There is a significant and growing group of consumers for whom defaulting on credit agreements is an accepted occurrence in everyday life. Won't pay rather than can't pay appears to be an emergent consumer philosophy. The different dimensions of fraud have also become more complex. For example, identity fraud relates to fraud across all accounts rather than just one or two, therefore multiple credit fraud could ensue.

Another characteristic of the new economy relates to the ways in which companies are handling default. When the numbers of defaulters were at relatively manageable levels, in-house credit departments could cope with the volume, and persistent defaulters would be taken to court for defaulting on their credit agreements. In the new economy there are so many defaulters that taking legal proceedings against those who cannot or will not pay is not a cost-effective option. New techniques have been introduced that attempt to track individual behaviour and try to recoup the debt when a customer's financial circumstances become more favourable. When all else fails, some lenders are parcelling up and selling off consumer debt to other companies. This is generating a debt sale market in personal finance, which we will return to in Chapter 6.

A final distinction is the construction of the credit markets. In the old economy of credit the broad distinction was between consumers who had access to mainstream credit and those who did not. In the new economy of credit there has been a growing sophistication of credit markets, to a point where multiple segments exist across a whole range of product categories. Furthermore, specialist sub-prime financial services providers have emerged to meet the needs of this new market. The next section of the chapter will assess some of these differences in more detail.

Mapping credit markets

A broad distinction is often made between the prime and the sub-prime sections of the market. However, this distinction is somewhat simplistic, since the sub-prime market is highly complex in its own right, as the discussion of alternative credit providers in the previous chapter demonstrated. Organizations and consumers within sub-prime markets can be classified according to whether they occupy a position within the 'new' or the 'old' economy of credit (see also Burton *et al.* 2004). There are considerable variations within these two categories with respect to consumer profiles, including their credit history, the products on offer, pricing strategies, delivery channels, the relative importance of credit scoring, the knowledge–control relationship, and levels of trust (see Table 4.2). We shall now assess the nature of these segments and the organizations that operate in this market.

The mainstream market

There is a greater degree of trust between financial institutions and individuals in the prime market compared with the other groups. This group of people are in full-time permanent employment. They are frequently married and are homeowners. These 'super-included' individuals have good credit histories, paying their bills on time, and they fulfil their credit commitments. These low-risk, creditworthy individuals have a range of financial products at their disposal. The development of sophisticated credit scoring systems has allowed asymmetries of information to be tackled 'at a distance', and these systems amount to reading consumers as text (Leyshon *et al.* 1998). These individuals, by virtue of their good credit histories, can be provided with credit facilities in a short space of time, and lenders will be vying for their business. However,

Table 4.2 Segmentation of the personal-sector credit market

	Prime	*Complex prime*	*Sub-prime*	*Non-status*
Customer profile	Middle and upper class, home-owners, married, full-time, permanent employment	Any socio-economic group	Any socio-economic group, but tend to be in less secure employment than the prime market	Lower socio-economic groups, living on local authority housing estates and in inner cities
Credit history	Unblemished	Intact but unusual	Impaired	Highly impaired or never been included in mainstream
Products	Wide range: overdrafts, mortgages, unsecured lending	Niche/ specialized lending mortgages and loans	Mortgages, car finance, consolidation loans	Limited range of small value loans
Pricing	Competitive	Risk-based	Risk-based	High interest
Delivery channels	Multiple	Internet, telephone and broker	Mostly telephone and internet	Direct, face to face
Credit scoring	Extensively used	Limited use	Extensively used	Rarely used
Trust relationship	High	High	Low	Low
Control relationship	At a distance	At a distance	At a distance	Face to face

under some circumstances consumers included in mainstream credit markets are not the most profitable consumers. Credit cards are a good example, with affluent customers paying off their bill at the end of the month rather than paying interest on roll-over balances. These customers cost the companies, since they are entitled to numerous freebies, including reward points towards goods, free air miles and free insurance.

Affluent consumers can play the system and source the best deal from mainstream financial institutions. These groups will also be the most know-ledgeable about financial services since they are media literate and are able to make informed choices based on a range of publicly available research in newspapers, magazines and websites (Burton 1994, 2002a). Moreover, middle-class consumers are more likely to have telephones and the computing equipment necessary to be able to substitute 'distanced' contact for face-to-face contact, and to take advantage of the keener rates and more advantageous conditions offered by providers using such distribution systems (Leyshon *et al*. 2004). In an era of risk-based pricing, these customers are the most blessed.

The complex prime market

Individuals in the complex prime market occupy a somewhat ambiguous position between the prime and sub-prime market. Individuals can be classified as part of the prime or sub-prime market dependent on lenders' criteria for different products. Consumer in the complex category can be drawn from any socio-economic group. Their credit history is intact but for one reason or another it is unusual. For example, an academic working on temporary contracts is a professional, earning a salary above the national average, but the fact that they are on a temporary contract would go against them. Another example might be a management consultant who undertakes contract work but would nevertheless earn a significant salary. The complex market tends to be a niche, specialist market that requires the input of an underwriter to make a decision on level of risk attached to particular borrowing requirements. The delivery channels tend to be via the internet, telephone or via a broker, although many complex cases have originally been processed as prime business and subsequently rejected part-way through the process because they do not conform to regular lending criteria. In this instance the application would be transferred to a sub-prime subsidiary if the parent organization has one. Complex prime customers enjoy a high-trust relationship since they do not have a blemished credit history, and in this respect they are not that much different in profile from customers in the prime section of the market.

The sub-prime market

The institutional structure of the new sub-prime economy of credit is very different from that of the old economy. New sub-prime institutions have emerged during the past ten to twenty years to meet the needs of credit-impaired consumers who have failed traditional credit-scoring procedures but whose financial history is not as impaired as that of those consumers who turn to moneylenders for credit (Burton *et al*. 2004). The terminology that is used to refer to new sub-prime business is still evolving. A variety of expressions have been used to refer to the business transacted in the new-economy sub-prime market, including non-prime, sub-prime, non-status, non-standard, near-prime, light adverse and heavy adverse. Within the industry, the term 'lending to iffy customers' has emerged to provide a vernacular description of the practices of companies within this part of the sub-prime market. In some quarters there has been a reluctance to use the term 'sub-prime' because of its overly negative connotations. Positive metaphors used to justify this part of the sub-prime market include 'challenging the status quo', 'championing the man in the street' and 'focusing on the ability of individuals to rebuild their credit record'.

The profile of consumers in this segment of the market can be highly diverse, since factors involved in credit default, including divorce and unemployment, can occur across any social class and age. The self-employed are also likely to be included in this category, since confirmation of income can in some circumstances prove difficult but is nevertheless an important 'passport' to mainstream lending. The credit histories of all consumers in this category are impaired in some respect. However, the concept of impairment covers a wide spectrum. On the one hand it includes individuals who have missed three mortgage payments in the past twelve months, while on the other it includes undischarged bankrupts. Risk-based pricing takes into account these wide variations. Typically, lenders will band criteria whether they relate to missed loan payments and/or county court judgments according to their severity, and typically charge an interest rate that reflects the degree of risk. An example of the types of criteria used to assess risk-based pricing for mortgages is provided in Table 4.3.

Organizations operating in the new sub-prime market are a mix of dedicated specialist providers, some of which have been offering these services since the 1980s, and mainstream financial institutions that have identified sub-prime

Table 4.3 Typical sub-prime mortgage lending portfolio

	Prime[a]	*Feather adverse*	*Light adverse*	*Medium adverse*	*Heavy adverse*	*Super-heavy adverse*
Bankruptcy discharged	No	No	No	No	No	Yes
County court judgments acceptable	£500	£1,000	£3,000	£7,500	£15,000	Unlimited
Defaults	Ignored	Ignored	Ignored	Ignored	Ignored	Ignored
Late payments – credit cards/ loans acceptable	Yes	Yes	Yes	Yes	Yes	Yes
Maximum loan to value	95%	90%	90%	85%	85%	85%
Missed mortgage payments	0 in 12	1 in 12 0 in 6	2 in 12 0 in 6	3 in 12 1 in 6	4 in 12 2 in 6	Unlimited
Mortgage defaults	No	No	No	No	No	Yes
Repossession	No	No	No	No	No	Yes

Note [a] Prime category used for comparative purposes only.

lending as a lucrative growth area. The specialist providers were often originally developed to service a particular niche market. For example, one of the pioneers in the United Kingdom was the Kensington Mortgage Company, which was originally established to provide specialist mortgage finance for bankrupts. Other companies in the market are relatively new entrants that are often subsidiaries of large mainstream lenders that perceived sub-prime as a lucrative addition to their portfolio. In the United States, Citibank, Morgan Chase and Wells Fargo all have sub-prime lending subsidiaries, albeit under different brand names. HSBC is also heavily involved in sub-prime lending through its purchase of Household and, along with Citibank's Citifinancial, is a leader in the market. For these two companies sub-prime lending has become a global phenomenon with operations in India, Asia, South America and Eastern Europe. Moreover, some non-financial institutions are also involved, for example GE Capital, a subsidiary of General Electric that provides consumer loans, many of which are sub-prime, in thirty-six countries (Lee 2004).

Sub-prime lenders offer a range of products, although in reality many organizations specialize in a few key areas, including consolidation loans, mortgages, car finance and credit cards. Most lending is secured: on homes in the case of personal loans and mortgages and on the car with respect to car loans. The ability of consumers to shop around in this market has become more of a reality in the past few years, since new entrants tempted by larger profit margins have moved into the market. The range of delivery channels in this market is not as wide as for mainstream offerings, but is IT-intensive, including telephone and internet provision, since these low-cost modes of entry present few barriers to new companies (Leyshon and Pollard 2000). Advertisements in the tabloids and on daytime television 'informercials' feature strongly in marketing campaigns (Burton *et al*. 2004).

Sub-prime lending is well established in the United States, particularly in relation to mortgage lending, where it was a niche market until the 1990s. Lee (2004) maintains that in the United States, sub-prime lending has gone mainstream, since it affects more and more Americans, and it has been exported overseas. The dollar value of sub-prime loans went up from $35 billion in 1994 to $150 billion in 1998. Moreover, the numbers of lenders specializing in sub-prime credit increased almost tenfold from 104,000 in 1993 to 997,000 in 1998. Some financial institutions not only have their own sub-prime mortgage subsidiaries but also provide an administrative service for other lenders. For example, Skipton Building Society has its own sub-prime division called Amber and has also established the third main credit-scoring bureau, Call Credit. However, it also provides a management service for other sub-prime mortgage lenders that are UK- and US-based through its Home Loan Management (HML) subsidiary. Thus, a new niche market has arisen in the management and administration of sub-prime mortgage portfolios.

Secured credit cards are another highly profitable area of business that is controversial even within the industry. Secured cards first emerged in 1982 but did not draw the attention of Citibank and other card issuers until the 1990s (Hudson 1996). Secured credit cards are targeted at consumers who are too poor or whose credit history is too shaky for them to obtain mainstream cards. Secured cards are promoted via direct mail, freephone telephone numbers, through radio, television, newspapers, magazines, in stores and within fringe banks in working-class communities. The cards are presented as one way in which customers can restore their creditworthiness, and are tempting in card-based societies such as the United States where to have one's credit card confiscated is on a par with being excommunicated by the medieval church (Calder 1999).

Secured cards are structured around the customer opening a savings account and receiving a bank card with a credit line equal to between 50 per cent and 100 per cent of the savings account balance. The cards are expensive to operate, requiring a processing fee with the application, high annual fees and either low or no interest paid on savings accounts, and the interest rates can run as high as 22 per cent. In effect, financial institutions are lending customers their own money and charging them significant fees and interest for doing so. Secured cards are among the most profitable segment of credit card portfolios, owing to the high interest rates, lack of default and annual fees. Citibank is the industry leader, and many secure cardholders are recruited from its mainstream turn-down list (Williams 2004).

Lord (2005) maintains that there are several reasons why the sub-prime market has grown in the United States. First, the rise in credit card debt and the ability of consumers to keep up payments fuelled a market for consolidation loans, a speciality of sub-prime lenders. Consolidation loans bundle up existing debt from a variety of sources and provide one loan to cover all outstanding advances. In some instances consolidation loans are secured against property, so if consumers fail to keep up repayments they could lose their home. Consolidation loans are frequently characterized by high upfront arrangement fees and high interest rates. They are marketed on the basis that consumers only have to deal with one lender, and the stressful situation of long-standing disputes with creditors can be brought to an end. Often, consumers add to their debt by taking the opportunity to take more credit and extending the term of the loan, thus accruing more interest. Second, higher bankruptcy rates in many Anglo-Saxon societies, which will be discussed in detail in Chapter 6, are also contributing to the growth of sub-prime lending. Although the stigma associated with bankruptcy has receded in recent years, consumers with a history of bankruptcy are frequently excluded from the mainstream financial services market. There is little option but to turn to sub-prime lenders for finance. A third reason for the growth was the securitization of retail mortgages via mortgage-backed security, which allowed sub-prime lenders to raise billions to back their lending and marketing activities. Fourth, the sub-prime mortgage market was extended to include the first mortgage market rather than the secondary market, where the business first became established. Finally, in the United States the Tax Reform Act 1986 encouraged consumers to transform non-mortgage debts into mortgage finance since it was the only form of tax-deductible interest.

Despite the presence of some reputable lenders within the sub-prime market, this area of business has attracted considerable criticism. There have been several books written in the United States from the perspective of investigative journalism that have highlighted some of the human devastation resulting from unethical, predatory lending. Authoritative accounts include Matthew Lee's (2004) *Predatory Lending: Toxic Credit in the Global Inner City*, Peterson's (2004) *Taming the Sharks: Towards a Cure for the High-Cost Credit Market*, Richard Lord's (2005) *American Nightmare: Predatory Lending and the Foreclosure of the American Dream* and Michael Hudson's (1996) *Merchants of Misery: How Corporate America Profits from Poverty*. These accounts provide one example after another of households being duped into loans with multiple fees including life insurance, disability insurance and unemployment insurance. Pre-payment penalties to end agreements are set so high that few can afford them, and some contracts can run for four to five years. Companies offer one refinancing deal after another to people who cannot afford them, keeping them in perpetual debt. Lee (2004: 2) maintains that in previous centuries this process was called 'debt peonage'; today we have the 'sub-prime serf'. Consolidation loans secured against homes where the loan to value ratio exceeds 125 per cent are not uncommon. When homeowners fail to keep up repayments, their homes are repossessed by the companies that financed them.

The non-status credit market

The non-status credit market largely comprises moneylenders, loan sharks, pawnbrokers and cheque cashers, who are engaged in a very traditional mode of delivering financial services. Moneylending can be traced back to antiquity, and concerns about its regressive social effects are reflected in strictures against usury that are contained within faiths such as Christianity and Islam. By the sixteenth century every level of society apart from the very poorest groups was involved in moneylending. For example, sixteenth-century shopkeepers (and haberdashers in particular) called themselves 'brokers' since they mediated between customers and moneylenders offering loans (for example, on clothes) at high rates of interest (Davies 1966). Moneylending is thus a relic form of the financial services sector (Leyshon *et al.* 2004). The traditional system of door-to-door collection is a mode of delivering financial services that was specifically developed to meet the needs of working-class people living in urban areas whereby premiums were collected by agents going from door to door on a weekly basis, thus enforcing financial self-discipline (Butt 1984; Knights and Vurdubakis 1993; Leyshon *et al.* 2004).

Contemporary consumers in this segment of the market are individuals in lower socio-economic groups who are in poorly paid unskilled or semi-skilled jobs or are unemployed. These are categories indicative of adults who do not make use of mainstream financial services in managing their affairs. Such individuals are more likely to be tenants than homeowners and live in inner cities and/or in public housing (Leyshon *et al.* 2004). They have credit histories that are highly impaired or have never been constructed with mainstream lenders. The products on offer in this section of the market are highly limited and are supplied by moneylenders or specialist retailers and take the form of small loans, typically of a few hundred pounds each. Often this form of finance is used to pay for day-to-day expenditure, including paying utility bills, and sometimes for special occasions such as holidays and Christmas (Kempson and Whyley 1999). Borrowing is usually of cash, but loans can be made through vouchers that can be used at a narrow range of retail outlets.

The use of mainstream credit scoring techniques in this market is highly constrained. Since many organizations are relatively new to the market, they do not have a complement of credit histories with which to compile scorecards. Credit-scoring bureaux that have not traditionally focused on this section of the market will be of little assistance in this respect. Credit-granting institutions therefore typically try to minimize the risk of default in other ways, including securing larger deposits and lending at lower loan-to-value ratios than in the prime market.

Interest rates and charges for credit from moneylenders tend to be much higher than from other sources. There are few alternative providers and all tend to be expensive. There has been considerable concern about the costs and terms of the credit they provide to their customers. To some extent the higher costs can be attributed to the high administrative overheads associated with the highly labour-intensive nature of the face-to-face delivery and the higher risks involved in the case of door-to-door collections. Whereas in the prime market it is assumed that consumers will repay on time and they are therefore penalized for not doing so, in the non-status market non-payment and late payment are factored into the pricing structure (Kempson and Whyley 1999: 6). Even good customers who repay on time are penalized by those who default.

Cheque cashers are another alternative credit provider in the contemporary urban landscape. The use of cheque-cashing outlets further impoverishes the disenfranchised, leaving them with no records or proof of payment and no ongoing relationship with lenders upon which they could build a credit history. Furthermore, individuals using this route can compromise their personal safety by carrying large amounts of cash.

Payday lenders are organizations that make small cash loans to individuals who need access to money quickly. In exchange for cash, the consumer writes a post-dated cheque to be cashed by the payday lender when the consumer's salary has been deposited in their bank account. The credit authorization process is quick and easy, and requires proof of employment, a phone number and a valid driving licence. There is little by way of paperwork, and less scrupulous attention is paid to borrowers' creditworthiness. For some consumers, payday loans can provide a useful stopgap when unexpected bills arise. For others, they can result in their falling deeper into an ever-increasing spiral of debt.

Payday lenders are most common in the United States, where they have emerged in ethnic minority and low-income neighbourhoods that have been abandoned by mainstream lenders. In 1992 only 300 payday loan outlets existed, compared to over 10,000 by 2000 (Manning 2000). Most payday loans total less than £250 ($500, ECU) and are typically to be repaid within a term of two to three weeks. The cost of the loan is around 20 per cent of the value borrowed. Research has indicated that payday loan consumers refinance or 'roll over' payday loans, thus ensuring a long-term relationship with one or more lenders (Graves 2003).

Pawnbrokers are one of the fastest-growing areas of lending in the United States. In 1985 there were a little under 5,000 pawnshops distributed across the country, but especially in the South. At the turn of the millennium the figure had risen to 14,000 outlets. Loans are typically provided for around 25–30 per cent of the appraised value of the pawned item. Approximately 30 per cent of customers default on their 'pawns' by failing either to 'renew' by paying the monthly interest, or to 'redeem' by paying the loan and interest. Although pawning can be an expensive method of raising cash, one advantage for borrowers is that pawns are not reported to credit bureaux, and delinquent payments and defaulted loans are treated as confidential. Thus, an individual's credit rating will not be affected. A variation on payday lending and pawn-broking is the car-title pawn, which is legal in twenty-five US states. The largest supplier, Title Loans of America, has over 300 stores nationwide. Car-title pawn outlets typically offer larger loans than traditional pawnshops ($300–$1,200), which are obtained by pledging a car title at monthly interest rates of between 2.5 per cent and 25 per cent. Consumers tend to use pawn titles for serious financial failings, including eviction or having essential services such as gas or electricity disconnected, or as a means of avoiding arrest for failing to pay child maintenance payments or income taxes. The car can be confiscated if two payments are missed (Manning 2000).

The rent-to-own industry is another aspect of the alternative sector and offers customers lacking access to credit and the ability to pay for goods at the point of sale access to new and used appliances, electronics and furniture. In the United States the number of rent-to-own stores stood at around 2,000 in the early 1980s; by the end of the 1990s the figure had reached in excess of 7,500. The British Thorn EMI group is a dominant player in the $14.5 billion market (Hudson 1996). Rent-to-own stores serve a variety of customers, from those who have been temporarily relocated by their employer and wish to rent on a short-term basis to those who complete the rent-to-own contract. However, the industry targets lower-income and credit-damaged consumers by not performing credit checks, making the application procedure quick and simple to understand. Manning's (2000: 202) assessment of Rent-A-Center's corporate advertising in the United States notes that it appeals to those on modest incomes, stressing 'free delivery, free setup, free service, no commitment'. Other appeals focus on the economics of renting compared with other ways of providing the same service. For example, in one advertisement a woman explains that it is more cost-effective to rent a washing machine and do her own laundry than to use a laundrette. In another ad a woman stresses the fact that she works every day and deserves to have nice things whether or not she has no credit history or a bad credit history.

Kolodinsky *et al.* (2005) indicate that most rent-to-own consumers in the United States are drawn from sections in society that have low incomes and low levels of educational attainment. Their research demonstrated that the total price paid by consumers on a variety of rent-to-own purchases was in excess of double the listed cash price of the products. Furthermore, the average monthly interest rate was 85.7 per cent, well above the legal threshold of 30 per cent. They also discovered that it was impossible for customers to identify the true cost of rent-to-own products, because only the cash price is revealed to customers.

The Basel II capital accord

The previous discussion demonstrates that credit markets have become more segmented and intricate within advanced societies over the past decade. Portfolios have become increasingly complex as lenders offer a more extensive assortment of loans to a wider range of borrowers, each comprising different levels of risk. It is apparent from the previous discussion that contemporary credit markets are characterized by a high degree of segmentation on the basis of risk. Lenders manage portfolios of consumer credit that can have different degrees attached to them. How different levels of risk are managed within the portfolio and what effect high levels of default have on the performance of the whole portfolio has become an important issue, given the adverse risk of default associated with sub-prime borrowing (Cowan and Cowan 2004). Despite the rapid growth in consumer credit, there remain large gaps in our quantitative understanding of retail portfolios (Allen, DeLong and Saunders 2004). Little academic research has been conducted in this field, and for this reason a special issue of the *Journal of Banking and Finance* entitled 'Retail Credit Risk and Management' was published (see Berlin and Mester 2004). Moreover, given the recent development of risk-based lending, many organizations do not have an extensive track record in risk management and measurement, which has caused some concern among regulators.

The significant growth in sub-prime lending has occurred in relatively stable, prosperous economic conditions. Exposure to risk in the event of an economic downturn and the effects on bank stability is something of an unknown quantity. However, there is evidence that lenders engaged in sub-prime lending are witnessing significant losses. In 2007, HSBC, one of the UK's largest banks, issued the first profit warning in its 142-year history. Its acquisition of Household, the US sub-prime mortgage lender, was the source of the bad debts, for which provisions of £10.6 billion had to be set aside, more than 35 per cent higher than in 2005. HSBC argued that other areas of Household's business, including credit cards, were profitable and that sub-prime mortgages were the difficult area. It was worrying that the defaults occurred relatively shortly after the downturn in the US housing market. These difficulties inevitably have a negative effect on the parent brand. After the debacle, HSBC was referred to by US pundits as a Highly Suspect British Company. Furthermore, poor-quality loans have forced nearly 30 sub-prime lenders in the US to close recently, and others are planning to exit the business (Johnson 2007).

Another pertinent issue in the retail lending landscape is the emergence of mortgage-backed securities, which allow banks to churn over business to make a quicker profit. Traditionally, lenders have raised cash on the money markets and lent it out at a higher rate; the difference between the two is the profit. However, in instances of mortgage and other long-term borrowing the payback time can be many years. Asset-backed securities allow banks to make loans and bundle them, creating stock or security in the company. The asset is the sum of mortgage payments being made by thousands of households, and the value of the mortgaged homes. The bundle is referred to as a mortgage-backed security, and can be sold on to other lenders. The new way of doing business was to lend high, cream off as much profit as possible by selling mortgage-backed securities to investors, then lend out and bundle up another security. Typically, an organization may provide mortgages to customers, keep the accounts for three to four months to ensure they repay, and then bundle up and sell on. Many lenders will have forward agreements over a specified timescale to sell a pre-specified number of accounts. The sale of sub-prime mortgage-backed securities in the United States increased from $11 billion in 1994 to $203 billion in 2003 (Lord 2005) (see Table 4.4). The selling of mortgage-backed securities does raise issues about the quality of the business being transacted. Some sub-prime lenders have been known to offer large loans to people who will have difficulty affording them, which will inevitably impact on the quality of the business. In 2006, 10 per cent of sub-primes packaged in the United States were in default, the highest figure in a decade (Beales and Spikes 2007; Jackson 2007).

The emergence of sub-prime mortgage-backed securities lends further support to the view that financial markets are 'now defined by a set of credit relationships with different time structures, etched in computer memories' (Corbridge and Thrift 1994: 11). The complexity of credit risk assessment in lending decisions has not gone unnoticed by bank regulators and has prompted

Table 4.4 Sub-prime mortgage securitization in the United States, 1994–2003

Year	Sub-prime loans made ($ billion)	Sub-prime loans turned into securities ($ billion)	Percentage of sub-prime loans securitized
1994	35	11	32
1995	65	18	28
1996	97	38	40
1997	125	66	53
1998	150	83	55
1999	160	60	37
2000	138	56	41
2001	173	76	44
2002	241	133	55
2003	332	203	61

Source: For sub-prime loans made, Federal Reserve Board. For securities, *Inside B and C Lending*, published by Inside Mortgage Finance Publications, cited in Lord (2005: 20).

tighter controls in this area. The Basel Committee on Banking Supervision is a committee of banking supervisory authorities that was established by the central bank governors of the Group of Ten countries in 1975. It comprises senior representatives of bank supervisory authorities in Belgium, Canada, France, Germany, Italy, Japan, Luxembourg, the Netherlands, Spain, Sweden, Switzerland, the United Kingdom and the United States. The committee usually meets at the Bank for International Settlements in Basel, Switzerland, which is why the regulatory frameworks the bank adopts are called the Basel Accords. There have been a number of accords over the years (see Van Deventer and Imai 2003) that have attempted to ensure that banks have robust methods of risk assessment in place, in order to foster confidence in the international banking system. The new standard for bank lending is called Basel II and is set out in a report entitled *International Convergence of Capital Measurement and Capital Standards: A Revised Framework* (www.bis.org) (Basel Committee on Banking Supervision 2004). This framework replaces the 1988 accord and is an attempt to further strengthen the soundness and stability of the inter-national banking system.

Experience has demonstrated that poor credit quality and credit risk assessment have been one of the major causes of bank distress in the case of individual banks and at the level of banking systems as a whole. Failure to identify and recognize deterioration in credit quality in a timely manner can aggravate and prolong the problem. For this reason, it is important that there are systematic and reliable measures of the concentration of risk in credit portfolios. Two sources of risk are evident in credit portfolios, *systematic* and *idiosyncratic*. Systematic risk is the effect of unexpected changes in macro-economic and financial market conditions on the performance of borrowers.

Idiosyncratic risk is the effects of risks that are peculiar to different organizations (Basel Committee on Banking Supervision 2006a).

The new framework is structured around ten principles that fall within two broad categories: supervisory expectations concerning robust credit risk assessment and valuation for loans, and the evaluation of credit risk assessment for loans controls and capital adequacy.

Supervisory expectations concerning robust credit risk assessment and valuation for loans

1   A bank's board of directors and senior management are responsible for ensuring that the bank has appropriate credit risk assessment processes and effective internal controls commensurate with the size, nature and complexity of its lending operations to consistently determine provisions for loan losses in accordance with the bank's stated policies and procedures, the applicable accounting framework and supervisory guidance.
2   A bank should have a system in place to reliably classify loans on the basis of credit risk.
3   A bank's policies should appropriately address validation of any internal credit risk assessment models.
4   A bank should adopt and document a sound loan loss methodology, which addresses credit risk assessment policies, procedures and controls for assessing credit risk, identifying problem loans and determining loan loss provisions in a timely manner.
5   A bank's aggregate amount of individual and collectively assessed loan loss provisions should be adequate to absorb estimated credit losses in the loan portfolio.
6   A bank's use of experienced credit judgement and reasonable estimates are an essential part of the recognition and measurement of loan losses.
7   A bank's credit risk assessment process for loans should provide the bank with the necessary tools, procedures and observable data to use for assessing credit risk, accounting for loan impairment and determining regulatory capital requirements.

Supervisory evaluation of credit risk assessment for loans controls and capital adequacy

8   Banking supervisors should periodically evaluate the effectiveness of a bank's credit risk policies and practices for assessing loan quality.
9   Banking supervisors should be satisfied that the methods employed by a bank to calculate loan loss provisions produce a reasonable and prudent measurement of estimated credit losses in the loan portfolio that are recognized in a timely manner.

10 Banking supervisors should consider credit risk assessment and valuation policies and practices when assessing a bank's capital adequacy (Basel Committee on Banking Supervision 2006b: 1).

The emphasis on more refined credit grading systems allows for a more accurate assessment of the characteristics of loan portfolios, the likelihood of defaults and, ultimately, the adequacy of loan provision in instances of loan losses. The committee stipulated that credit risk ratings should be removed and updated whenever relevant new information is received and credit risk ratings should be changed accordingly. The process should be undertaken at least once a year and far more frequently with respect to 'larger, complex, high risk or problem credit' (Basel Committee on Banking Supervision 2006b: 5). The assessment process should include circumstances that affect the repayment of individual loans, including significant financial difficulty on the part of the borrower, the probability of bankruptcy or other financial reorganization of the borrower, and any breaches of contract such as a default or delinquency in interest or payment concessions granted by the lender for economic or legal reasons.

The accord places a great deal of emphasis on identifying loan loss in a timely manner, and the taking of appropriate action. While it recognizes that historical trends and economic conditions are an important starting point for assessing risk at institutional level, alone they are not sufficient, given the proliferation of new areas of lending. The accord maintains that there needs to be a consideration of a wider range of factors that could result in loan losses in the portfolio, factors that could be different from those obtaining in historical experience. A number of features are relevant in this respect:

- changes in lending policies and procedures, including underwriting standards and collection, charge-off, and recovery;
- changes in international, national and local economic and business conditions and developments, including the condition of various market segments;
- changes in the trend, volume and severity of past due loans and loans graded as low quality, as well as trends in the volume of impaired loans, troubled debt restructurings and other loan modifications;
- changes in the experience, ability and depth of lending management and staff;
- changes related to new market segments and products;
- changes in the quality of the bank's loan review system and the degree of oversight by the bank's senior management and board of directors;
- the existence and effect of any concentrations of credit, and changes in the level of such concentrations;

- the effect of external factors such as competition and legal and regulatory requirements on the level of estimated credit losses in the institution's current portfolio; and
- changes in the credit risk profile of the loan portfolio as a whole (BIS 2006: 9).

The accord has imposed a tight regulatory framework on lending criteria that takes a more cautious approach to risk assessment. In theory, it should mean that lending criteria should become stricter and some of the consumers who were marginal cases with respect to being able to borrow may subsequently be excluded.

Conclusion

The concepts of the 'old' and 'new' economies of credit provide a valuable device for illustrating changes in the consumer credit lending environment. The finer segmentation of the lending market into prime, complex prime, sub-prime and non-status presents a realistic picture of the operation of contemporary credit markets. The non-status credit options are the ones that have attracted the most controversy since they deal with the most disadvantaged consumers in society and are the outlets that are the most exploitative in terms of pricing. Pawnshops and moneylenders are a persistent feature of the financial services landscape. These outlets are a stark reminder of the deeply fractured nature of consumer society. However, it is the applications of credit scoring that were discussed in the previous chapter that have allowed lenders to more precisely define consumers according to the risk that they present to the business. Sub-prime lending inevitably involves a higher degree of risk. This issue has not gone unnoticed by the regulators. The Basel II Accord will have a significant impact on future trends in consumer societies since lenders are put under pressure to calculate in detail the degree of risk for their credit portfolios.

Questions

1 What features characterize the 'old' and 'new' economy of credit?
2 Explain the differences between the prime, complex prime, sub-prime and non-status credit markets.
3 What do you understand by the term 'mortgage-backed securities'?
4 What changes does the Basel II Accord require with respect to credit portfolios and how may these changes affect consumer society?

Further reading

Berlin, M. and Mester, L.J. (2004) 'Retail credit risk management and measurement: an introduction to the special issue', *Journal of Banking and Finance*, 28: 721–725.

Burton, D., Knights, D., Leyshon, A., Alferoff, C. and Signoretta, P. (2004) 'Making a market: the UK retail financial services industry and the rise of the complex sub-prime credit market', *Competition and Change*, 8, 1: 3–26.

Graves, S.M. (2003) 'Landscapes of predation, landscapes of neglect: a location analysis of payday lenders and banks', *Professional Geographer*, 55, 3: 303–317.

Hudson, M. (ed.) (1996) *Merchants of Misery: How Corporate America Profits from Poverty*, Monroe, ME: Common Courage.

Kolodinsky, J., Murphy, M., Baehr, A. and Lesser, S. (2005) 'Time price differentials in the rent-to-own industry: implications for empowering vulnerable consumers', *International Journal of Consumer Studies*, 29, 2: 119–124.

Lee, M. (2004) *Predatory Bender: America in the Aughts / Predatory lending: toxic credit in the global inner city*, Bronx, NY: Inner City Press.

Lord, R. (2005) *American Nightmare: Predatory Lending and the Foreclosure of the American Dream*, Monroe, ME: Common Courage.

Peterson, C.L. (2004) *Taming the Sharks: Towards a Cure for the High-Cost Credit Market*, Akron, OH: University of Akron Press.

Williams, B. (2004) *Debt for Sale: A Social History of the Credit Trap*, Philadelphia: University of Pennsylvania Press.

5 The marketing of consumer credit

The role of marketing is central to many accounts of the development of consumer society. As Bauman (1998: 31) notes, 'consumer society is not one of delayed gratification; it's a "now" society. A wanting society, not a waiting society.' In this environment, marketing plays a central role, since the function has responsibility for developing new products and strategically placing them so that they will be an attractive proposition for consumers. The marketing of credit has become a highly controversial process. On the one hand, financial institutions have to lend to consumers to stay in business and enhance their profitability. However, consumers and consumer groups object to high levels of interest and upfront fees, and unethical marketing practices that encourage consumers to take on more credit than is perhaps prudent. This chapter will begin by charting the historical root of marketing as a business function and assessing the development of financial services marketing. The second section will explore the changing nature of consumer research and how it has been influenced by debates surrounding consumption and consumer society.

In the remainder of the chapter the discussion will focus on specific aspects of credit. The first theme is marketing and the democratization of credit, and we shall explore the ways in which the huge growth in credit has facilitated equal access to credit. The fourth section of the chapter will focus on advertising, specifically the ideology that surrounds the language of credit and debt in advertising. Credit and consumer segmentation will be the theme of the fifth section, and a number of issues surrounding the targeting of credit to vulnerable groups will be raised. The sixth section deals with the current extensive use of the direct marketing of credit. In the seventh section the concept of new product innovation will be explored within the contemporary credit market. The final section will address unfair sales tactics associated with the marketing of credit.

How modern is modern marketing?

It used to be a widely held view within the marketing community that modern marketing practices are a relatively recent phenomenon. The predominant view was that the Production Era pre-dated the Marketing Era, with the latter being a much more sophisticated approach that integrated marketing within organizations. The groundswell of opinion was that organizations gave little thought to marketing, and it only developed relatively recently. The inspiration for the Production Era–Sales Era–Marketing Era model came from a case study of the evolution of marketing at the Pillsbury Company (Keith 1960). According to Keith, the Production Era at Pillsbury occurred from the firm's foundation in the 1860s and lasted until the 1930s. This era was characterized by management's emphasis on production rather than distribution. The Production Era was followed by the Sales Era, which incorporated the hard sell, backed by research and advertising. By the 1950s the organization had moved to the Marketing Era of sophisticated customer orientation.

The Production Era of marketing is usually dated from about 1870 until 1930, and its main features are as follows:

- Firms focused their attention largely on physical production, straining to overcome age-old constraints on supply with new technologies and more efficient management techniques, and distribution was a secondary concern, left to independent wholesalers and retailers.
- Output consisted of limited product lines whose conception and design reflected production requirements more than research into customer needs; insight into customer needs was not crucial, because
- demand exceeded supply; disposable income and desire for any available products grew rapidly and without pause among the broad populace, and
- there was little competition in each product market; hence,
- wholesalers and retailers did not have to develop sophisticated methods because 'products sold themselves'; wholesalers and especially retailers were peripheral to the business enterprise, whose locus was manufacturing firms (Fullerton 1988: 108).

The view that modern marketing evolved from a production era was questioned by Fullerton (1988) in his seminal article published in the *Journal of Marketing* entitled 'How modern is modern marketing? Marketing's evolution and the myth of the "Production Era"'. There is mounting evidence that the Production–Sales–Marketing Era model is not an appropriate way to conceptualize marketing's development as a business function. Nevett (1985) has demonstrated that the need to undertake media research was acted upon by advertisers and their agents in mid-nineteenth-century Britain, but the methods used were fairly primitive by today's standards. Alexander (1970) has provided evidence to indicate that one-price pricing and enticing window displays were strategies adopted by some urban shops before 1850. Redlich (1935) traces most twentieth-century advertising vehicles to their sixteenth-century origins; the difference is that contemporary advertising tends to be different in its pervasiveness and impact. In short, the development of modern marketing requires a more sensitive approach to unearth its origins than had hitherto been suggested within the marketing community.

Fullerton provides a different periodization of marketing's development, seeing it as taking place through four eras: the *Era of Antecedents*, the *Era of Origins*, the *Era of Institutional Development* and the *Era of Refinement and Formalization*. The *Era of Antecedents* is the term to describe the gestation period before a breakthrough in business thinking and practices occurred that would lay the foundations for future marketing developments. The gestational period was estimated to begin about 1500 in Britain and Germany and the 1660s in North America. The dominant value system sustained the view that commerce was little better than criminality; finance and distribution systems did not exist, and the means of production and the transport infrastructure were primitive. Powerful forces in the form of religious, political and social influences resisted attempts to increase low levels of consumption. Approximately 75–90 per cent of the population were self-sufficient; mass markets did not exist, but entrepreneurs did cultivate a market for luxury goods among the nobility.

In the *Era of Origins*, modern marketing begins – starting in Britain about 1750 and in Germany and the United States around 1830. Fullerton maintains that 'this period marked the beginning of *pervasive* attention to stimulating and meeting demand among *nearly all of society*' (1988: 122). This period began with the onset of the Industrial Revolution. Improvements in production and transportation, combined with the migration of the rural population to urban centres, provided the basis for large mass markets. Consumers were targeted and products were manufactured to appeal to potential buyers. As competition intensified between firms, marketing activity increased. The era was complete in Britain by 1850 but continued in the United States and Germany until 1870.

The *Era of Institutional Development* was a period when a marketing infrastructure was developed in Britain, Germany and the United States. It commenced from 1850 onwards in Britain and 1870 in the other two countries. The era was completed in all countries by 1929. Mass production required a system to stimulate demand for the goods produced. The physical separation of production and consumption necessitated appropriate distribution and communications infrastructure. New institutions that focused on advertising, market research and retailing helped marketing become an integrated part of daily life.

The *Era of Refinement and Formalization* occurred in all three countries from around 1930. This era was the start of modern marketing as we know it, with the development of new retailing formats such as supermarkets, and developments (including containerization) that assisted physical distribution and logistics. Market analysis became more sophisticated, with the gathering, measuring and evaluating of market information. Marketing activities began to be formally organized into marketing departments.

The ways in which credit supported consumption in the latter part of the nineteenth and early part of the twentieth century have already been documented (in Chapter 2). However, what needs to be acknowledged is that the marketing of financial services *per se* has a much more recent history and that this is relevant to our understanding of the marketing of credit by mainstream financial institutions. The development of services marketing as opposed to product marketing as a distinctive approach to marketing theory and practice can be dated from the mid-1960s (Fisk and Tansuhaj 1985). A landmark was the publication of the first text on the topic, *Services Marketing*, in 1974 (Rathmell 1974). The move to a service-based economy required a new approach to marketing that took into account the unique characteristics of services. The marketing of financial services literature came a few years later, with the publication of *Marketing Financial Services* (McIver 1980), *Financial Marketing and Communications* (Newman 1984), *Marketing Financial Services: A Strategic Vision* (Donnelly, Berry and Thompson 1985), *Marketing Financial Services* (Ennew, Watkins and Wright 1990) and *Retailing of Financial Services* (McGoldrick and Greenland 1994).

Marketing developed as a powerful force in financial institutions during the early 1980s, owing to a combination of deregulation of credit markets, new entrants in the market, and the problem of Third World debt, which made many lenders seek out business opportunities nearer to home (Howcroft 1985). During this period, marketing departments were established in some financial institutions for the first time. There were also cultural shifts within financial institutions from an administrative to a sales and marketing orientation. The marketing of credit to personal-sector consumers intensified in this period, assisted by the deregulation of financial markets (Burton 1994). Some of the ways this has occurred will be discussed later in the chapter.

The changing nature of consumer research

The development of theories of consumer society has been paralleled by the introduction of alternative perspectives on consumer research and consumer behaviour in marketing. Belk (1995) has provided a valuable overview of these changes in his assessment of old and new perspectives in consumer behaviour research, as summarized in Table 5.1. When marketing was first taught in US business schools at the beginning of the twentieth century it was highly influenced by economics and was largely taught by economists. This approach to studying consumer research has tended to foreground the concept of rational economic man. According to this interpretation, consumption and consumer behaviour are largely determined economic constraints. The model of the consumer in some of the early consumer research centred on an information-processing, rational consumer whose purchase decisions were largely determined by price. The consumer is little more than an abstract individual who is required in a commodified world where money is the main instrument of exchange. Economists do not tell us why consumers make the decisions they do. Indeed, this approach to understanding credit use by consumers is still observable in the forecasting and credit risk literature, which largely operates with a rational view of the consumer as someone who can be reduced to a statistical variable (see Chapters 3 and 4).

In the 1950s the economic approach to studying consumer behaviour began to be questioned by the emergence of motivational research. This genre of research was conducted by industry within the confines of marketing research advertising and specialist research agencies and by academics. Motivational research used techniques from psychoanalysis to examine the latent emotional meanings of a variety of consumer goods, with the focus remaining on how to distribute and sell goods more effectively (Stern 1990). The instrumental nature of motivational research and its focus on manipulating consumers were reflected in Vance Packard's (1957) book entitled *The Hidden Persuaders*. Anxiety about the potential of marketers manipulating the subconscious desires of consumers was a central factor in the decline of motivational research.

Another major factor to pre-empt the decline of motivational research was the 'scientific revolution' and the rise of positivism in the social sciences during the 1960s. Consumer research embraced scientific experimentation, borrowing methods and concepts from psychology. The focus in consumer research turned towards various persuasive techniques and the effects of what has became known as the marketing mix: product, price, promotion and distribution. Although the influence of psychology brought an additional perspective to consumer research, it was largely along the lines of a re-rationalized view of the consumer. The dominant view was of the consumer as information processor. Consumer research remains dominated by economic and psychological approaches; however, there are some indications that things are changing.

Table 5.1 Old and new perspectives in consumer behaviour research

Old perspective	New perspective
Positivist	Non-positivist
Experimental/surveys	Ethnographies
Quantitative	Qualitative
A priori theory	Emergent theory
Economic/psychological	Sociological/anthropological
Micro/managerial	Macro/cultural
Focus on buying	Focus on consuming
Emphasis on cognitions	Emphasis on emotions
American	Multicultural

Source: Belk (1995: 61, figure 2.1).

The new consumer behaviour literature has a much broader base in its focus on alternative philosophies of science, a more macro focus on consumer well-being and the effects of marketing and consumption activities on culture (see also Arnould and Thompson 2005 on twenty years of consumer culture theory research). In the 1980s a number of anthropologists, sociologists and literary critics joined marketing departments, reflecting an interest in consumption and the consumer in many disciplines, as was noted in the previous section. The shift to neo-positivist methods opened up new issues and spaces for alternative discourse (Hirschman and Holbrook 1992; Brown 1995; Brown and Turley 1997; Stern 1993, 1998). Emergent sub-fields included macro-marketing, social marketing, consumer policy and marketing history. This different orientation had implications for conceptualizing the consumer. As Belk (1995: 59) notes,

> Removed from the sterile assumptions of the laboratory or anonymous scaled attitude measures, the new consumer behaviour precipitates the unavoidable conclusion that consumers are not mere automatons who receive information inputs and produce brand choice outputs that maximize satisfaction. Rather they are socially connected human beings participating in multiple interacting cultures.

Some of this new literature focused on the symbolic meaning of consumption, the role of property and possessions in defining the self, and the role of consumption festivals and rituals. Another strand of research can be broadly termed critical perspectives and has embodied critical theoretic, feminist, Marxist, postmodern and poststructural approaches drawn from other social science disciplines. Some of the scholarship generated by these diverse strands of theory included the gendered nature of consumer behaviour, materialism and consumer culture, consumer resistance to the marketization of everyday life, and dysfunctional consumer behaviour including alcohol use, smoking, eating disorders, compulsive buying, and gambling.

Despite the plethora of alternative spaces that have opened up over the past two decades, credit and its role in consumer society have rarely been addressed within the consumer behaviour literature as serious topics of analysis in their own right. As a result, most of the current literature on consumer credit is written from outside of consumer research. Of the few accounts that do exist, most focus on credit cards and are somewhat dated. Hirschman (1979) notes that consumers tend to spend more when credit cards are available, while Garcia (1980) provides a descriptive account of credit card users. Bernthal, Crockett and Rose (2005) provide a more recent study that treads the well-worn path of credit cards as lifestyle facilitators. They draw the unsurprising conclusion that credit cards can facilitate consumption, generating a trajectory of freedom and achievement. Alternatively, they can take on the characteristics of a debtor's prison and be used as a coping strategy in a trajectory of constraint. Henry

(2005) provides some insights into money management strategies across different social classes but does not directly address the issue of credit or debt.

Marketing and the democratization of credit

The democratization of credit idea is not a new concept. It first appeared in 1914 in an article in *Current Opinion* (see Austin 2004) and promoted the view that people of small means should be able to borrow small loans with dignity from banks in the same way as the wealthy, cutting out loan sharks. Nearly a century later the democratization of credit is an issue that remains on the agenda. The lack of appropriate access to credit is a powerful reminder that not all individuals are active participants in consumer society on an equal footing. In our rush to celebrate the positive aspects of consumer society, there has been a neglect of poor consumers (Bauman 1998).

Kempson and Whyley (1999) argue that individuals in lower socio-economic groups suffer exclusion from financial services (including credit) in a range of ways. First is *access exclusion*, where access is restricted to mainstream financial services as a result of branch closures and adverse risk assessment practices (see Chapter 3). A second method of exclusion is *condition exclusion*, where individuals are excluded from using mainstream products because of the conditions attached to them. For example, operating a current account can be expensive if individuals have to keep minimum balances to avoid paying charges, and charges can be expensive. A third form of exclusion is *price exclusion*, whereby individuals are priced out of the market. Lee (2003) indicates that the biggest increases in bank charges in recent years are the ones that poor people may incur, for example returning direct debits, exceeding overdraft limits, and so forth. The final area of exclusion is *marketing exclusion*. This feature refers to the lack of attention mainstream financial institutions have given to consumers in lower socio-economic groups (Burton *et al.* 2004). In fact this observation of excluding individuals who are viewed as less profitable is applicable across marketing *per se*; it is not a characteristic unique to financial services (Hirschman 1993).

How far consumer societies have come to attaining the *democratization of credit* ideal is a contentious issue. On a positive note, lenders who are willing to lend to a wider range of customers could be viewed as positively contributing to the *democratization of credit*. To some extent this has occurred as mainstream lenders have broadened their customer base. Lyons (2003) maintains that since the mid-1990s, low-income families in the United States have been able to obtain their desired debt levels. This finding was apparent across all households regardless of permanent earnings, age, gender or race. Those experiencing the greatest gains were black households and households with low permanent earnings. A further study by Bird, Hagstrom and Wild (1999) that examined credit card debt of the poor and non-poor found that between 1983 and 1995 the proportion of poor households with a credit card more than doubled. The average balances of the poor rose by almost the same percentage as for the non-poor. While there was little evidence that higher levels of debt had negative consequences in terms of increasing the financial strain in poor households, nevertheless they may have contributed to households living beyond their means. Potentially, the higher levels of debt made these families more vulnerable to an economic slowdown. Gramlich (2000) indicates that mortgage lending to low-income borrowers increased by nearly 75 per cent between 1993 and 1998 compared with 52 per cent for upper-income households. A large-scale study conducted by Lee (2003) gives a rather different impression by indicating that poor people's access to credit products witnessed only a slightly positive increase during the 1990s.

It is the case that for some consumers the benefits of increased competition in the market have enabled them to obtain credit from a wider range of mainstream lenders and in some instances borrow more in real terms. They will have benefited from investments lenders have made in the context of increasing service quality levels in credit card processing (Collier 1991), the credit authorization process (Leung and Lai 2001), expert systems for fraud alert (Leonard 1995), and so forth. However, as we have seen from the material presented in Chapter 4, the significant increase in business for individuals in lower socio-economic groups has been through a range of alternative suppliers that are sometimes subsidiaries of mainstream lenders. Many of these new entrants have a competitive advantage over mainstream institutions in terms of their location, opening hours and operational policies, and they often provide services in the mother tongue of consumers. They do not conduct traditional credit scoring, loan decisions are often made within an hour, loans are paid in cash and they take cash payments (Lee 2003). In this respect these providers are meeting the needs of consumers, but there are higher costs attached to them.

To return to the issue we started out with concerning the democratization of credit, consumer societies have not enabled poor people to access mainstream credit at affordable prices. The democratization of credit remains elusive and poor people are using much the same methods of accessing credit as they did in the middle of the nineteenth century (see Chapter 1). What we have witnessed is the continuation of a parallel system of credit: one for the well off, another for the poor. In many instances, mainstream financial institutions are supporting the alternative market and exploiting individuals who have no other choice but to use it. From the lender's standpoint their policies could be viewed as inclusive, since they are doing business with consumers they had previously excluded. In this respect they are selling the idea of their own virtue (Kennedy 2004). However, the justification is a difficult one when consumer credit is a lucrative area of business. Companies such as General Electric generate more revenue from their credit company subsidiaries, in this case GE Capital, than they do from their manufacturing operations (Manning 2000).

Credit marketing, ideology and the language of debt

A central concern surrounding the negative consequences of consumer credit and debt is the way in which credit has been advertised, and the policy of some financial institutions to deliberately target vulnerable consumers in their desire to extract the maximum amount of profit from those who can least afford it. Advertising has long been linked to the concept of ideology, from the original work of the Frankfurt School to contemporary cultural theory. Eagleton (1991) provides one of the most comprehensive assessments of ideology. Ideology is viewed as a system of beliefs and values that emanate from, and promulgate the worldview of, the dominant group in society. The maintenance and promulgation of the dominant group's ideology are used to sustain and legitimate their power over the perception of social reality, social relations and institutions. Eagleton (1991: 5) notes that ideology may be used by dominant groups to legitimate their social control through at least six different strategies:

> A dominant power may legitimate itself by *promoting* beliefs and values congenial to it: by *naturalizing* and *universalizing* such beliefs so as to [make them appear] self-evident and inevitable: by *denigrating* ideas which might challenge it: by *excluding* rival forms of thought . . . and by *obscuring* social reality in ways convenient to itself.

The last strategy is referred to as *mystification*, and often takes the form of masking or suppressing external social challenges to the dominant group's control.

Advertising can be classed as ideology in the sense that it provides consumers with a particular representation of reality (Dyer 1992). Elliott and Ritson (1997: 197) argue that the most important function of advertising is to legitimate the consumer's activities, thus allowing consumption without 'guilt, suspicion or resistance'. However, it is also clear that advertisements potentially offer different readings dependent on the characteristics of the reader and the context in which the advertisement was viewed. Demystification occurs when existing ideologies are challenged and become a site of consumer resistance (Hirschman 1993; Crockett and Wallendorf 2004). There is another important issue to note with respect to credit advertising, and that is that information and persuasion are usually inextricably linked. Wernick (1991: 405) describes this as a promotional culture where 'the line between what is incidental as advertising and what is ostensibly its primary content, as information and entertainment, is reduced at most to a matter of level and degree'. This promotion by lenders of the liberating effects of credit, obscuring the grave consequences and language of debt, represents an ideology that is being challenged by significant numbers of consumers.

However, conflating the issues of information and promotion is also an activity in which consumer organizations are becoming embroiled. Aldridge

(1997) notes that the Consumers' Association in the United Kingdom is supposed to promote independent, impartial advice to subscribing consumers about a range of products through its *Which?* magazine. Yet it launched its own Which? Visa Card in September 1996 with the slogan 'Using the Which? Card will identify you as a discerning customer'. Furthermore, in a subsequent edition of *Which?* magazine, the Which? Visa Card was promoted as the best credit card on the market. Aldridge interprets this episode as a clash between promotional and anti-promotional cultures.

Historically, whether advertising contributes to an increase in consumer credit is a theme addressed by Olney (1991) for the United States in the 1920s. She demonstrates that although durable goods were advertised more frequently in the 1920s than before World War I, advertisements grew markedly larger during the period. However, manufacturers were no more aggressive in marketing their goods with credit. The availability of credit terms is not mentioned any more frequently in the print advertising of the 1920s than earlier. Nor did manu-facturers use pricing as a marketing strategy; indeed, advertisements for durables were less likely to use the goods price in the early 1920s than in the periods before or afterwards. Prior to World War I the marketing of credit in the form of the 'easy payment plans' was most often mentioned in advertise-ments for pianos. However, after the war easy payment plans were most frequently mentioned in advertisements for domestic appliances, particularly electrical appliances, but even in this case they accounted for only 25 per cent of the advertisements. If manufacturers were using credit as a way to market their products, it was not manifestly apparent in advertisements. Yet by the end of the 1920s, up to 90 per cent of durable goods were purchased with credit, and household debt doubled during the decade. By the 1930s the advertising of credit had become widespread.

One criticism of the contemporary credit industry is that it has promoted overly positive images and metaphors of credit that have tended to obscure the negative consequences of debt. This is particularly true in the case of credit cards, where the emphasis is on convenience, enabling consumers to settle bills any time any place anywhere. This is not surprising when one considers that advertising tends to be an unreliable source of information because it comes from a biased source, namely the producers of the product or service being advertised (Dyer 1992). Klein (1999) provides an interesting overview of credit card advertising in the United States. Credit card advertising is directly linked with the desire for symbolic goods in a competitive society. He argues that marketing and advertising act as an antidote to alienation in the workplace, and credit cards facilitate the achieving of fantasies and dreams. Advances in technology have served to speed up the purchase process via plastic cards and therefore provide an immediate gateway to the consumer society. Klein charts the development of the credit card from a product that was initially marketed to the very affluent to a mass-market product that reached saturation point in the mid-1980s. The bottom line is that the credit card companies have always stressed the aspirational approach: that you can afford to buy what you want; the card brings your dreams within reach.

Advertising's purpose is to attract our attention and make us favourably predisposed to the product on offer. Advertising language is loaded language. The gap between consumers' lived experience and dominant cultural meanings manipulated by lenders is starting to grate with many less well off consumers. As Williams (2004: 55–56) maintains, 'the portrayal of credit cards as benign, helpful companions appeared to match the experiences and perceptions of more advantaged customers'. The metaphors continue when lenders want to recruit new consumers: 'As they solicit our business we become valued, pre-approved, preferred, creditworthy, select customers, or *members*, "worthy" of relationship banking, affinity cards, and grace, in timeworn metaphors from domestic and religious life.' Credit cards in particular are promoted as offering 'options', 'freedom' and 'control'. For existing consumers, the flattery of 'pre-approval', 'valued customers', 'selected from your community for a very special offer' is all too familiar.

When consumers look as though they are becoming less creditworthy, a whole new vocabulary tends to emerge. As Martin (2002: 162) observes,

> One thing that the large consumer credit houses possess is the means to badger people in default. . . . Redlining, declined credit, and other forms of exclusion only bring added work and in that regard opportunity for disciplinary contact with financial regimens. Poverty in this regard is not simply a lack, but an excess of attention.

Tom Ryan, the comedian, points out that 'pre-ruined' might be more appropriate terminology when consumers have maxed out on their card and have the limit raised without their permission once it has reached its ceiling. Lenders may raise interest rates to 'penalty rates', and 'excess charges' may be incurred for going over one's limit. Offers of debt consolidation, 'low-interest starter loans' and 'convenience' cheques are terminology that are used in aggressive strategies to market credit to those already in debt who can least afford it. Invariably the so-called new offers have higher interest rates and more punitive terms and conditions than the original debt. There is a deliberate policy to put the blame on to the consumer and make them feel inferior in situations of default.

There is a need for a counter-narrative alternative to the ones developed by lenders in their advertising campaigns. The messages should be akin to public health messages that credit and debt can damage your health, ruin personal relationships and cause long-term harm. As Williams (2004: 57) succinctly states, debt does not allow us to 'Master the moment' or 'Be everywhere we want to be', but drains resources, drags us and our future down, propels inequality, and masks race, class, gender and generational differences while exacerbating tensions, divisions and inequities that run precisely along those axes. Oganizations develop strategies to target customers who are unlikely to pay off their bills at the end of the month rather than those who use them for convenience. The convenience users are highly unprofitable since they pay no interest and benefit from free insurance and other freebies. As was mentioned earlier, industry jargon to refer to convenience customers is 'deadbeats', hardly a flattering description of some of the most affluent consumers.

Much of the contemporary scholarship on credit and debt has focused on credit cards. Yet for most people their mortgage is the biggest credit commitment that they will ever make. The meaning of homeownership is emotive for many people, and home is a source of ontological security (Saunders 1986). In this respect a home loan is unlike other areas of consumer credit. For many people the home is an important investment for the future, an inheritance that they can leave to their children and kin. Drentea and Lavrakas (2000) draw attention to the distinction between *normative* and *non-normative* debt. Normative debt takes the form of mortgages and car loans, which are deemed to be necessities in many advanced societies. Furthermore, normative debt enjoys positive associations with 'stability, responsibility and being a tax-paying member of the community' (2000: 518). Normative debt is often viewed positively, and is productive. By contrast, non-normative debt is associated with frivolity and lack of constraint, such as credit card spending.

For many people, housing has been a good investment and delivered significant financial gains. The higher multiples of salary that lenders are willing to let consumers borrow testify to the importance stakeholders place on owning one's home. Interest-only mortgages are another development to allow cash-strapped borrowers to take out larger loans than might perhaps be prudent. The gamble consumers are willing to take is that by the time the mortgage term ends, property prices will have increased so as to enable them to pay off the principal. Another recent development has been the introduction of self-certification mortgages that do not require borrowers to provide proof of their salary. For a premium interest rate, to take account of the higher rate of risk, consumers can take out significant multiples of their salary in the expectation that they will be able to keep up with the payments. Significant problems have occurred because individuals enter into consolidation loans that are secured on their property (see Chapter 4). Lenders have developed particular advertising strategies to attract these consumers by advertising on daytime TV, positioning themselves as friendly, approachable and unobtrusive – in other words, characteristics that are oppositional to those of mainstream lenders.

Credit and consumer segmentation

Consumer segmentation is an important technique that enables marketers to divide up the population into meaningful groups that have characteristics in common in order that products can be developed to meet their needs and wants. Traditionally, market segmentation has used a range of traditional criteria, including socio-economic group, age and gender. More recently, other features have been included, such as lifestyle variables and psychographics. However, postmodernists within the marketing community have argued that consumers' wants and needs are in such a constant state of flux that they defy marketers' attempts to profile them (Brown 1995).

Financial institutions have become more sophisticated in the way they market themselves, playing closer attention to segmentation targeting and positioning. A more strategic focus is crucial in the highly competitive market for credit. In Chapter 3, attention was drawn to some of the new ways in which lenders have used state-of-the-art data-mining techniques to assess the behaviour and profitability of some consumer groups. New segments and niche markets are one way to extract maximum amounts of profit in a mature marketplace. Because of their more sophisticated information systems, lenders are in a far better position to respond to opportunities and simultaneously reduce risk because of data they can acquire from credit-scoring bureaux. There are two main growth markets that lenders have targeted over the past decade, namely students and consumers in the lower socio-economic groups. However, it is the targeting of these two groups that has raised ethical issues. Marketers like to believe that they take the moral high ground and promote a morally indifferent or neutral stance in order to prevent a backlash of public opinion (Desmond 1998). Furthermore, scholarship in the field of ethics in finance and financial services is not highly developed (see, for example, Boatright 1999). But there are mounting criticisms in these two areas of business.

Seducing students

From the early 1990s onwards, financial institutions began to market themselves aggressively to young people, especially those in further and higher education, who were perceived to be the lucrative consumers of the future. Williams (2004) describes the way lenders have approached the student market as 'seducing students', which seems to be a fairly apt description of the scenario confronting young people in many Anglo-Saxon countries. Curtis (2004) goes further by suggesting that the university is a contemporary version of the debtors' prison for many students. Return on relationships and customer lifetime value became an important measure of marketing success. It has been estimated that 70 per cent of college students in the United States have and use credit cards (Grable and Yoo 2006). They are an incredibly attractive segment that renew each year as different cohorts of students begin their studies. Students have all the hallmarks of long-standing consumers, since many turn out to be incredibly loyal, keeping their first credit card brand for fifteen years. On arrival at college or university they are rarely committed to any specific brand; from a financial service perspective they are akin to 'virgin territory'. This attribute often goes hand in hand with their not being perhaps quite as savvy as established financial services users (Braunsberger, Lucas and Roach 2004).

Advertisements for credit, whether for credit cards or overdrafts, make strong links between credit, adulthood, maturity and autonomy. Slogans on credit cards focus on students taking charge of their life, emancipation from parents, and enjoying freedom and flexibility. Other subtle features are that guardians and parents do not have to co-sign application forms, stressing independence and confidentiality (Williams 2004). The freebies are also a significant aspect of marketing to this group of young people. It has long been recognized that there is little brand differentiation in the minds of consumers where banks are concerned. One bank is perceived as being pretty much like another, and this is reflected in the ways in which consumers have chosen the financial institutions with which they deal. Banks will be chosen on the basis of what upfront deals are promoted.

Student loans to pay for tuition fees have merely exacerbated the problem of debt for many young people. Education has long been viewed by those who are less well off in society as a way out of poverty and of improving their life chances. The philosophy of free higher education has become symptomatic of a bygone age in many advanced societies and has added to the debt burden of young people, a burden that they continue to harbour for many years thereafter. In some respects, student loans have unique qualities that are not applicable in other areas of credit. This sentiment has been shared by Salehi (1997) when she reflects on the experiences of students in the United States.

With most long-term debts the borrower is able to calculate total costs and interest rates, and the decision to borrow is based on some knowledge of the borrower's projected income and expenses. However, when students borrow to finance their education, they take on debt incrementally and they cannot know at any point either the full price of the education or what the real burden of the debt they are assuming will be. With the current high levels of tuition increases in England, students' expenses can rise dramatically while they are still in university or college. Moreover, students have no way of knowing what their future job prospects will be, or even whether they will graduate (see Williams 2004: 79).

There is also evidence that students facing financial stress are more likely to drop out and/or take on paid work to reduce their debt burden, which in turn affects their studies and their enjoyment of extra-curricular activities (Grable and Yoo 2006). Furthermore, research has demonstrated that there are racial differences in both financial behaviour and financial stress brought about by increasing levels of debt. Comparing African-Americans to non-Hispanic whites, Grable and Joo (2006) found that African-Americans have more credit card debt on average and are subject to more financial stress.

While financial institutions use the lack of parental involvement in their offspring's financial affairs as a positive advertising strategy in order to generate more credit business from students, the reality is that parental involvement can prove a stabilizing influence. Research by Palmer, Pinto and Parente (2001) has demonstrated that involvement by a parent or guardian as co-obligator tends to lead to lower credit card balances, pre-acquisition parental involvement leads to a lower total balance and post-acquistion parental involvement has the opposite effect. A far more serious lesson would be learned by young people whose parents could not or would not bail them out; they would essentially be allocated to sub-prime lending markets from the beginning of their credit trajectories and would find it difficult to escape – not to mention the social stigma that goes hand in hand with that scenario.

Manning (2000) has also identified another worrying trend relevant to student debt. Some students can obtain credit more easily than their families, especially if their parents have a poor credit history. In some instances the abundance of credit handed out to students is propping up their families. This little-commented-upon trend is not confined to families in lower socio-economic groups. Middle-class parents are increasingly asking their children to provide loans on their credit cards when their own credit lines dry up as a result of divorce, health problems or debt relations within the family.

Marketing credit to students has been described as 'predatory marketing', since many students are not experienced in financial affairs (Manning 2000: 161). Desperate students have even been found to use credit cards to bet on the stock market to reduce their debts. University debt has serious implications for obtaining some types of work on graduation. For example, most financial institutions will credit-score potential employees before offering a job. In extreme cases, indebtedness is compounded by problems finding a job on graduation within a reasonable timescale. Furthermore, under the current bankruptcy legislation in the United States, credit card debt is dischargeable whereas student loans are not. This feature has led some to argue that college students filing for bankruptcy may be penalized more than other debtors.

Profiting from the poor

The second segment that has attracted attention has been poorer customers who are outside the banking system. The predatory lending practices of alternative lenders were discussed in Chapter 4. The industry providing financial services for the bankless is worth in excess of $5 billion a year in the United States and makes Visa and MasterCard appear like 'kindly nonprofits' (Hudson 1996). The industry brings into stark contrast inequalities in the cost of social credit to consumers in different social groups. In this respect little has changed: contemporary patterns and access to credit display some synergies remarkably similar to those found in the seventeenth century, as discussed in Chapter 1.

Williams (2004: 123–124) has explored the strategies that consumers use to work fringe banking. They pawn televisions and VCRs between cheques and redeem them when they can. They cash their cheques at America's Cash Express and pay their bills with money orders and moneygrams they purchase there. They use the poor person's telephone, the pager, or a temporary cellphone, and sometimes 'rent' grossly overpriced furniture, cars and appliances for as long as they can. And this debt poisons the credit careers that more and more define our autobiographies as citizens. When a person cannot get a job, a car, an apartment, a mortgage or a bank account, and is thrust into the world of cash only, it is almost impossible for them to find their way out.

The high cost of credit and charges makes it impossible for some consumers to repay. But lenders would argue that it is good business to extend credit in order that consumers can just meet minimum payments and pay the maximum amount of interest. There seems to be an acceptance that the wealthy are entitled to interest and charge-free credit, and that the poor should pay more to subsidize the rich. The social relations bring to mind David and Goliath: they are always oppressive; wiping the slate clean and starting over is always illusive. No wonder that so many consumers are turning to bankruptcy as the only way out. Moreover, discrimination in credit markets leads Austin (2004) to argue that black people's money is worth less than white people's money both socially and materially. Vulnerability to predatory lenders that target women, minorities, low-income earners and senior citizens has meant that these consumers have been confined to the cash economy. Austin comments:

> A belief in black intellectual inferiority masks investments in black people, their property and their communities that seem riskier than comparable investments in whites. A belief that black borrowers are stupid or incompetent will lead to more refusals to lend, higher interest rates, demands for more information, and higher transaction costs in credit transactions involving blacks. Some blacks have internalized these notions.
>
> (2004: 1251)

New product innovation

The development of an increasing number of differentiated credit products has been an important feature of the past decade. There has probably been more product innovation and segmentation of existing products in the past twenty years than in the whole previous history of consumer credit. Klein (1999) argues that post-Fordist differentiation has facilitated various credit card categories: travel and entertainment (T&E; American Express, Diners Club and Carte Blanche) and bank cards (BankAmericard and Mastercharge). Credit cards have been designed to promote different images and have been aimed at various niches to appeal to various groups of consumers. MasterCard's image tended to focus on the average consumer and family living; Visa concentrated on travel and self-actualization; and American Express was usually oriented towards the business traveller.

By the mid-1980s the image of credit cards was transformed from the post-Fordist (differentiated product) to a postmodern image-driven financial instrument with the development of the prestigious platinum and gold cards. During the same period affinity cards were introduced, which were associated with good causes. Affinity cards were successful for two reasons. First, they acted as an incentive for consumers to take on an additional card or switch from a previous card. According to Visa, affinity card solicitations produced two or three times the number of applications of regular cards. The second reason for their success was that consumers use their affinity cards more often and they spend more on them. The postmodern reshaping of cards continued with additional strategies that included not charging annual fees and giving free air miles and insurance. Emphasis on the traits of the smart shopper who attracts lots of benefits by using their card but pays no interest began to emerge.

Credit cards have been marketed through the use of celebrity endorsements; then there is the emotional appeal of affinity cards that promote particular charities; finally, there are strategies that exploit materialistic instincts, such as co-branded cards that offer free air miles and other products. New product innovation on credit cards has become particularly confusing with respect to price. More sophisticated pricing strategies that have been introduced include tiered systems for charging interest rates, transfer rates and standard rates, and higher charges for cash advances. Furthermore, each offer can have a limited time-span (Manning 2000).

Mortgages are another area of credit that has witnessed a huge increase in product differentiation. The difference between prime and sub-prime mortgages, and the segmentation within the sub-prime category, were discussed in Chapter 4. In addition to these categories there have been a whole host of others. Buy-to-let mortgages have become increasingly popular as consumers have become more willing to invest in the housing market. In some respects housing has become a safer investment than pensions, given the poor performance of some pension funds and the collapse of others. The lifetime mortgage has become another popular option, as consumers who have retired and paid off their mortgage may wish to remortgage and withdraw some equity to make their retirement more comfortable. Equity withdrawal has been an important trend within the mortgage market *per se*, as individuals take advantage of higher property prices to fund existing consumption.

The days when customers were faced with a straight choice between a repayment or an endowment mortgage have disappeared. Some of the main mortgage lenders offer hundreds of variations of mortgage terms and conditions to cover all the options likely to appeal to potential borrowers. Some of the variations include prime versus sub-prime, repayment versus endowment, fixed rate periods, discount rates, tracker rates, interest-only options. Some of the controversial developments have been in self-certification mortgages whereby borrowers can purchase mortgages of many times their annual salary. Other recent developments are where lenders are willing to provide mortgages equivalent to far higher multiples of the customer's salary or joint salary than was previously the case. Another growth area linked to the buoyancy of the mortgage market is subsidiary services such as insurance against illness or unemployment. These are presented as options for most customers but are often a prerequisite for higher-risk customers, which increases the cost of borrowing.

Credit and direct marketing

One of the ways in which marketing has been transformed over the past decade is through the extensive use of direct marketing. A huge range of textbooks have emerged to satisfy the insatiable need to know how to conduct direct marketing. Just a few of the offerings that say very similar things in much the same way include Tapp's (2005) *Principles of Direct and Database Marketing*, Sargeant and West's (2001) *Direct and Interactive Marketing*, O'Malley, Patterson and Evans' (1999) *Exploring Direct Marketing*, and McCorkhell's (2000) *Direct and Database Marketing*. Tapp's (2005: 4) definition of direct marketing is as follows:

> Direct marketing is a method of marketing based on individual consumer records held on a database. These records are the basis for marketing analysis, planning, implementation of programmes, and control of all this activity. A key ingredient is the company database that can hold huge amounts of personal information about transactions and purchasers that will enable marketers to make appropriate approaches to particular groups of consumers with a view of obtaining a higher response rate.

In-house databases can be bought to supplement existing data, which is particularly valuable if an organization wishes to attract individuals who have a different profile as compared with existing customers. Major lifestyle databases are produced by Experian and Equifax, which also happen to be the two major credit scoring bureaux, in addition to others such as CACI. A second aspect is that marketers make a direct approach to the customer via a telephone call, email, a mobile phone text message, a letter, or some other one-to-one medium with the aim of generating a direct response.

Approaches are often couched in terms of people being a loyal or long-standing customer and therefore meriting special offers or discount as a reward for customer loyalty. Indeed, many direct marketing techniques are viewed within the wider remit of relationship marketing or customer relationship marketing, which attracted huge attention in marketing circles in the 1990s. An advantage of direct marketing from the marketer's viewpoint is that the activity can be undertaken from any location; no expensive high street locations are necessary. An even bigger advantage of direct marketing is that the results of marketing initiatives can be fairly precisely measured in terms of the return on investment. A response to a direct approach might generate a request for more information or an order. This information can be subsequently added to the database and used to direct future promotions.

Direct marketing has not been without its critiques. There have been concerns that the activity is socially irresponsible and wasteful. Anyone who has received multiple mail shots through the letter box in one day is likely to agree with that sentiment. Furthermore, the one-to-one interaction, often at one's home or place of work, could be construed as an intrusion of privacy. There are also privacy issues about the selling of mailing lists. In theory this should not happen, since data protection legislation should protect consumers from this, but evidence suggests that from time to time lists do get sold. The philosophy underpinning direct marketing is that consumers want a relationship with producers, but it is fairly evident that many consumers would prefer to do without the intimacy.

Direct marketing as a distinctive way of relating to consumers has emerged as an important method of marketing credit. While marketing academics promulgate the view that direct marketing is new, that is far from the truth. We learned in Chapter 3 that financial institutions and retailers from the 1840s onwards used lists of customers to assess creditworthiness and as a way of targeting existing customers. In the 1960s, credit card companies were sending out huge direct mailings. The development of credit scoring necessitating use and manipulation of huge datasets goes back to the 1940s. Lenders send unsolicited mail offers of personal loans, mortgages, credit cards, consolidation loans, and equity withdrawal from home loans. This practice continues as lenders mail out huge numbers of pre-approved personal loans, introductory offers to switch credit card companies and mortgage provider, and 'sales' on loan interest rates that usually coincide with clothes sales in the shops. In many areas of marketing the direct effects of marketing efforts cannot be accurately calculated since there can be other contributory factors in a customer's decision to purchase a particular product. In the case of direct marketing, lenders are able to calculate returns on their investment from huge mailings based on projected response rates and the purchase of products.

A difficulty lenders face is sending offers of credit products to consumers who subsequently apply for products but are then refused. A recurrent problem is how to know which customers should be mailed to maximize the response while minimizing the risk and simultaneously minimizing the number of respondents rejected at application in order to avoid jeopardizing existing customer relationships. From experience, organizations know that customers who are more likely to respond to credit appeals tend to be those who have a higher credit risk. A further problem relates to the enormous amount of data that need to be organized before the mailing can proceed and the availability of means with which to undertake the task effectively. For many large financial institutions, resolving this situation requires the development of increasingly sophisticated models (Bennett, Platts and Crossley 2004).

The timing is also vital, since lenders know that people may be more amenable to adopt credit at times of financial stress, including Christmas and the holiday season. Other types of lending occur in cycles, for example car loans if individuals change their car every two or three years. If lenders are aware of this pattern of behaviour, mailshots can be sent to promote their offer. Another important variable is stage in the life cycle, since it has traditionally been the case that individuals setting up their own home and starting families tend to be the highest users of credit. This is in contrast to retired individuals who may have paid off their mortgage, whose children have flown the nest and who have good pensions. To some extent this model is being disrupted, since many young people are taking on significant amounts of debt to pay for their education and are being faced with huge mortgage burdens due to house price inflation. Modelling which consumers to approach, the best time to do so, for what purpose and how much to offer has become a very precise science.

The direct mass marketing of credit as we know it today emerged in the United States in the late 1950s with the advent of the credit card. In order to generate mass adoption of a new product, unsolicited cards were mailed in one wave after another in an attempt to get people hooked. In 1958, BankAmericard undertook the first mass mailing of 60,000 unsolicited credit cards to existing Bank of America customers. Over the subsequent twelve years, nearly 100 million unsolicited credit cards flooded US households. There was public outrage when cards were intercepted and used illegally. On the defensive, banks speculated about the perpetrators of the crimes. Some argued that prostitutes were to blame by lifting men's wallets; others claimed that merchants were copying charge slips in order to counterfeit cards. Other wrongdoers in the frame included criminal gangs, which generated a whole cottage industry in manufacturing fake cards. Even postal workers were implicated in intercepting cards so they could sell them on the black market (Williams 2004). Some of these issues are still apparent in contemporary consumer society.

Unfair sales tactics

A persistent criticism in relation to the marketing of credit is unfair sales practices. The concept of pushy salespeople who dupe individuals into purchasing goods and services that they do not need or want has been a fairly persistent image that has dogged marketing for years. This sentiment is reflected in the title of an article published in the *Journal of Marketing* in the 1950s entitled 'Would you let your daughter marry a marketing man?' (Burton 2001). This negative perception is intensified in relation to the marketing of credit products, since there is a tradition of providing incentives for salespeople based on the volume and value of products sold. Another difficulty is the level of education of consumers – specifically, a general lack of understanding of financial services within the population, with credit being no exception. The lack of understanding of concepts such as APR (annual percentage rate), for example, is one that has proved fairly persistent.

According to the Lord (2005: 21–22) HUD/Treasury Report, predatory lending 'involves engaging in deception or fraud, manipulating the borrower through aggressive sales tactics, or taking unfair advantage of a borrower's lack of understanding about loan terms. These practices are often combined with loan terms that, alone or in combination, are abusive or make the borrower more vulnerable to abusive practices'. In some instances, financial literacy problems are exacerbated by literacy difficulties (Wallendorf 2001; Leyshon *et al.* 2004). As far as mortgages are concerned, Lord notes the following:

- Loan 'flipping' refers to the practice of repeatedly refinancing a borrower's loan over a short period and charging high fees, which sometimes include pre-payment penalties. The lender and often a mortgage broker will charge a fee each time. Recurrent flipping reduces the equity left in the house, and sometimes borrowing can exceed the value of the house. Loans to the value of 125 per cent of the value of the house are not uncommon.

- Balloon payments have become a relatively common method of financing many types of purchases, from cars to houses, over the past decade. Huge payments appear at the end of the term of the loan to make the payments at the start more affordable for consumers and easier for lenders to sell. Frequently, customers have to take out another loan to cover the balloon payment at the end, thus extending the term of the loan and adding further interest. Balloon payments are legal, provided the terms of the loan have been properly explained to the customer. In practice, borrowers often claim that they were misled or did not understand the terms.

- Excessive fees and 'packaging' are frequently cited in the context of predatory lending, with consumers required to pay out more in fees than would be expected, or perhaps justified on the basis of interest rates, borrowers' incomes and credit rating. Extra costs, including various sorts of insurance, are frequently packaged into the loan without consumers being fully aware of the conditions or costs incurred. The pre-payment penalty sometimes called an early completion fee is a common penalty that means if consumers sell the house or pay off a loan within a short space of time, they have to pay significant extra costs for the privilege.

- Lending without due regard for the borrower's ability to repay has become a very important issue and touches on corporate social responsibility in lending. Allowing consumers to load themselves up with debt is unethical, although some lenders adopt this strategy to enable them to repossess homes when lenders are unable to repay. Affordability has become an important economic and political issue in lending decisions and will be discussed in more depth in Chapter 7.

• Outright fraud occurs in instances where unscrupulous lenders deliberately falsify a borrower's income or the value of a home in order to clinch the deal. As a consequence, the consumer could be left with a loan that they cannot afford to pay and are unable to refinance, since reputable lenders will steer well clear of fraudulent loans.

Conclusion

There has been much discussion about the marketing of credit. It has become a highly controversial activity, given the greater numbers of consumers who are finding themselves in greater levels of debt from which they cannot escape. These developments have generated a discourse around the issue of corporate social responsibility and the ethics of target marketing to vulnerable consumers. However, in the past decade financial institutions have invested considerably in new product development and systems that enable customers to choose the right product for them and to be able to access it in a speedy manner. For most consumers, the potential for acquiring different types of credit for a wider range of suppliers has never been greater. Entrepreneurial customers can play the systems and search out the best deal by playing off one lender against another. For those with blemished credit records or those who have never created a credit record for themselves, there are also many choices, but these are mostly inferior to the services and prices offered by mainstream lenders. The choices available to disadvantaged consumers are little different from the sources of credit that were available to consumers centuries ago (see Chapter 1). Despite the revolution in the marketing of credit that we have witnessed in recent years, the ideal of the democratization of credit remains elusive.

Questions

1 How useful is Fullerton's assessment of the development of modern marketing for our contemporary understanding of the marketing of credit?
2 To what extent have consumer societies witnessed the democratization of credit?
3 How does the ideology of advertising obscure the language of debt?
4 Why can marketing to students be construed as predatory lending?

Further reading

Arnould, E.J. and Thompson, C.J. (2005) 'Consumer culture theory (CCT): twenty years of research', *Journal of Consumer Research*, 31, March: 868–882.

Austin, R. (2004) 'Of predatory lending and the democratization of credit: preserving the social safety net of informality in small loan transactions', *American University Law Review*, 53, 6: 1217–1258.

Belk, R. (1995) 'Studies in the new consumer behaviour', in Miller, D. (ed.) *Acknowledging Consumption*, London: Routledge.

Fullerton, R.A. (1988) 'How modern is modern marketing? Marketing's evolution and the myth of the "Production Era"', *Journal of Marketing*, 52, January: 108–125.

Klein, L. (1999) *It's in the Cards: Consumer Credit and the American Experience*, Westport, CT: Praeger.

Lyons, A.C. (2003) 'How credit access has changed over time for U.S. households', *Journal of Consumer Affairs*, 37 (2): 231–255.

Packard, V. (1957) *The Hidden Persuaders*, London: Longmans Green.

6 Credit and consumer misbehaviour

Consumer misbehaviour is a relatively under-researched area. Far more attention has been given to the positive aspects of consumption. Consumer misbehaviour where credit is concerned is not new. Evidence presented in Chapter 1 demonstrates that as long as credit has existed, there have been some consumers who have refused or have been unable to pay their debts. What is perhaps different about contemporary consumer society is the scale of consumer misbehaviour, the variety of forms it can take and the responses of creditors. In social contexts where lenders and borrowers were personally known to each other, there was an underlying moral and ethical commitment to repay the debt. However, given the impersonal, institutionalized nature of credit authorization, that moral obligation is somewhat distanced. Default and delinquency in credit relationships can be understood within a broader context of consumer misbehaviour in consumer societies.

The chapter will begin by providing a historical overview of consumer financial misbehaviour. In the second section a conceptual overview of different dimensions of consumer misbehaviour will be given and the relationship of consumer misbehaviour to consumer culture will be assessed. In the third section, credit and consumer deviance will be explored, prior to assessing consumer bankruptcy as an extreme form of misbehaviour in the fourth section. As a consequence of increased levels of default, lenders are developing various techniques for recouping debt, and some of these will be discussed in the penultimate section. The final section of the chapter will assess the relatively recent emergence of a debt sale market in personal finance. This market has emerged within the past ten years and operates as a mechanism whereby lenders relieve themselves of outstanding loans for the best price they can achieve on the open market.

Historical perspectives on financial misbehaviour

Financial misbehaviour has a long history where credit and debt are concerned. Individuals failing to pay their debts have existed for as long as credit has been extended. What has changed over time is the numbers of consumers who fail to repay, the reasons they give for not doing so, and the punishment meted out to wrongdoers. Things have changed somewhat over the past four hundred years, but a review of historical accounts illustrates that debt was considered a very serious crime, and the punishments for it were very severe. The Romans had some very unpleasant ways of dealing with debtors. Under the Law of Twelve Tables, creditors were literally given their pound of flesh; they were able to cut up the debtor's body into pieces according to their individual claims (Aris 1985). During the second and third centuries, debtors could be sold into slavery abroad by their creditors. Alternatively, there was an arrangement called *nexum* whereby the debtor would have to work in bondage until the debt was paid off. *Nexum* was abolished in the fourth century and creditors were required to take creditors to court. If found guilty, they would be interned in a private prison or have to go and serve in the army. If they were imprisoned, the costs of sustaining the prisoner fell to the creditor, which resulted in private arrangements being made for the debtor to work off the debts. *Nexum* emerged again via a different route (Brunt 1971).

The fate of debtors was not that much better in England several centuries later. In 1623, James I required debtors to be 'set upon the pillory in some public place for the space of two hours and have one of his or her ears nailed to the pillory and cut off' (quoted in Barty-King 1991: 17–18). The worst-case scenario was that debtors were sentenced to death. Concealing possessions from creditors was considered a very serious crime. In 1761 a debtor called John Perrott was hanged at Smithfield in London for trying to conceal part of his effects.

Probably the most comprehensive historical account of credit and debt in the United States is provided by Bruce Mann (2002) in his text *Republic of Debtors: Bankruptcy in the Age of American Independence*. He notes that the world of imprisoned debtors is largely uncharted territory, and the few accounts within the small literature that exists often fail to penetrate the prison walls. This is not because of lack of remonstrations by the imprisoned but rather because of the failure of the authorities to take note and act. The treatment of debtors in eighteenth-century America reflected practices that had been imported from England. He notes, 'imprisonment for debt was an unquestioned piece of the cultural baggage of English immigration in the seventeenth century. It could hardly have been otherwise for a practice that had existed in England for three hundred years' (Mann 2002: 81). So ingrained was imprisonment for debt in the culture of early America that opposition did not appear until the 1750s. Every colony and subsequently every state permitted imprisonment for debt. Debtors could be imprisoned on arrest for failure to pay a creditor before a formal judgment had been reached. The vast majority of colonies permitted insolvent debtors to be bound in service to their creditors. Typically, this was for a seven-year period, the standard term for indentured servants. Some creditors hoped that the threat of prison would frighten the debtor into disclosing concealed wealth, or that a family member would step in to protect them. In practice this rarely happened, since most imprisoned debtors were insolvent because their businesses had failed for one reason or another. Even if the debtor had the means to repay one creditor, once other creditors sued for what they were owed, the debtor was unable to buy his freedom by repaying the first creditor in the queue and ignoring the rest.

Unlike in England, there were no debtor's prisons in America before the Revolution. Debtors and criminals were thrown together, as were men and women, in the same prison. Women did go to prison for debt, but most debtors were prostitutes who had been 'imprisoned by brothel owners for small boarding debts when disease or age limited their usefulness' (Mann 2002: 91). However, some women who were innocent were also known to have joined their debtor husbands in prison – whether out of necessity is not clear. Mixed-gender prisons shocked visitors from England and Ireland, where segregation existed as a matter of decency. They also created problems for married debtors whose spouses relinquished their support on the basis of debauchery. Unlike criminals and paupers, debtors were required to provide their own food, fuel and clothing. In many respects, running into debt was a greater crime than robbing people on the highway, rape, or arson. Needless to say, hunger, degradation and abuse were rife as debtors starved to death or committed suicide. This prompted reform movements to provide relief in the form of food and clothing. Despite these efforts the dreadful conditions remained, and the conditions for debtors imprisoned in New York were compared unfavourably with those found in the Bastille in Paris. In 1800 it was the view of some reformers that imprisonment for debt was a form of 'capital punishment wielded by private creditors with the acquiescence of the state ... the creditor unconstitutionally possesses [absolute power] over the life, liberty, and property of the debtor' (Mann 2002: 105–106).

Unsurprisingly, given the brutal regime in prison, debtors attempted to avoid it at all costs. In England some protection came in the form of the ancient custom of ecclesiastical sanctuary. Sanctuary became known as 'Alsatia' after Alsace, part of France that for centuries had given refuge to the disaffected. In London the precincts of the Collegiate Church of St Martin-le-Grand, founded in 1065, gave sanctuary to refugees from the law. The precincts continued to give shelter to debtors until 1967. More famous was Whitefriars in London, which performed the same function and acted as the basis for some novels that portrayed the area as seedy and threatening, somewhere nobody was trusted. The protection given by Alsatia was not just confined to England. In Scotland the precinct of Holyrood Abbey in Edinburgh performed the same function. Up until 1560, anyone in fear of capture could take refuge, and after the Reformation it remained a safe sanctuary for debtors (Barty-King 1991).

Another relevant theme in consumer financial misbehaviour is fraud. Historical accounts of fraud are thinner on the ground than those concerned with consumer credit and debt. One insight is provided by McGowen's (2005) account of the Bank of England and the policing of forgery between 1797 and 1821. While the punishment for debtors described above was fairly severe, the penalty for being convicted of forgery was death, and an execution usually followed a guilty verdict. The severity of the punishment did not deter individuals from being involved in the activity. Some estimates claim that there were more than 120 major distributors of fraudulent coin in London in 1797. Many were old hands who were well acquainted with inadequacies of the law and the extreme difficulties of proving guilt. The naïve and inexperienced were caught out, but their fate did little to curtail the trade. In 1797 the bank had to suspend cash payments as a consequence of fiscal challenges arising from the long war with revolutionary France. It was forced to suspend the acts that restricted the issue of notes under £5 and supplied large numbers of £1 and £2 notes to maintain circulation. Forgery of these new notes was a simple business for well-established fraudsters, since the notes were little more than 'a printed form with a number, a date and a clerk's signature' (McGowen 2005: 85). The notes were perceived as an easy source of profit, and within a relatively short period an increasing number of forged notes were being passed to bank cashiers. Small changes to the design occurred in 1798, and a wavy watermark was introduced in 1800. But each of these changes brought only temporary respite as the numbers of forgeries steadily increased.

Throughout the eighteenth century the responsibility for detecting crime and the capture and prosecution of offenders lay with the victims of the crime. The Bank of England was no exception in this respect, and the pursuing and prosecuting of forgers was left to the bank's solicitors. They had the task of dealing with not only the legal aspects of each case but also the policing. In doing so they placed advertisements in newspapers and sought the cooperation of local magistrates and the police force. Providing rewards delivered some results, but prosecutions brought were the tip of the iceberg. Only the development of dense local networks curbed the problem.

Historical accounts provide a context for understanding contemporary developments in consumer financial misbehaviour. The greater surveillance of contemporary consumers has facilitated a more detailed assessment of their shortcomings. A greater range of consumer deviance is also apparent in contemporary consumer culture. In the next section the relationship between consumer misbehaviour and consumer society will be considered and then the concept of consumer financial misbehaviour will be addressed in more detail.

Consumer misbehaviour and consumer society

Fullerton and Punj (1998) maintain that consumer misbehaviour has developed as an integral part of modern consumer culture. They argue that it has been shaped by the very marketing values and practices that legitimate consumption practices. They note that

> [c]onsumer misbehaviour is a significant phenomenon which affects the experiences of *all* consumers. It is in fact an *inseparable* part of the consumer experience. Many consumers misbehave at least some of the time. Those consumers not themselves misbehaving, are all inevitably victimized by others' misconduct.

Fullerton and Punj define consumer misbehaviour as acts by consumers that 'violate the generally accepted norms of conduct in consumption situations, and thus disrupt the consumption order' (1998: 394). Central to defining consumer misbehaviour are the rights of marketers to establish boundaries concerning the physical and financial property of products and services, and their right to control the consumption process.

The motives for consumer misbehaviour are many and varied, and scholars in several areas of the social sciences have contributed to the debate. Some of the important areas of debate concern the sociology of deviance (Montanino 1977), criminology (Vold and Bernard 1986) and psychologically abnormal behaviour (Phillips 2006), in addition to specific consumer misbehaviours (Phillips, Alexander and Shaw 2005). Motives for consumer misbehaviour can be classified in a range of ways. One cause that has been identified is *unfulfilled aspirations*: if individuals cannot achieve their goals legitimately, they will do so by other means. Among particular groups in society this can result in misbehaviour such as theft and shoplifting. A second theme within the consumer behaviour literature is *deviant thrill seeking*. For some consumers there is a thrill attached to defying legal and moral norms of behaviour and challenging structures that have been put in place to keep order. The risk of being caught merely adds to the excitement. In this respect, deviant thrill seeking can be viewed as a perverse variant on hedonic consumption (Arnold and Reynolds 2003). A third motive for consumer misbehaviour concerns an *absence of moral constraints*: the lack of strong internal inhibitions against conduct not perceived to be wrongdoing or immoral by the perpetrator despite being viewed as unacceptable by others. In some instances errant consumers refuse to acknowledge any sense of moral responsibility or remorse whatsoever.

A fourth source of misbehaviour centres on *differential association*. This view suggests that deviant behaviour is learned within particular groups in society. Groups that deviate from the prevailing norms in society can have their own identity and consumption patterns. Consumer misbehaviour can be an integral part of in-group rituals among teenagers and adult repeat offenders. Differential association and its subsequent effect on consumer misbehaviour could be construed as dysfunctional effects of consumer socialization. *Pathological socialization* is a fifth source of consumer misbehaviour. This feature concerns the negative feelings that large institutions and the power that they wield can prompt in the minds of consumers. Research has demonstrated that consumers often find large companies more legitimate targets than smaller companies. Explanations for this behaviour relate to the perceived social distance between consumers and organizations. The larger the distance, the more likely organizations are to be considered a legitimate target of consumer misbehaviour. A penultimate reason for consumer misbehaviour relates to what have been described as *provocative situational factors*. Particular situations or circumstances can prompt consumers to misbehave. Enticing displays may result in shoplifting; crowding and heat may trigger aggressiveness to other consumers and marketers. A final cause of misbehaviour is *calculated opportunism*. In this instance, consumers assess the risks as against the rewards of misbehaviour. Consumer misbehaviour follows a rational path that differs from mainstream consumer decision-making only because of the consumer's lack of ethical constraints. These seven reasons are not exhaustive, but they do indicate that many aspects of consumer misbehaviour are linked to the culture of consumption.

Consumer misbehaviour is highly diverse and can be gender specific. Fullerton and Punj (1998) identify thirty-five types of misbehaviour, which can be classified into five different categories: that directed against marketer employees, that directed against other consumers, that directed against marketer merchandise, that directed against the marketer's financial assets and that directed against the marketer's physical premises. Misbehaving consumers come from a variety of socio-economic groups and backgrounds. Individuals who might be classified as outright deviants are included, but so are middle-class, stable people from privileged backgrounds. Within contemporary consumer culture teenagers tend to be disproportionately involved in store-related misbehaviour, while males have traditionally been responsible for vandalism. Various other types of misbehaviour, including credit card and cheque fraud, tend to involve adults, because of the regulation surrounding these products.

The financial cost of consumer misbehaviour can be considerable, but it is largely met with ambivalence from marketers and consumers alike. Research has demonstrated that consumers are largely indifferent towards misbehaviour that involves illegally appropriating financial assets and property. Likewise, marketers display considerable ambivalence towards aberrant consumer behaviour, an ambivalence that Fullerton and Punj (1998) suggest borders on tolerance. The cost of consumer misbehaviour frequently equates with the cost of doing business. Inevitably these costs contribute to higher prices for all consumers, which reduces the overall efficiency of the marketing system. Another reason for tolerance on the part of organizations relates to some of the negative consequences of admitting there is a problem and damaging the brand.

Credit and consumer deviance

The relationship between consumer misbehaviour and consumer culture is a valuable framework in which to discuss credit, debt and consumer deviance. Much of the existing consumer misbehaviour research focuses on retailing and the development of new retailing formats that provide opportunities for shoplifting (Phillips, Alexander and Shaw 2005). Far less attention has been paid to various aspects of credit and debt and consumer misbehaviour, yet it is an important issue that has considerable significance to individuals, lenders and the wider economy. Much attention has been given to the concepts of consumer power and sovereignty in consumer society (Abercrombie 1994; Keat 1994), but the concept of the unmanageable consumer (Gabriel and Lang 1997) has rarely surfaced within discussions of consumer credit. In the case of financial services, many aspects of consumer misbehaviour are hidden from consumers since they could reveal flaws in the system. Fraud would be one example where to reveal details could prejudice future security. For the most part, preventing consumer misbehaviour where credit is concerned has centred on using sanctions such as blacklisting through credit reference agencies. For the vast majority of consumers the threat of being blacklisted and relegated to the sub-prime market is an effective control mechanism. Despite some of the serious sanctions that consumers face for not repaying their debts, greater levels and new methods of consumer resistance are being witnessed. Three types of consumer behaviour have been identified: non-culpable default, fraud and serial default.

Non-culpable default

To some extent, non-culpable (non-intentional) default has always existed and will always exist. Since time began, individuals have fallen on hard times as a result of an unpredictable combination of social and economic circumstances. As the discussion of the sub-prime market in Chapter 4 demonstrated, the ways in which people default include non-payment of mortgage instalments, the ignoring of county court judgments and the non-payment of council tax. Many of these defaulting episodes are caused through loss of income because of relationship breakdown or unemployment (Burton *et al.* 2004). For example, Lyons and Fisher (2006) identify significant debt repayment problems among divorced women with children after divorce. Their difficulties are due to various interrelated factors, including lower levels of household income. Typically, women were awarded custody of children, which affected their ability to work, and they faced increased expenditure on childcare payments. Absent fathers often would not pay maintenance, or paid inadequate amounts. Furthermore, many married women do not establish credit histories for themselves when they are married and subsequently have problems borrowing when they get divorced. These types of financial difficulties can be problematic for many people during some period of their life but are frequently resolved rather than being persistent or recurring.

Serial default

Serial default occupies a 'grey' area between non-culpable default and criminalized fraud. Some consumers are taking on credit commitments that they do not meet and are repeating the process with one lender after another. Some types of lender are more vulnerable to this type of default than others. For example, most door-to-door moneylenders do not use credit scoring prior to lending, since most customers who use this method of obtaining credit have never constructed a credit history for themselves with mainstream lenders (Burton *et al.* 2004). Moneylenders are often unaware whether a customer is trustworthy or not until they have loaned them the money and they generate a repayment record.

Serial default on a large scale has been detected fairly recently, as a result of recent developments in information technology. The extensive pooling of credit data, along with the use of the more extensive and sophisticated data-mining techniques, has enabled financial institutions to detect individuals who repeatedly fail to repay their debts. It is members of this group, who systematically fail to repay on purpose, who have been labelled serial defaulters. The ability to detect serial default is an important intelligence development for mainstream financial institutions. Until recently they only had access to their own customers' default rates and patterns of default.

The concepts of 'insolvency' and 'bankruptcy' that were largely confined to the discourse of business are increasingly being used in the context of households and individuals. Bankruptcy and insolvency can be one extreme outcome of serial default. Until fairly recently, defaulting behaviour tended to be researched in the context of specific financial products, including credit cards and mortgages. However, credit-scoring bureaux are increasingly identifying patterns of individuals defaulting on a range of mainstream financial products, with some individuals in the prime market becoming 'serial defaulters'. This point is made by a senior official at a leading credit scoring bureau:

> [I]f somebody is not prepared to pay you £100 for a mobile phone, the chances are they're not prepared to pay you £1,000 for a personal loan. So if you look at the incidence of default on mainstream financial products and mobile phones, they're very highly correlated. People who default on one tend to default on the other. Bit of a sweeping generalization but it is predictive. And the same argument has always been made to us about mail order data. . . . At one time we had millions and millions of mail order customers and we had all their records on the database but they tended to be very low value, £50–£100. People said, 'oh, I'm not interested in a £100

default', but when you do the analysis, the incidence of default on people with £5,000 personal loans is very closely related to the default made on £100 mail order accounts. If they're prepared to default in one area they will default in another area. So it is a strong indicator.

Fraud

Fraud as a criminalized activity is an extreme form of consumer resistance that occupies a position at the opposite end of the spectrum from non-culpable default. Fraud may be linked to the notion of entitlement on the part of disenfranchised consumers, a criminal reaction against perceived victimization, injustice or inequality created by a retailer, manufacturer, lender, or the culture of consumption itself (Chin 1997). One of the most significant problems in retailing is fraud. The three biggest sources of fraud are cheque fraud, payment card fraud and counterfeit money. In the United Kingdom these three sources account for 77 per cent of fraudulent transactions. Electrical, furniture and carpets are the sectors most at risk from cheque fraud. Payment card fraud is most visible in internet, catalogue, telephone and TV shopping, and has been a barrier to the widespread adoption of online shopping (Fernie 2004: 270).

Fraud in its various guises is running at epidemic proportions as financial institutions attempt to tackle the latest breach of their security systems. Fraud includes obtaining credit by deception, for example by providing an incorrect address. Fraud is having some serious consequences for consumer confidence. As mentioned above, credit card fraud is hampering the development of new retail formats, including internet shopping (Burton 2002b). As more consumers have financial accounts, more and more credit and debit cards are in circulation, and the greater the risk of fraud becomes. By 2002, cyberbazaars offering credit card numbers in bulk for as little as $100 for 240 cards thrived on the internet. Hackers break into merchants' computer systems; they fence the cards, make purchases and get cash advances (Ritchel 2002). More regular occurrences are illegitimate cash advances where withdrawals are made from ATMs and the cardholder is responsible for proving that fraud has taken place.

The newest and most serious cases relate to identity theft rather than the fraudulent use of accounts or cards, and represent an additional area of consumer vulnerability in consumer societies (Langenderfer and Shimp 2001). In the United Kingdom, identity fraud is one of the fastest-growing crimes. In the United States, where identity theft had been more prevalent, the incidences appear to have peaked as consumers have become more aware of personal security. There has been a steady decline in reported cases since 2003. In 2006, 3.7 per cent of people surveyed said that someone had stolen their identity in the previous twelve months, down from 4.7 per cent in 2003. Thieves used victims' existing bank or credit card accounts or opened new ones. The total losses from the crime fell in 2006 to $49 billion, compared to $56 billion in 2005 (Leland 2007).

Consumer bankruptcy

Perhaps the most extreme form of consumer deviance as far as credit is concerned is bankruptcy. Since Elizabethan times the law has drawn a careful distinction between bankrupt traders and insolvent debtors. In recognition that traders could not operate without credit, the law has offered protection against the honest but unfortunate trader. Creditors could have full access to his goods and possessions but not to his body (Aris 1985). Ramsay (1997) makes the useful distinction with debt, generally defined as owing money to another party. Insolvency is commonly referred to as a state in which liabilities (debts) exceed assets or of being unable to pay liabilities as they become due. Whereas indebtedness and insolvency are non-legal states, bankruptcy is a legal state in which the debtor enters into a legal arrangement with the court to dissolve or repay debts. There has been a considerable increase in the numbers of consumer bankruptcies in Anglo-Saxon countries, and numbers of repeat offenders are on the increase. In Canada, third, fourth and fifth repeat bankrupts are becoming more common (McGregor and Berry 2001). These findings seem to suggest that more consumers are using bankruptcy as a strategic option in order to wipe their slate clean of debts and start over. Skeel (2001: 1) argues that 'US debtors treat it as a means to another, healthier end, not as the end'. To some extent this viewpoint is reflected in the US legislative process. The 1978 Code made bankruptcy more respectable by referring to bankruptcy debtors as debtors, not bankrupts, thus partly removing the stigma of the latter. By contrast, Griffiths (2000) notes that as far as Australia is concerned, many consumers do not choose to go bankrupt and that proceedings are initiated by concerned creditors rather than debtors.

Moreover, there is a growing trend to differentiate between various types of bankrupts, with some instances being deemed worse than others. In Britain the distinction has been made between culpable and non-culpable bankrupts, in which levels of blame and fault are differentiated (Burton *et al.* 2004). This distinction has been around for several years in the United States with the distinction between Chapter 7 and Chapter 13. Chapter 7 is the more serious state and requires the liquidation of assets, whereas Chapter 13 has more of a rehabilitation status. In Chapter 7 the debtor surrenders non-exempt property and wealth to the court. Creditors are obliged to cease efforts to collect all debts and a plan is formulated to liquidate assets and distribute the proceeds to creditors. Debtors give up all their non-exempt assets in return for keeping all future income. Chapter 7 debtors cannot refile for bankruptcy again for six years. In Chapter 13, debtors can keep their existing property and outstanding debt is rescheduled, with the exception of mortgage debt, which cannot be rescheduled. Under most circumstances debtors are relieved of paying some of the outstanding debt, and court approval of the plan does not require the agreement of the creditors. Furthermore, the use of Chapter 13 does not preclude individuals from obtaining a discharge in a Chapter 7 case (Domowitz and Sartain 1999).

Given the fairly rapid increase in the number of bankruptcies, one might have expected a significant amount of research to have been conducted on this aspect of consumer misbehaviour. However, in reality research identifying underlying reasons for this extreme form of credit default is lagging behind trends in consumer behaviour. This is partly due to the fact that bankrupts are often ashamed and do not want to talk about the subject. It is a period in their lives that they would rather forget (Aris 1985). We probably know most about the situation in the United States, through the lens of two large-scale studies that were published as two major reference works: *As We Forgive Our Debtors: Bankruptcy and Consumer Credit in America* (Sullivan, Warren and Westbrook 1989) and *The Fragile Middle Class: Americans in Debt* (Sullivan, Warren and Westbrook 2000). Contrary to what might have been expected, the first of these studies revealed that bankrupts 'were not a substratum of day labourers or housemaids but people with the characteristics of the middle class, though with lower class incomes' (Sullivan, Warren and Westbrook 1989: 2). This finding was also repeated a decade later, with petitioners being firmly located in the middle class in terms of their education and employment.

There were some significant gender differences in bankruptcy filing over the period. In 1981, 27 per cent of petitions were from men filing singly, and this figure remained around the same a decade later. By contrast, the proportion of women filing alone had nearly doubled from 17 per cent to 30 per cent. The average age of 38 remained fairly static. An analysis of the ethnic composition of bankrupts revealed that blacks are over-represented, while other ethnic groups were under-represented. The main difference between bankrupts and the rest of the population relates to their financial characteristics. In the more recent study, families were living on half the median family income of the population, and nearly one-third fell below the poverty line. Many of those filing for bankruptcy could not possibly have repaid their debts.

Sullivan, Warren and Westbrook (2000) found that the reasons for bankruptcy fell into four main categories. Two out of three petitions indicated that it was due to job problems: unemployment or underemployment. Nearly 20 per cent cited medical costs resulting from illness or injury, which were compounded by loss of income. Fifteen per cent of the sample indicated that the break-up of a marriage had been the primary cause in filing for bankruptcy. The key to financial recovery from divorce is remarriage, and this factor is particularly true for women, who tend to have responsibility for children. Only 5 per cent cited problems with credit card debt, which is possibly a lower figure than might have been expected, given the significant literature on the relationship between credit cards, consumption and debt (Ritzer 1995; Klein 1999). A smaller-scale study in the United States conducted by Domowitz and Sartain (1999) concluded that health problems leading to substantial medical debt are the main factors in bankruptcy decisions, and at the margins, credit card debt relative to income is important. Homeownership discourages bankruptcy, and higher marriage rates, employment rates and income encourage the choice of Chapter 13 bankruptcy (rehabilitation) over Chapter 7.

McGregor and Berry (1997) identify a similar range of contributory factors in consumer bankruptcy in Canada. These have included changes in labour markets, corporate downsizing, employment status, ageing, marital status, family type, and number and type of dependants. In Australia, unemployment has been the primary cause of consumer bankruptcies since 1992, followed by liabilities on guarantees, domestic discord, ill health, gambling and adverse litigation (Griffiths 2000).

The increase in bankruptcies has led to more systematic assessment of the ideology that underpins bankruptcy laws. Ramsay (1997) identifies three main paradigms that inform the legal framework for bankruptcy legislation. The first is a *response to deviant behaviour* by individuals who require help in learning acceptable norms of credit behaviour. A second is informed by *consumer protection*, specifically consumers who underestimate the future risks associated with present consumption using credit. A third orientation is underpinned by a philosophy of *providing a safety net*, perhaps in the form of social welfare, for the financial consequences that may have led to the bankruptcy, including poverty or persistent debt overcommitment.

McGregor and Berry (2001) used the framework proposed by Ramsay to analyse bankruptcy policy in Canada, the United States and Sweden. Although there were obviously some differences in the legal frameworks operating in these countries, there were some important overriding similarities. They conclude that none of the three countries offers an example of one of the paradigms identified by Ramsay. The countries took approaches that had elements of all three philosophies and none took exactly the same approach. They conclude:

> It is clear, however, that the prevailing punitive features of each law seem to mitigate any protective or welfare motives. A focus on education and prevention (hence protection) is mentioned in the objectives of the laws but seems to be lacking, replaced instead with punishment in actual implementation. There is little evidence of the welfare model at all as defined by Ramsay, that is a safety net for financial consequences associated with life's transitions, prevailing poverty or ongoing debt-overcommitment. . . . In general, the plight of the debtor is overshadowed by the rights of the creditor.
>
> (2001: 216)

Slight differences between the three countries in their approaches were identified. For example, US law is more pro-debtor than Canadian, and Sweden is definitely pro-creditor. McGregor *et al.* conclude that 'all countries could take lessons from each other leading to a combined protective and welfare approach rather than just a punishment approach'.

Techniques for recouping debt

Techniques used for recouping debt are as old as credit itself, yet the debt collection process has rarely attracted attention. Rock (1973) argues that debt collection is a central but neglected area of social control. Strategies have traditionally varied according to the type of lender. Loan sharks in the nineteenth-century United States were astute psychologists in using stigma against delinquent borrowers. Often violence, lynching and rape were included in the loan shark's repertoire (Williams 2004). Other approaches included having money stopped out of wages and sending removals trucks bearing the words 'delinquent borrower repossession' to visit the debtor's home. One of the most imaginative ploys was the use of 'bawlerouts', usually a female with a loud voice who visited the debtor at their place of employment and bawled out details of the debt in front of colleagues (Germain 1996). Bawlerouts were such an integrated part of popular culture that Forest Halsey wrote a novel entitled *The Bawlerout* that was published in 1912.

The inability to precisely predict consumer behaviour has led to a re-evaluation of lenders' credit management procedures. In the case of persistent debtors the emergence of a debt sale market has replaced in-house debt collection departments and seeking commitments to pay through the courts, practices that were widely used in the old economy of credit referred to in Chapter 4. Recent trends in credit management procedures have included lenders acting more swiftly, with some cases being passed to bailiffs when an individual is only two months behind on payments. An emergent trend is to be more aggressive in dealing with early delinquency, with customers being contacted earlier and more frequently in the very early stages. In many cases late payment charges are threatened and imposed. Other techniques include 'resting', where organizations recognize the futility of aggressively demanding payment from customers who are clearly not able to pay at a particular point in time, but return to make further demands in the future (Credit Services Association 2003).

In their wide-ranging study of credit management practices, Dominy and Kempson (2003) identified three organizational approaches to arrears management: holistic, hard business, and one-size-fits-all. Creditors favouring the *holistic approach* invest in systems to enable their staff to discover the circumstances of people who fall into arrears and their reasons for non-payment. On the basis of the information provided by consumers, organizations adapt their arrears management and debt recovery approaches. Only when they believe that a consumer is deliberately avoiding paying when they are able to pay are the courts used. The *hard business approach* was adopted by organizations whose philosophy to credit management was to recover outstanding arrears at minimum cost. Organizations seek to reduce costs by avoiding interventions where there is little chance of success. These creditors work to the letter rather than the spirit of the law, and are generally less successful than organizations that adopt the holistic approach. Creditors that use the *one-size-fits-all approach* apply a standard set of procedures for all customers regardless of their circumstances. Organizations in this category frequently rely on the courts to provide information on a customer's circumstances rather than having established systems to capture this information for themselves. Mainstream financial institutions are represented in the business and holistic approaches, though some sub-prime lenders (especially those offering secured loans) operate a one-size-fits-all policy.

Few studies of debt collection exist. One of the few to attempt to investigate the whole process and the behaviour of actors involved is provided by Rock (1973) in his account entitled *Making People Pay*. He suggests that the typical debtor is a passive deviant, since the source of the deviancy is the inability or refusal to engage in the desired behaviour. Furthermore, he suggests that in many instances the social deviancy is managed in such a way that few debtors undergo a significant transformation of identity. In many areas of deviance the agencies involved endeavour to demonstrate that they are morally superior in relation not only to the deviants but also to the community which they manage. This is not strictly true of contemporary debt collectors, and in this respect conventional theories of deviance are reversed. Rook maintains that some 'aspects of credit lending and recovery are regarded as more deviant than the actions of defaulters' (Rock 1973: 24).

The debtor who fails to repay the debt is made to go through a series of experiences. Many instances of social control revolve around various rites of passage, as we discussed in Chapter 3 with respect to credit scoring. That said, the official regulation of default does not provide for such a ritual. The unceremonious nature of the debt collection process lacks drama which might otherwise make it highly visible. Rather, Rock (1973: 7) points out that '[d]ebtors are redeemable deviants who are held to require management because they have *failed* to perform certain acts. Those acts can be performed at almost any time in the enforcement career. Defaulters are thus conditionally deviant'. At any time, debtors can repay their debts, and at such time they will cease to be deviants. Because of their special status, conditional deviants require a different approach, one that avoids 'degradation' and 'ostracism'. Low visibility is a feature of the collection and communications process, and as a consequence it has been relatively unreported. The media play an important role in raising awareness of and structuring deviance, but cases of enforcement are rarely considered newsworthy. Given the low profile of the debt collection process, one might assume that few people would know about the mechanics of the process unless they had been personally involved. In fact, this assumption was supported by Rock's study of consumer knowledge of debt collection in London.

The debt sale market in personal finance

The preceding discussion has demonstrated a substantial increase in credit to support consumption in contemporary consumer society. Furthermore, it has been noted that the expansion in credit has been accompanied by higher levels of consumer default. A few missed payments can be easily caught up over a relatively short space of time. However, so significant are some rates of consumer default that new forms of institutional arrangements have been introduced by credit providers to deal with this problem. The focus of this section is the relatively new development of a debt sale market in personal finance. Although this market was first developed in the 1990s, relatively little is known about its operation. By contrast, a secondary debt market for corporate credit has been in existence for a significant period of time. The securitization of mortgage and credit card credit is also well established. A secondary debt market for personal-sector credit has emerged within the past ten years as a result of higher levels of consumer default. When in-house collection processes have been exhausted and redress through the courts is not viewed as an appropriate option, some lenders sell debt on to another organization to collect.

Ingham (2001) maintains that debt has become increasingly 'depersonalized' and transferable, and has included the transformation of a personalized bilateral debt relation into the means of paying a third-party creditor. He argues that debts paid by other debts are forms of money that are unique to capitalism. Trends in the area of personal finance are a variation of Ingham's concept of third-party debt. Lenders sell on their debt, sometimes through intermediaries, for the best rates they can achieve on the open market. In the United States, bad loan debt is often sold 'to law firms that specialize in taking unlucky debtors to court (rather than breaking their kneecaps like the old loan sharks)' (Williams 2004: 2).

The process of selling and negotiating a price for debt is rarely straightforward. Pricing is a complex issue, since it involves creditors taking a calculated gamble on the movement of interest rates and the percentage of the debt that is likely to be eventually recovered. While we have some knowledge of business-to-business dealers in the financial services sector (Farley, Hayes and Kopalle 2004) and the factors that influence dealer pricing of consumer credit (Bertola, Hochguertel and Winfred 2005), we have little understanding of the process of the selling and pricing of consumer debt. In some instances lenders sell the names of debtors for as little as 1 per cent of the debt's total value. Under these circumstances, agencies keep any cash they acquire from continuing to pursue the debt, making a profit if they can extract more than 1p in the pound. In 2003, 20 million cases were passed to debt collectors in the United Kingdom, but because of multiple delinquency, precise numbers of people in debt are difficult to establish (Dominy and Kempson 2003).

There are other costs to debt sellers apart from those of a financial nature. For example, damage to the brand may occur as a result of lenders being involved in what might be perceived by some customers to be unethical business practices. Moreover, large debt sale could be construed as an absence of appropriate controls in credit authorization practices and dubious policies in the area of corporate social responsibility. Furthermore, mainstream lenders that are the primary sellers of debt could be tarnished by the activities of companies to which they sell the debt, which are largely outside their control. This has led to mainstream institutions 'churning' their sub-prime subsidiaries when problems emerge, in an attempt to protect their image and credibility in the marketplace (Burton *et al.* 2004). For some of these reasons, some large lenders do not sell on their debt and prefer to write it off instead.

The institutional networks and webs of credit and debt are becoming increasingly complex as a result of the buying and selling of consumer debt. The buying and selling of corporate debt is well established, whereas the securitization and selling of personal-sector debt (mortgages, credit cards, personal loans) is of more recent origin. To date, personal loans have been largely exempt from securitization, but this is likely to occur in the not too distant future as more sophisticated risk models are developed (Allen, DeLong and Saunders 2004). Mainstream lenders and credit card companies are some of the biggest sellers of consumer debt. However, organizations in the public sector are also engaging in selling debt. For example, in the United Kingdom the debt sale of student loans by the government is increasingly common.

Debt-collecting agencies offer a variety of services, including credit scoring, door-to-door collection, computerized dialing systems, decision support to assess the likelihood of debtors repaying, bailiffs, car recovery, surveillance and absconder tracing. In the United Kingdom the debt collection market is very fragmented, with many small companies being established as a result of the low barriers to entry, with respect to start-up costs and expertise. From time to time there have been complaints about bailiffs using undesirable tactics to seize property from individuals who owe money. Mounting consumer concerns have resulted in tighter regulation and the view that debt collectors should move away from being hired heavies and be professionals who have a degree of legal knowledge and can provide advice. In defence of the industry, the Credit Services Association (2003) indicates that 17 million cases were handled by its members in 2003, and only 80 complaints from debtors were lodged. However, these statistics are probably not representative of all of the consumers in the United Kingdom who had problems with the debt collection service industry.

In the United States the numbers of complaints against such organizations have witnessed very significant increases over the past decade. The Federal Trade Commission, which enforces the federal law that governs debt collection practices, received 66,627 complaints about third-party collectors in 2005, many more than in any other industry and nearly six times the number in 1999. In some cases consumers were not even responsible for the debt for which they were being chased, and many thousands of others were being harassed where the debt could not be verified. Furthermore, some consumers are getting caught in the debt sale process itself. In some instances, lenders have agreed that bank charges were not valid, but debt cases continued because the bank had sold the debt to a collection agency, so in effect it was out of the bank's hands. The Federal Trade Commission enforces the Fair Debt Collection Practices Act 1977. The Act prohibits abusive, deceptive and unfair tactics by collection agencies. In July 2005 the commission won $10.2 million, the biggest ever judgment for illegal collection practices, against National Check Control of New Jersey. The company was prosecuted for overstating the amounts that consumers owed and threatening them with arrest and prosecution (Chan 2006).

It is not surprising that consumers (and consumer groups) are becoming concerned about the process of buying and selling of debt from one organization to another without the debtor's knowledge or consent. Debt can be sold on to any number of organizations, and there are clearly ethical issues surrounding consumers accepting loans from one lender and having to repay another. This is particularly the case when the debt is sold to organizations that are inferior to the original lender. Further down the debt recovery chain are bailiffs, who can use undesirable tactics to seize property from individuals who owe money. One form of consumer resistance to debt sale has emerged in the form of websites that are designed to warn consumers of industry tactics. One example is the US-based site 'I hate debt', which provides an in-depth account of the 'hidden' side of the debt collection industry and the debt sale market (see www.ihatedebt.com). Other sites are of a more general nature, dealing with a range of consumer affairs and highlighting organizations that have a reputation for treating consumers unfairly. One such site is www.consumerist.com, which gives financial services a high profile.

The response of the debt collection industry to these criticisms has been to establish trade associations to give itself some respectability. One such group in Britain is the debt sellers and buyers group of the Credit Services Association. As one might have expected, most of the members are buyers of debt rather than sellers, since large national and multinational financial institutions are the main sellers in the market. Debt buyers tend to be small organizations or wealthy individuals. One negative consequence of establishing trade associations is the problems that can emerge if one of the members is found guilty of inappropriate behaviour. This has happened in Britain, and even though the company concerned was excluded, it still reflects badly on other members and the industry in general. One of the negative consequences associated with debt sale is the tarnishing of the original lender's brand, and for this reason some financial institutions prefer to write debt off rather than sell it on.

There are clearly consumer policy issues arising from the debt sale industry. Since it is a fairly new phenomenon, some of the parameters of the industry, the organizations involved and some of the processes undertaken are relatively under-researched. There appears to be little by way of formal regulation in place to protect the consumer interest. As levels of consumer debt rise and more lenders engage in debt sale, it is an area of consumer policy that may come more to the fore in the near future. Furthermore, it is a difficult area to research. Consumers are often ashamed that they are in debt, so do not want to draw attention to the dilemmas that they find themselves in, and debt collectors are often unwilling to share the details of their working practices for fear of attracting criticism. The new Consumer Credit Act 2006 in the United Kingdom tightened up the debt administration industry and credit information services by requiring that they obtain a licence to operate. However, disappointingly, it does not 'introduce, or codify, any duty for lenders to act responsibly towards debtors or any requirement as to the form in which an agreement is to be made' (Smith and McCalla 2006: 29).

Conclusion

This chapter has focused on the concept of consumer financial misbehaviour. It is probably true to say that financial misbehaviour has existed as long as credit has been extended but that the characteristics of perpetrators have changed over time in response to economic and social conditions. There is much more research to be undertaken to unravel the history of credit and debt. Existing historical accounts of the fate of debtors in the eighteenth- and nineteenth-century United Kingdom and United States paint a picture of brutality, with debtors being regarded as worse than serious criminals. For some activities such as forgery, the punishment was death, which similarly points to the seriousness of financial misbehaviour. In many countries, individuals are still punished by imprisonment for unpaid debts. In this respect there are important continuities with a brutal past.

The roots of consumer misbehaviour in consumer societies have many sources and can take a variety of forms. Consumer financial misbehaviour has been categorized in terms of non-culpable default, serial default and fraud. The most extreme form of financial misbehaviour is consumer bankruptcy, and it is increasing in most advanced societies. Multiple bankruptcies are becoming more common and testify to the reduction in the stigma of the process. Lenders are resorting to a wider variety of methods to recoup debt. The debt sale market in personal finance is one strategy that has attracted considerable attention, since many consumers are unhappy about borrowing from one organization and having to pay back another. Consumer resistance has taken the form of websites aimed at protecting consumers from abuses by debt collectors.

Questions

1   What are the main reasons for consumer misbehaviour in consumer society?
2   Explain the main types of consumer financial misbehaviour.
3   Assess the techniques that lenders use to recoup debt.
4   What do you understand by the debt sale market in personal finance?

Further reading

Fullerton, R.A. and Punj, G. (1998) 'The unintended consequences of the culture of consumption: an historical-theoretical analysis of consumer misbehaviour', *Consumption, Markets and Culture*, 1, 4: 303–423.

Griffiths, M. (2000) 'The sustainability of consumer credit growth in late twentieth century Australia', *Journal of Consumer Studies and Home Economics*, 24, 1: 23–33.

McGowen, R. (2005) 'The Bank of England and the policing of forgery 1797–1821', *Past and Present*, 186, February: 81–96.

McGregor, S.L.T. and Berry, R.E. (2001) 'Analysis of Canadian, American and Swedish bankruptcy policy', *International Journal of Consumer Studies*, 25, 3: 208–227.

Mann, B.H. (2002) *Republic of Debtors: Bankruptcy in the Age of American Independence*, Cambridge, MA: Harvard University Press.

Phillips, S., Alexander, A. and Shaw, G. (2005) 'Consumer misbehavior: the rise of self-service grocery retailing and shoplifting in the United Kingdom c. 1950–1970', *Journal of Macromarketing*, 25, 1: 66–75.

Ramsay, I. (1997) 'Models of consumer bankruptcy: implications for research and policy', *Journal of Consumer Policy*, 20: 269–287.

Sullivan, T.A., Warren, E. and Westbrook, J.L. (1989) *As We Forgive Our Debtors: Bankruptcy and Consumer Credit in America*, Oxford: Oxford University Press.

Sullivan, T.A., Warren, E. and Westbrook, J.L. (2000) *The Fragile Middle Class: Americans in Debt*, New Haven, CT: Yale University Press.

7 Consumer credit and the politics of consumption

Many accounts of consumption tend to focus on cultural accounts of consumer behaviour. Hilton (2003) argues that cultural considerations should be placed within the wider economic and political context in which consumption takes place. The consumption of credit in advanced societies is a highly political issue in more ways than one. Indicators such as consumer confidence, spending, and the building of new homes are just some of the ways in which the health of national economies is being measured. Tax cuts and other stimulants are introduced in anticipation that consumer spending will prevent a recession. The strength of the housing market is an important factor in determining whether interest rates go up or down. The success of Japan as a new democracy after World War II was driven by the development of a mass consumer culture. Recent criticism has come as a result of the country failing to spend itself out of a protracted recession (Cohen 2004). In these respects the politics of consumption is tied to the economics of consumption and the success or failure of national economies (Bertola, Disney and Grant 2006).

Other aspects of the politics of consumption are the ways in which, through their consumption, individuals have developed their political consciousness, shaped their political organizations and challenged the process of government. Political mobilization around the issue of consumption has focused on advanced Western societies, but this scholarship has recently been extended to post-socialist societies (Mandel and Humphrey 2002). Some scholars have suggested that particular issues have had a higher profile than others. For example, Sayer (1999) argues that poverty, inequality and social justice, 'the politics of distribution', which once dominated political agendas, have been sidelined by the '(cultural) politics of recognition' (1999: 54) involving the previously neglected issues of gender, sexuality and the environment.

The focus of this chapter is to explore the relationship between consumption, public policy and the consumer interest. In the first section the dynamics of the politics of consumption will be assessed within the context of advanced industrial societies. In the second, the relationship between credit, consumer policy and consumer society will be discussed, especially in the context of the power differences between producers and consumers. A prominent theme in contemporary discourse is the issue of sustainable consumption. The third part of the chapter will address the relationship between credit and sustainable consumption. The fourth section will concern the important relationship between debt and personal well-being. The commodification of debt advice is a relatively new development that will be discussed in the fifth section. The final three sections of the chapter focus on affordability, consumer education, and secrecy and privacy concerns.

The politics of consumption

Hilton (2003) argues that consumption has inspired important socio-political movements over the past hundred years. At the core have been the consumer's right to safety, the right to be informed, the right to choose, the right to be heard and the right to recourse and redress (Aaker and Day 1978). Some scholars argue that organized consumer action has a much longer history that in some instances dates back many centuries. Thompson (1971: 79) claims that in eighteenth-century Britain there was a 'highly-sensitive consumer-consciousness' around what were illegitimate practices in marketing and within important industries, including milling and baking. A popular consensus emerged around social norms and obligations of key institutions and individuals within the community. Taken together, the ensuing philosophy constituted a 'moral economy of the poor'. In the United Kingdom, views of consumption and understanding of prices impacted upon early socialist thought. For example, the demand for reasonably priced quality goods was a cornerstone of the cooperative movement. Consumer representation has been embedded in state infrastructure since the World War I Consumers' Council had an impact on the Food Council dating back to 1925 and the Agricultural Marketing Boards in the 1930s. Over time the cooperative movement's role as the spearhead of consumerism has waned and the Consumers' Association has taken up the mantle, with its membership peaking in the late 1980s (Hilton 2003).

Consumerism was a mobilizing force throughout the twentieth century. The defining feature over recent years is the strength of the movement and its ability to disrupt the activities of large corporations in some sectors of the economy. Abbinnett (2007) provides a useful overview of the differences between various strands of anti-capitalist discourse and political activism that have arisen from the global organization of capital. The classic accounts written by the first wave of scholars involved in highlighting the unequal power relations between producers and consumers included Ralph Nader's (1973) *The Consumer and Corporate Accountability*, Vance Packard's (1957) *Hidden Persuaders*, Stuart Ewen's (1976) *Captains of Consciousness* and Herbert Marcuse's (1964) *One-Dimensional Man*. What might be considered the second wave comprises those who have more recently developed a more explicit anti-capitalist agenda in accounts such as Naomi Klein's (2000) *No Logo*, George Monbiot's (2000) *The Captive State: The Corporate Takeover of Britain* and Lasn's (1999) *Culture Jam: The Uncooling of America*.

In many societies, consumerism has been a middle-class phenomenon, but equally it has not been a minority interest, whether in the context of supporting legislative change or in its contribution to single-issue campaigning. The diversity of consumer politics has negated a coherent collective consumer conscience and a definition of what constitutes the consumer interest. Nevertheless, focusing on the politics of consumption is a way of understanding the relationship between material culture and citizenship. Hilton and Daunton (2001: 3–5) argue that four main themes have tended to inform the politics of consumption. First, the issue of morality is embedded in many discussions of consumption. A core debate has been the 'moral, social and economic desirability' of consumption *per se*, whether some goods and services are more damaging than others (alcohol, tobacco, drugs), and where the boundaries lie between necessity and luxury. A second theme concerns who has the authority and who is entitled to speak on behalf of the consumer, since many different 'faces' of the consumer can exist at any one time (Gabriel and Lang 1997). In reality the answer to this question is the complex interaction of various interest groups. These include active consumers, whether in an organized forum or not, commercial and political organizations that attempt to define the parameters of the consumer for their own ends, and other sites of specialist knowledge within and outside modern governments.

A third theme relates to the market structures that constitute the environment in which consumer needs and wants are satisfied, or not as the case may be. Issues such as the number of competitors in the market, the private versus public provision of goods and services, and collective versus individual consumption are all relevant to the consumption choices of individuals and households. A final debate, and one at the core of discussion of material politics, is the relationship between the consumer, citizenship and the state. At different historical periods of time, the state, through the medium of regulation and legislation, has influenced, if not determined, particular markets, protected individuals within specific markets and promoted consumer activism in others. Consumers too have created their own notions of citizenship that may provide a point of resistance against government and state action. Daunton and Hilton maintain, 'In short, the relationships between states and consumers are constantly being negotiated, forever developing new notions of citizenship' (2001: 5).

Credit, consumer policy and consumer society

It is against the political backdrop of the changing nature of consumerism in society that the financial services sector needs to be understood (Burton 1994).

The adequacy of consumer policy in consumer societies is highly dependent on the model of the consumer that is adopted. Many accounts of consumer society focus on the view that consumers are educated and reflexive, and that the challenge for producers is to continually react to the ever-changing needs of demanding consumers. According to this interpretation, consumers have become more powerful than producers. Support for this viewpoint emerges from the changing discourse of the consumer (du Gay and Salaman 1992). Patients, students and borrowers are reinvented as consumers, and the needs of consumers are written into mission statements and customer charters.

A rather different perspective is that the discourse of the powerful consumer is somewhat misplaced. Within important sectors of the economy there is a significant concentration of power within a relatively small number of organizations. Within the United Kingdom and many other advanced societies this observation is as true of retailing as it is in the financial services sector. Retailers and manufacturers are powerful producers of consumer culture, and while discourse of consumer choice abounds, retailers determine the product choices that are available for individuals to purchase. In this respect, retailers are a powerful force in determining popular culture and can result in unequal or asymmetric power relations between retailers and consumers.

A recent example in the United Kingdom drawn from the financial services sector related to overcharging. A website that focuses on financial advice (moneysavingexpert.com) provided a template of a letter to enable consumers to complain and request a refund of unlawful bank charges. The existence of the website was published by national newspapers. Over a million letters had been downloaded between November 2006 and February 2007. The protest generated 10,000 claims a day by customers that were sent to their bank, while the Financial Services Ombudsman was receiving 5,000 enquiries a week (Hickman 2007). Collectively these activities generated what became known as a *reclaim culture*. Some consumers did manage to obtain a refund of their charges, but after a relatively short time the banks began charging customers for the investigative work that was required on their account to determine whether refunds were in order. Clearly, the thought of paying an upfront fee would put cash-strapped customers off pursuing a claim.

An alternative perspective is that neither the consumer sovereignty thesis nor the powerful producer thesis is a sufficiently sensitive basis for understanding consumer–producer relationships. An alternative scenario is that consumers are more knowledgeable about some goods and services than others and therefore need greater protection in certain areas of consumption than in others. Certainly, some financial services are complex and difficult for some consumers to understand, and it is for this reason that financial institutions are among the most highly regulated organizations in advanced societies. Within the existing literature the credit choices available to low-income consumers who are most vulnerable from extortionate interest rates, high charges, and dubious terms and conditions have rarely been addressed in academic research (Karpatkin 1999; Bazerman 2001). Aldridge (1998) argues that it is not just lack of financial capital that is the problem for these groups but the cultural capital that is required for their acquisition. Nor is it just individuals within certain socio-economic classes that find financial services difficult to comprehend; to some extent this is a problems across all social classes. In Chapter 6 it was noted that the majority of bankrupts are drawn from the middle class. The information asymmetries between financial institutions and their consumers are exploited by lenders. Financial institutions could develop financial education as an important marketing strategy, but most choose not to (Burton 2002a). In short, Martin's (2002) financialization of everyday life thesis may be a requirement of living in a consumer society, but the reality is that most consumers fall far short where financial competence is concerned.

The view that consumer protection policy needs redesigning and rethinking in view of the changing nature of consumption and consumer society is gaining considerable support. In particular, there is recognition of the need for new policies to govern and regulate the new digital and media age in the public interest. The question of who will regulate is a pertinent issue, as Poster (1995: 84) indicates: 'Nation-states are at a loss when faced with a global com-munications network. Technology has taken a turn that defies the power of modern governments.' Consumers have to trust regulators to act in their interests, but they do not always do so, in the face of pressure from industry groups, and the financial services sector is no exception (Mitchell 1991; Burton 1994).

One consequence of the expansion of credit in consumer society is the need for greater levels of consumer awareness and education, and more counselling services. Financial literacy is an issue with which many advanced societies are grappling. In many countries there is a comparative lack of social policy with respect to credit, whether in terms of government provision (since most credit is provided commercially), questions about access, or regulation (Edwards 2000). Furthermore, credit marketing and consumer protection have not received significant amounts of attention, and therefore techniques of control over abuses in marketing behaviour are relatively underdeveloped.

One of the most valuable accounts in this area is Ison's (1979) *Credit Marketing and Consumer Protection*, but is somewhat dated, having been written nearly thirty years ago, before the extraordinary boom in credit occurred. Nevertheless, some of his observations have contemporary relevance. Ison (1979: 333) maintains that

> Strength and sophistication in sanctions have not always been features of consumer protection legislation. One explanation is, of course, the incidence of political power. Following the industrial revolution, the rising pre-eminence on the political scene of those controlling industry and

commerce brought not only the wholesome notion of free trade, but also the more dubious ancillary doctrines of *laissez-faire* and *caveat emptor*.

In the mid-1960s Borrie and Diamond (1964: 16) questioned the concept of *caveat emptor* and its divergence with consumer culture:

> It may be a cherished adage of the consuming public that the consumer is always right, but in the eyes of the law this saying has never been significant. Far greater emphasis has been placed by the courts on the maxim *caveat emptor* – let the buyer beware.

In contrast to the might and lobbying power of huge corporations there is little by way of a sustained, powerful lobbying force in the consumer interest. Consumer organizations have witnessed considerable expansion, and the internet has facilitated new websites that have provided a focus for consumer resistance, but these forums have to work hard with limited resources to cover a wide variety of policy areas. In the financial services sector the power of organizations is even more significant, given that many sub-sectors are self-regulated (McGee 1992).

Ison (1979) maintains that the advantage of self-regulation is that if remedial action is required to correct a problem, it can be resolved promptly with industry agreement rather than the industry having to risk confronting government action. This can be particularly the case with issues of a technical nature that can be quickly resolved within the industry. However, there are a number of disadvantages of self-regulation. First, the democratic process is overridden when acceptable levels of integrity are given to one side of the marketplace. Second, there are often conflicts of interests between self-regulatory organizations and consumers, and giving producers the upper hand could result in abuses of power. For example, it is in the interests of lenders to limit the competition in the market so that they can obtain a greater share of business, with the potential to charge higher interest rates and fees. Obviously, anti-competitive practices are not in the consumer interest. Third, members of self-regulatory organizations often exchange technical and marketing information with each other. This results in important information circulating within the industry rather than having a wider remit that could act as a force for change. Fourth, when industry bodies do become involved in consumer protection issues, it is often for reasons that bode well for the success of the venture. For example, abuses in marketing will often generate a public outcry for government action. A self-regulatory organization may be compelled to act, but only as long as the issue stays in the headlines.

The power difference between huge multinational banks and individual consumers is vast. As a result, few individuals seek redress through the courts. This feature is as true of the United Kingdom as it is in the United States and

Canada. Furthermore, the marketing of consumer goods and services is part of the private law of contract. The courts treat contracts as evidence of the terms upon which the parties were dealing. However, this analysis fails to reflect the realities of mass production and distribution, which means that consumers often trust the agent or member of staff to provide or interpret information for them and do not read the small print themselves. One of the major problems involved in sub-prime lending has been lack of consumers' awareness of the implications of the contracts they were signing, and, as a consequence, many lost their homes. Proving deceit in the form of misinformation by salespeople is very difficult, especially when it is one person's word against another; the discussion may have been lengthy, and could have occurred several months previously. In short, theories of consumer society have made little by way of significant contribution to debates about consumer policy and protection. In part this is because of the emphasis on consumer autonomy, sovereignty and fun aspects of consumption rather than on the ordinary and the mundane (Gronow and Warde 2001).

Consumers, credit and sustainable consumption

The concept of sustainability has been used in a variety of ways in contemporary discourse, spanning areas as diverse as the environmentally sensitive nature of production and consumption, and economic sustainability in localities and regions. The World Commission on Environment and Development (1987) defined sustainable consumption as patterns of consumption that meet the needs of the present without compromising the ability of subsequent generations to meet their own needs. Fuchs and Lorek (2005) maintain that there are *weak* and *strong* approaches to sustainable consumption. The *weak* approach refers to an increase in the overall efficiency of existing consumption through technological developments that act as a filter to its harmful effects. A *strong* approach requires changes in consumption *patterns* and consumption *levels*. Fuchs and Lorek provide three examples to illustrate the differences between weak and strong sustainable consumption approaches:

> (1) Weak sustainable consumption could mean driving a car that will use 3 litres rather than 10 litres of gasoline per 100 kilometres. Strong sustainable consumption, in contrast, can mean going by train rather than by car or travelling less far or less frequently. (2) Important improvements in efficient consumption related to housing can be reached through proper insulation, efficient heating systems, and the construction of low energy houses. For strong sustainable consumption, behavioural factors such as airing and the choice of adequate room temperature are important. In addition, a strong sustainable consumption perspective would problematize the societal trend to continuously increase the square meter living space per person. (3) In the consumption cluster of nutrition, technological

efficiency measured in yield/area is mostly accompanied by environmental pressure (e.g., energy-consuming fertilizers, groundwater pressure, or the controversial effects of genetically modified organisms). Strong consumption measures, in contrast, could include a reduction in meat consumption and an emphasis on regional products.

(2005: 262–263)

There is something of a consensus around the view that current levels of consumption by affluent consumers in rich and poor countries are unsustainable. Yet progress towards sustainable consumption over the intervening years has been slow, despite its being in the long-term interests of consumers and consumer groups to promote these developments (Thogersen 2005). The role of consumer knowledge in supporting the sustainable consumption agenda is receiving more attention within contemporary debates, although some might argue that it has been marginalized (Lash, Szerszynski and Wynne 1998). Recent debates have included the expert–lay divide and the role of the public realm as an alternative forum for generating public knowledge (Wynne 1998), grass-roots organizations as a source of social values about sustainable development and sustainability (Grove-White 1998), and translating philosophical and political awareness into meaningful consumer action (Szerszynski 1998).

Despite the burgeoning sustainable consumption literature, little attention has been directed at the role of consumer credit in underpinning some of these developments. Consumers do not have complete freedom in their consumption patterns, and that equally applies to sustainable consumption. Financial considerations can be a significant factor in decisions to act on sustainable consumption appeals. For example, the purchase of more expensive environmentally friendly and organic food products is positively correlated with income (O'Donovan and McCarthy 2002). The willingness to purchase goods that are more environmentally friendly products also increases with income (Alberini *et al.* 2005), and the opposite is also true, with cash-strapped consumers being unable to afford these goods (Tanner and Wolfing Kast 2003). Cohen (2007) maintains that the relationship between philosophical debates on sustainability and credit concerns appropriate levels of affluence and distinguishing between opulent and frugal lifestyles. Consumer credit has the power to support or negate sustainability initiatives within households and elsewhere in the economy – for example, the extent to which credit is being used to upgrade household appliances to more efficient ones, and to buy costly fair trade products that might otherwise be beyond one's budget. Conversely, it is not clear to what extent substantial credit repayments are forcing consumers to downsize their consumption in the longer term, negating capital investments that could improve the energy and materials efficiency of their lifestyles. Far more attention needs to be paid to the extent to which sustainable consumption is being underpinned by levels of unsustainable credit.

There are some groups in society that are radically changing their consumption patterns, reducing their levels of consumption and associated levels of credit and debt. They are resisting the disease of 'affluenza' by deliberately failing to sustain previous levels of consumption, as a political act of resistance. Schor (1998) maintains that consumers can become locked into a cycle of overwork to sustain patterns of overconsumption. In an attempt to keep up with or do better than the Joneses, they generate consumer aspirations that are unsustainable and can result in anxiety, frustration and dissatisfaction. Consumer resistance to financialization and the resultant overwork and consumption can take the form of downshifting whereby individuals decide to lead simpler lives, have simpler tastes and have more time for themselves and to enjoy life.

Schor's (1998) account of downshifters illustrates that many of them are switching careers; others are working part time, starting home-based businesses, or leaving full-time work altogether to spend more time with their families. The price for changing their lifestyle is earning less money, forcing them to change their consumption patterns. Schor maintains that

> [t]hey don't shop as much, they make more of what they need themselves, and they spend less money in the world of commodified leisure. Their birthday parties don't have magicians or clowns; the kids play pin-the-tail-on-the-donkey and fish for coins in the bathtub. . . . They drive a seven-year-old car or maybe take the bus to work. Their patronage of restaurants drops off precipitously. They stop going to first-run movies. But for virtually all of them, these changes are worth it.
>
> (1998: 22–23)

A prominent trend among downshifters is their desire to align their lifestyle with their values. Lives may become out of synch because people do not have time for things that are important to them, because they do not believe in the work they are doing, or because the relationship between money, identity and consumption has become meaningless.

Schor acknowledges that downshifters are not the first movement of this type in history. Quakers, transcendentalists and hippies have supported the philosophy of leading frugal and alternative lifestyles. However, these were small, ideologically coherent groups that were 'much more self-consciously anticonsumerist than most of today's downshifters' (1998: 23). Downshifters are not dropping out, nor are they 'back to the land types', nor do they live together. They do not share a religion. Their occupational status is fairly mainstream and they are drawn from urban and suburban populations. What they do have in common is that they represent a significant counter-trend to the ideology that has dominated advanced Western societies, of bettering and improving one's social status.

Schor is not the only investigator to note this changing orientation among some groups in society. One of the first to do so was Elgin (1981) in his text *Voluntary Simplicity: Toward a Way of Life That Is Outwardly Simple, Inwardly Rich*, which promoted frugal consumption, ecological awareness and personal growth. The Simple Living Network is a forum that brings together like-minded people (www.simpleliving.net). Furthermore, research that has compared voluntary simplifiers and regular people in the same geographical area has demonstrated that simplifiers were happier according to a variety of criteria (Kasser 2002). It is not surprising that this view is being popularized through accounts such as Shira Boss's (2006) *Green with Envy: Why Keeping Up with the Joneses Is Keeping Us in Debt.*

The downshifting ideology is one that could be promoted more positively in contemporary culture. Cross (1993) maintains that part of the problem is finding an appropriate language that expresses the alternatives without condemning or embracing people whose lives are consumed by working and shopping. He notes:

> They need to understand why consumerism works and yet how its 'comforts' frustrate and are but poor substitutes for social solidarity and self-expression. Less dependence on goods might free us from heteronomy at work and manipulation at play. It should also help overcome ecological waste and danger. But intellectuals must join with the people in finding a language and a practice that expresses this alternative.
>
> (1993: 212).

Credit, debt and personal well-being

The desirability of sustaining current levels of consumption has given rise to a rather different set of concerns centring on the relationship between credit, debt and personal well-being. There is a considerable literature that has demonstrated a strong association between socio-economic status, health and mortality, but in general we know little about the relationship between measures that tap into well-being such as debt, assets, financial hardship and wealth. There is mounting evidence that credit and debt can cause some consumers considerable amounts of stress (Brown *et al.* 2005). The relationship between debt and suicide is relatively long-standing. Dossey (2007) provides accounts of whole families committing suicide as a result of financial distress in the early eighteenth century. Suicides linked to the inability to cope with debt have become an unwelcome but regular feature in the media in many advanced societies.

Measures of financial well-being have traditionally focused on objective and easily measurable indicators, including income and net worth. Yet individuals with good incomes and reasonable levels of net worth can find themselves in financial difficulties as a result of a combination of unpredictable circumstances. Alternative approaches to measuring financial health have emphasized subjective indicators of well-being, including calculating financial stress levels, understanding consumer financial behaviour and knowledge, ways of determining financial solvency, attitudes towards risk tolerance, and levels of consumer financial education (Xiao, Sorhaindo and Garman 2006).

Drentea and Lavrakas (2000) have examined credit card debt as a means of assessing financial well-being, since people use credit cards to purchase products and services that they would normally not be able to afford. In this respect, credit card debt may give a more comprehensive assessment of financial well-being than income, because it may tap into long-term deprivation. They argue that studying the relationship between credit card debt and health is important for three reasons. First, consumers may use cards to pay for basic necessities such as food, household bills, clothing and medicine. Credit card debt accumulates over time and the interest payments are high; it is therefore indicative of extended financial hardship. Second, high levels of debt may prevent individuals from spending money on items that would improve their health, such as food, healthcare and treats that would improve the quality of their life. Third, the stress of owing money and the increased stress associated with the knowledge of paying high interest rates could result in reduced levels of personal well-being. The relationship between race, debt and well-being is an issue that is of relevance to the discussion. For example, it is fairly well established that African-Americans as a group have, on average, worse health records and a lower life expectancy than whites. Furthermore, African-Americans also carry proportionately high levels of debt. It is not clear the extent to which debt can explain the differences in the relationship between health and race.

The results of Drentea and Lavrakas's study indicated that the financial strain associated with a high debt/income ratio were associated with ill health. They also found that debt/income ratio had a stronger effect on ill health than income did. In addition, lack of finances had an impact on health behaviours and risks. However, neither the level of credit card debt nor stress about levels of debt was associated with race. Drentea and Lavrakas's (2000) work was one of the first attempts to provide a link between debt and well-being, and in this respect it provided a platform that other scholars could build upon. A limitation of their work was that it focused on one source of debt, credit cards, as opposed to total debt.

There is an expanding area of research that demonstrates a significant relationship between financial stress and family well-being (see Xiao, Sorhaindo and Garman 2006 for an overview). Financial stress has been linked to depression and having negative employment-related effects. Financial stress has been positively related to both reduced performance at work and absenteeism (Kim, Sorhaindo and Garman 2006). Studies of unemployed youths in

Australia have demonstrated that financial strain is positively related to general psychological distress. Coping strategies to deal with financial stress, such as alcohol abuse, can exacerbate the problem. There also appear to be racial or ethnic and nationality differences in levels of financial stress. For example, research in the United States among white and African-American students found that African-Americans reported higher levels of financial stress (Worthington 2006; Grable and Yoo 2006).

The old adage 'When poverty comes through the door, love flies out of the window' seems as true today as it ever was. Research has demonstrated that financial strain can cause problems in personal relationships, including marriage problems, instability and marriage breakdown (Sullivan, Warren and Westbrook 2000). Moreover, in some instances marital problems can lead to bankruptcy, and the reverse is also true, with bankruptcy leading to marital breakdown. The effects of divorce and personal bankruptcy can be severe and long term, especially if the individual does not remarry (Fisher and Lyons 2006). Financial strain can be particularly severe and prolonged for divorced women who have caring responsibilities for children, and this has led to a discussion about the most suitable method for allocating welfare benefits. Coping with financial strain after the birth of a baby is not uncommon. The ability to cope can be the result of behavioural, psychological, and financial characteristics. C.M. Walker (1996) found that strategies developed by new mothers to cope with reduced financial circumstances included being less materialistic, being aware of how much things cost, and avoiding impulse buying.

What most of the recent investigations of credit, debt and personal well-being have demonstrated is that some of the dysfunctional and somewhat hidden costs of consumer society can be enormous. To date, there has been little discussion of what this all means in policy terms with respect to the economics of individuals taking time off work, the effect on social and interpersonal relations, and ill health within advanced societies.

The commodification of debt counselling

Concerns over levels of consumer financial knowledge have caused anxiety for academics and policymakers. Some of the main themes that have arisen include low levels of financial literacy across most social groups, consumers' lack of interest in financial affairs, and the mis-selling of some financial products, including mortgages and pensions (Burton 1994). A similar set of concerns have been reported in the context of credit and debt with respect to consumer awareness of APR, the cost of credit and the awareness of alterative credit suppliers. Yet Martin (2002) maintains that the need for financial skills has never been greater, and consumer education and consumer financial literacy have become part and parcel of the financialization of everyday life. As the use of financial services has become widespread and more deeply embedded in contemporary consumer society, consumers are increasingly required to take responsibility for tasks that might previously have been undertaken by financial service professionals.

Despite financialization arguments supporting the idea of more educated consumers, greater numbers of individuals and households are finding themselves in debt. Debt counselling was first established as a specialist area of expertise in the United States in the 1970s and is now well established in many advanced societies. There is an established literature to support this work in the form of debt advice workers' handbooks (Buswell 2001; Wolfe *et al.* 1998; Blamire 1984). The maturation of this literature is reflected in its segmentation, with texts providing debt advice for use by social workers (Ryan 1996) and professionals working with ex-offenders (Gibbons 2001). Innovative computer programs have also been developed to assess debt portfolios and subsequently suggest repayment options, enabling consumers to decide how to distribute the extra payments most effectively. Some educational institutions are also developing partnerships in order to help inform and educate at-risk groups, including minorities, single parents, divorced people and others (Lown 2005).

There has been a tradition in the United Kingdom and the United States of providing free debt advice for consumers who need help in managing their financial affairs and negotiating with creditors. The larger numbers of customers finding themselves in debt has increased the demand for debt advice. For example, in the United States between 1988 and 1998, the number of consumers entering non-profit debt management programmes nearly doubled (Manning 2000). Similar patterns are evident in other countries, including the United Kingdom (Hinton and Berthoud 1988). The demand for advice has been so great that organizations offering free provision have found it difficult to meet the demand. As a consequence, a new market centring on the commodification of debt advice has emerged during the past decade. Commercial agencies that provide debt advice and associated assistance for a fee have emerged, but they have not been without their critics, who highlight the exploitative nature of the provision.

Xiao, Sorhaindo and Garman (2006) maintain that new competitors have entered the market but that they fail to provide an appropriate service. Research in the United States indicates that many non-profit credit counsellors are essentially unqualified call centre sales staff, with debtors receiving little or no counselling. Agencies are making large profits by steering consumers into debt management plans that have high upfront fees regardless of individual need and circumstances (Lown 2005). Some of the newer non-profit organizations advertise extensively on television to attract as many people as possible, charging exorbitant fees that are subsequently funnelled into affiliated for-profit companies. Furthermore, debt elimination scams are proliferating on the internet. In return for fees ranging from $3,000 to $20,000, debt elimination websites offer to help consumers challenge the validity of their loans (Consumer Affairs 2004). Another service touted to vulnerable consumers is debt repair, which involves removing details of credit records that have a negative impact on a consumer's credit history. Debt repair in this sense is not legal. In the United Kingdom this misleading practice has recently been addressed within a wide-ranging review of credit legislation. Smith and McCalla (2006: 42) note:

> The particular mischief that is sought to be addressed is the practice of misleading desperate or otherwise vulnerable consumers into believing that, for a fee, they can have their credit records cleaned, by the removal of adverse entries whether or not the entries are valid.

Debt repair in this context does not exist; it is not legal. Services of this nature are little more than a scam.

Richard Lord (2005), in his book *American Nightmare*, provides some graphic examples of how consumers are forced into deeper debt by appealing debt management programmes that offer to consolidate debt and provide lower monthly payments. Some schemes even provide extra cash, adding to the debt burden of consumers who are already in severe financial difficulties. Many consolidation loans are provided to homeowners, and loans are secured against debtors' homes. Indeed, for many companies providing consolidation loans, homeownership is a prerequisite. Failure to keep up payments can culminate in homes being repossessed and in extreme cases can lead to bankruptcy (see Burton *et al.* 2004). Unscrupulous organizations often provide loans in excess of 100 per cent of the value as a deliberate way of overextending debtors in order to repossess the property when they can no longer make the payments. In this respect, consolidation lenders are another form of predatory financial service supplier, plundering individuals who are already in financial difficulties.

The proliferation of commercial organizations that provide debt advice is a cause for concern. The regulation of debt advice has taken something of a back seat to the highly regulated advice that lenders are required to provide to consumers before they purchase a financial service product. Perhaps the nature of this imbalance should be readdressed in view of some of the developments in the commodification of debt advice.

Affordability in credit modelling

An important social and public policy issue that has arisen, given the larger numbers of consumers who are finding themselves in financial difficulties, is why lenders have authorized the giving of more credit to individuals who were already having problems meeting their existing commitments. This issue of overindebtedness is significant, given the very good quality credit-scoring data that lenders already have at their disposal. This debate has given rise to the role of affordability in lending decisions and the sanctioning of credit. Regulators and some lenders have addressed the issue by giving a higher priority to affordability by finding ways of integrating affordability into the credit-scoring process. In the United Kingdom a government task force on tackling over-indebtedness stressed the need for investment and more sophisticated scoring techniques to identify overcommitment. Suggestions included the view that systems should be developed using all available data to assess the borrower's ability to repay. A customer's disposable income is often calculated by assessing income and expenditure, and for most lenders these are the overriding factors in the decision to grant credit. However, the question remains whether a detailed assessment of a customer's income and expenditure always leads to an appropriate lending decision.

The lack of attention paid to 'affordability' and 'overindebtedness' in the credit-scoring literature is illustrated by a recent literature search of the *Web of Knowledge* and *Science Direct* that yielded no positive results (Finlay 2006). Wilkinson and Tingay (2004) maintain that a number of initiatives by practitioners have been designed to assess affordability. However, the data and methods of analyses used to do this vary between companies. There are a number of dilemmas involved in defining affordability. On the income side of the equation these relate to the dilemmas concerning the use of gross or net income, and whether to include overtime, bonuses and commission. Perhaps the greatest difficulty concerns what constitutes expenditure. A judgement has to be made whether to include just large items such as mortgage or rent, or whether fixed-term credit agreements should also be included even if they have only a short time to run. Other dilemmas concern revolving credit, specifically whether the credit limit is the measure, the monthly payment or the average balance over a specified period. Then there are other regular payments that potentially could be included, such as life insurance, endowments, maintenance, and so forth. Confirmation of all of these details to the satisfaction of the lender is another barrier that needs to be overcome. Wilkinson and Tingay argue that 'all in all, defining affordability, let alone verifying and assessing it, gives a very hazy picture' (2004: 64).

To test whether assessment of affordability adds real value to the lending decision, Wilkinson and Tingay (2004) conducted an empirical investigation into a mass-market financial institution with a sizeable unsecured loan book. The portfolio used for the analysis had a mass-market, high-risk customer base since it was this group that would be susceptible to affordability problems. The rejection rate was high, and customers were offered terms through risk-based pricing. The data confirmed that affordability factors are significant but that the customer's residential status was more predictive of credit risk than any of the affordability factors. Furthermore, the benefits to the lender in terms of reducing default were disappointing. The reason why affordability added only marginally to the quality of the lending decision was that the decision was closely correlated with more traditional and reliable information from the application form and credit bureau data.

The predictability problem has also been highlighted by Finlay (2006). Customer affordability and level of indebtedness are unlikely to be static properties, which, it might be argued, invalidates the models. For example, if a customer's loan is about to terminate a short time after the modelling, the affordability levels will change. A second issue is that income and expenditure are also likely to change in real life, for example through salary increases or an individual being made redundant. Third, expenditure always expands to take into account any excess income, and this raises the question of whether only essential expenditure should be used in affordability calculations.

The issue of affordability in the context of consumer credit is a very contentious one, and the statistical models that have been built to assess affordability appear to offer limited explanations. However, it is desirable that affordability in lending is placed higher up the agenda, since the numbers of consumers in difficulties and higher bankruptcy rates suggest that more conservative credit limits might have been prudent.

Consumer education

There has been considerable attention directed at the impact of consumer education and information on the development of reflexive consumers in advanced societies. In most societies, financial institutions are among the most regulated in the economy – and for good reason, given the pivotal role of money as regards the well-being of individuals and society. Given the evident vulnerability of financial services consumers, many advanced societies have developed an infrastructure to educate adults and children. A wide-ranging review of consumer education provision in the United Kingdom demonstrated that aspects of financial education were by far the most dominant theme. Indeed, the maturity of the consumer education market is evident in the targeting of different segments of consumers with different educational programmes. Credit and debt were given a particularly high profile (Office of Fair Trading 2006). Examples include a national debt line, a one-day credit workshop provided by a prominent credit-scoring bureau, a consumer credit counselling service and personal financial education in schools (www.oft.gov.uk.nr).

In recent years there has been an explosion in the number of self-help texts that have focused on credit and debt management for consumers who would rather deal with their problems themselves in the privacy of their own homes. These books tend to be no-nonsense practical accounts of how the credit industry operates, various tricks of the trade, and knowing some of the legal issues associated with credit and debt. The books provide a positive, proactive approach to dealing with debt, as some of the titles indicate: *How to Cope with Credit and Deal with Debt* (Andrews and Houghton 1986), *The Complete Idiot's*

Guide to Beating Debt (Strauss and Jaffe 2000), *The Credit Repair Kit* (Ventura 1998), *The DIY Credit Repair Manual* (Rose 1998), *Repair Your Credit and Knock Out Your Debt* (Michael 2004), *Credit Hell* (Dvorkin 2005), *Credit Repair Kit for Dummies* (Bucci 2006) and *Deal with Your Debt* (Weston 2006). These texts are an important addition to consumer education initiatives, since we know that many people in debt are too ashamed to ask for advice. Many debtors struggle on their own for weeks, months, even years, with the situation getting worse all the time. It is a case of swallowing some of the little pride they have left before asking for help (Hinton and Berthoud 1988).

The subject of credit and debt is given a high profile within financial education initiatives, and for good reason, since they can have major implications on people's lives. For example, many organizations in the financial services sector will not hire people with poor credit histories. Difficulties can arise in renting or buying one's own home, or purchasing a vehicle, or indeed any transaction where personal trust and credit go hand in hand (Lyons and Fisher 2006). However, the provision of consumer education is a controversial activity. Lenders are often best placed to provide education, since they are most knowledgeable about their consumers' financial health. Lenders can also provide the relevant details at the time that they need it. However, many lenders have a vested interest in not doing so because of the profit motive of securing new business. Lenders have much to gain by hiding poor terms and conditions of credit rather than focusing on transparency. It would be a very ethical lender that referred consumers to other lenders that could provide a better deal in what is a highly competitive marketplace. This issue raises the conceptual distinction between education and information. Consumer education is generic and would provide transferable knowledge that consumers could use in different contexts. Lenders are more concerned with providing product-specific information about their own range of products to secure a sale. Some financial institutions have been criticized for providing events that were advertised as education seminars but in fact were little more than a glorified sales pitch (Burton 2002a).

Another point of controversy concerns the sources of funding of consumer education initiatives. It is becoming increasingly common for financial institutions to fund education initiatives, whether in the context of education in schools, adult education or educational seminars. One interpretation of these initiatives is that financial institutions are taking corporate social responsibility seriously, and investing resources in genuinely trying to resolve the problems of excessive credit and debt. Lenders have a vested interest in ensuring that consumers repay their debts, since if they fail to do so it will result in losses of revenue due to default. The growing acceptability of bankruptcy as a way out of debt has resulted in net losses to creditors being counted in tens of billions of pounds or dollars or euros. For example, in the United States, losses to creditors as a result of bankruptcy have grown twice as fast as consumer instalment credit since 1980 (Domowitz and Sartain 1999). On the other hand, cynics would argue that consumer education is little more that another marketing initiative, enhancing consumers' awareness of the brand in the belief that familiarity and perceptions of trustworthiness may encourage a sale.

Whether consumer education does deliver changes in behaviour is debatable and, furthermore, very difficult to measure. The underlying assumption is that consumers are unaware of the consequences of their actions and that consumer education will prompt a change in behaviour through heightened understanding. However, research has demonstrated that consumers can use a number of types of rules to constrain expenditure. These include the matching rule, where consumption in any particular period has to be matched by available income. Setting credit balances up to a certain limit and not overstretching them is another strategy. Using mental accounts via budgeting so that one does not overspend on tempting products can be useful. Increasing credit limits results in a greater likelihood that the consumer will make a purchase. We also know that credit limits influence spending to a greater degree for consumers with lower credibility: younger consumers and less educated consumers. However, consumers are myopic in that they do not consider the future when making current spending decisions. Very often they have not developed willpower and pre-commitment strategies, and fall prey to tempting purchases even in the absence of present liquidity (Soman and Cheema 2002).

An examination of consumer credit and debt in its historical context indicates that the crux of the issue is the culture of consumer societies. Calder (1999) maintains that contemporary explanations of credit and debt in the United States have remained remarkably similar and are much the same today as they were in the 1920s, the 1950s and the 1970s. He notes:

> It begins with the unhappy tale of how a 'typical' middle-class family fell thousands of dollars in debt as it struggled to keep up with the Joneses. Then comes the observation that American consumer debt is larger than the combined gross domestic product of six or seven foreign countries. There follows a paragraph of handwringing over the demise of the 'Puritan ethic', followed by finger-pointing at bankers and retailers for the indiscriminate issuance of credit cards to teenagers, toddlers, dead people, and the occasional house pet. Then comes a litany of specific worries: first, that generous credit leads to overbuying, which leads to inflation, which causes recession, which brings on a wave of defaults and repossessions, which aggravates the recession, and so on (a kind of economic domino theory). Second, that installment credit is deceptively expensive, as the rhythm of regular payments lulls consumers into a state of appalling ignorance about the total cost of their loans, until all that matters to most of them is the size of the monthly payments. Third, that consumer credit has turned America into a nation of bankrupts. . . . It is an old tired analysis,

its chief merit being that stories about profligate spenders up to their eyeballs in debt still sell magazines and attract viewing audiences for television news shows.

(1999: 294)

He believes that consumers do not take the critics very seriously, and when exhorted to refrain from using credit, they approve of the doctrine but practise the contrary. Education does increase awareness of some of the difficulties associated with overextending credit and getting into debt, but the lure of goods and services in a competitive consumer society is a difficult addiction to give up. It seems that significant numbers of consumers would rather deal with the consequences of debt than avoid getting into debt in the first place. Work hard, play hard, is the mantra. The car bumper sticker stating, 'I owe, I owe, off to work I go' reflects the resignation with which debt is accepted in everyday life.

Secrecy and privacy concerns

Secrecy and privacy concerns have become a consumer policy issue, especially since so much financial data is held on consumer behaviour across a wide range of lenders. Furthermore, credit-scoring bureaux operate as huge data warehouses and have far more data about consumers than individual lenders do. Ritzer (1995) maintains that the invasion of privacy as a private or public issue rarely concerns credit card companies unless a public outcry occurs and the government threatens to become involved. Furthermore, there is little to indicate that other lenders take a different view. Yet credit reports contain significant amounts of precise information about millions of individuals and their credit history. These details include previous addresses, links to other individuals and their credit history if a home has been shared, all the loans and cards that have been used going back several years, details of missed payments, outstanding balances, details of county court judgments where individuals have been taken to court for non-payment of bills, bankruptcy status, the number of times credit has been scored within a specific timescale, and so forth.

All credit-scoring bureaux will have access to this detailed information; there is little difference between any of them. Another limiting factor of contemporary credit-scoring systems is that at present they are country specific. However, it is only a matter of time before this will change. Feasibility studies have already been conducted with a view to developing a single European scorecard, but the attempt failed because of the economic and social diversity, which could impact on the level of bad debt (Platts and Howe 2004). If these issues can be overcome, the credit-scoring bureaux will be even more powerful in the future. Lenders that use scoring data presume that the data are an accurate record of consumer credit history. However, the huge amounts of data entry involved in updating databases inevitably leads to inaccuracies, and this has resulted in significant numbers of consumer complaints. These complaints tend to emerge when consumers have been denied credit for no apparent reason. Estimates in the United States indicate that 2 million people are affected by mistakes relating to credit card data alone. Until fairly recently, credit records that were held by credit-scoring bureaux were confidential; however, they are currently available on the internet for a small fee.

Another issue concerns affinity cards, a term used to describe the arrangement whereby credit card companies link up with good causes and pay a proportion of the total spent on the card to the nominated organization. A problem with these arrangements is that customers are not always informed precisely how much is being given to the good cause. Some card issuers have secrecy clauses in their agreements. In some instances consumers *are* aware of how much is donated, and have complained about the small percentages involved. Affinity cards may be regarded as little more than a gimmick, a marketing ploy to develop new business rather than a genuine charity-led initiative.

Ritzer argues that current trends in financial data collection, storage and use turn Simmel's theory of the relationship between money and secrecy upside down. While money in its currency form allows for more secrecy than previous varieties, card payments reduce the possibility of secrecy. Lenders are able to detect when, where and how we spend our money. There are obviously commercial benefits to having access to this information, particularly with respect to behavioural and profitability scoring, since lenders can examine patterns in the consumer behaviour data that they hold. Perhaps a social benefit is being able to trace people, whether they are missing persons or criminals.

Conclusion

The politics of consumption is an important strand in the broader debate about consumer society. This is particularly true of financial services organizations, which tend to be among the most highly regulated institutions in the economy. A number of different consumer policy issues have been discussed in this chapter. The expansion of credit has certainly had a positive effect on the lives of many consumers. However, the downsides of credit and debt in consumer society, though less exciting than the hedonistic aspects, deserve more attention. Sustainability has attracted a huge amount of attention in both popular and academic discourse, yet the extent to which sustainability initiatives are being underpinned by unsustainable levels of credit remains an unresolved issue. The relationship between credit, debt and personal well-being requires more attention than it currently receives. Objective indicators of credit and debt tend to make the headlines, but subjective factors such as their effect on physical and mental health are important. The stress connected to debt can wreck families and ruin careers, and can result in higher medical bills for the individuals and society. Consumer financial education has a high profile in many advanced societies. Far more effort is being directed towards educating consumers about the technicalities and implications of entering into credit agreements. This provision is a positive move in the right direction. However, the question needs to be asked whether or not it should be regarded as a panacea and treated as such.

Questions

1   What do you understand by the term 'politics of consumption'?
2   How persuasive are issues of consumer sovereignty in the credit relationship?
3   What implications do debates about sustainable consumption have for the future of credit in consumer societies?
4   Why has there been such an increase in self-help guides focusing on debt management?

Further reading

Bazerman, M.H. (2001) 'Consumer research for consumers', *Journal of Consumer Research*, 27, March: 499–504.

Cohen, M.J. (2007) 'Consumer credit, household financial management, and sustainable consumption', *International Journal of Consumer Studies*, 31, 1: 57–65.

Dossey, L. (2007) 'Debt and health', *Explore: The Journal of Science and Healing*, 3, 2: 83–90.

Drentea, P. and Lavrakas, P.J. (2000) '"Over the limit": the association among health, race and debt', *Social Science and Medicine*, 50, 4: 517–529.

Fisher, J.J. and Lyons, A.C. (2006) 'Till debt do us part: a model of divorce and personal bankruptcy', *Review of Economics of the Household*, 4, 1: 35–53.

Karpatkin, R.H. (1999) 'Towards a fair and just marketplace for all consumers: the responsibilities of marketing professionals', *Journal of Public Policy and Marketing*, 18, 2: 118–122.

Schor, J. (1998) *The Overspent American: Upscaling, Downshifting and the New Consumer*, New York: Basic Books.

Wilkinson, G. and Tingay, J. (2004) 'The use of affordability data: does it add real value?', in Thomas, L.C., Edelman, D.B. and Crook, J.N. (eds) *Readings in Credit Scoring: Foundations, Developments, and Aims*, Oxford: Oxford University Press, pp. 63–71.

Xiao, J.J., Sorhaindo, B. and Garman, E.T. (2006) 'Financial behaviours of consumers in credit counselling', *International Journal of Consumer Studies*, 30, 2: 108–121.

Bibliography

Aaker, D.A. and Day, G.S. (1978) 'A guide to consumerism', in Aaker, D.A. and Day, G.S. (eds) *Consumerism: A Search for the Consumer Interest*, New York: Macmillan, pp. 2–18.

Abbinnett, R. (2007) 'Untimely agitations: Derrida, Klein and Hardt and Neri on the idea of anti-capitalism', *Journal for Cultural Research*, 11, 1: 41–56.

Abercrombie, N. (1994) 'Authority and consumer society', in Keat, R., Whiteley, N. and Abercrombie, N. (eds) *The Authority of the Consumer*, London: Routledge, pp. 43–57.

Agnew, J. (1993) 'Coming up for air: consumer culture in historical perspective', in Brewer, J. and Porter, R. (eds) *Consumption and the World of Goods*, London: Routledge.

Alberini, A., Rosato, P., Longo, A. and Zanatta, V. (2005) 'The effects of information on willingness to pay: a contingent valuation study of S. Erasmo in the lagoon of Venice', in Krarup, S. and Russell, C.S. (eds) *Environment, Information and Consumer Behaviour*, Cheltenham, UK: Edward Elgar, pp. 215–247.

Aldridge, A. (1997) 'Engaging with promotional culture: organised consumerism and the personal financial services industry', *Sociology*, 31, 3: 389–408.

Alexander, D. (1970) *Retailing in England during the Industrial Revolution*, London: Athlone Press.

Allen, J. and Pryke, M. (1999) 'Money culture after Georg Simmel: mobility, movement, and identity', *Environment and Planning D: Society and Space*, 117: 51–68.

Allen, L., DeLong, G. and Saunders, A. (2004) 'Issues in the credit risk modeling of retail markets', *Journal of Banking and Finance*, 28, 4: 727–752.

Andreeva, G., Ansell, J. and Crook, J. (2004) 'Impact of anti-discrimination laws on credit scoring', *Journal of Financial Services Marketing*, 9, 1: 22–33.

Andrews, A. and Houghton, P. (1986) *How to Cope with Credit and Deal with Debt*, London: Unwin.

Aris, S. (1985) *Going Bust: Inside the Bankruptcy Business*, London: André Deutsch.

Arnold, M.J. and Reynolds, K.E. (2003) 'Hedonic shopping motivations', *Journal of Retailing*, 79, 2: 77–95.

Arnould, E.J. and Thompson, C.J. (2005) 'Consumer culture theory (CCT): twenty years of research', *Journal of Consumer Research*, 31, March: 868–882.

Aughterson, K. (ed.) (1995) *Renaissance Women: A Sourcebook*, London: Routledge.

Austin, R. (2004) 'Of predatory lending and the democratization of credit: preserving the social safety net of informality in small loan transactions', *American University Law Review*, 53, 6: 1217–1258.

Avery, R.B., Calem, P.S. and Canner, G.B. (2004) 'Consumer credit scoring: do situational circumstances matter?,' *Journal of Banking and Finance*, 28: 835–856.

Baritz, L. (1982) *The Good Life: The Meaning of Success for the American Middle Class*, New York: Harper & Row.

Bartos, R. (1989) *Marketing to Women*, Oxford: Heinemann Professional Publishing.

Barty-King, H. (1991) *The Worst Poverty: A History of Debt and Debtors*, Stroud, UK: Alan Sutton Publishing.

Basel Committee on Banking Supervision (2004) *International Convergence of Capital Measurement and Capital Standards: A Revised Framework*, Basel: Bank for International Settlements.

Basel Committee on Banking Supervision (2006a) *Studies on Credit Risk Concentration*, Basel: Bank for International Settlements.

Basel Committee on Banking Supervision (2006b) *Sound Credit Risk Assessment and Valuation for Loans*, Basel: Bank for International Settlements.

Baudrillard, J. (1998) *Consumer Society: Myths and Structures*, London: Sage.

Bauman, Z. (1992) *Intimations of Postmodernity*, London: Routledge.

Bauman, Z. (1998) *Work, Consumerism and the New Poor*, Buckingham, UK: Open University Press.

Bazerman, M.H. (2001), 'Consumer research for consumers', *Journal of Consumer Research*, 27, March: 499–504.

Beales, R. and Spikes, S. (2007) 'HSBC to unveil US bad debt provisions', *Financial Times*, 5 March: 21.

Beatty, S.E. and Ferrell, M.E. (1998) 'Impulse buying: modelling its precursors', *Journal of Retailing*, 74, 2: 169–191.

Beck, U. (1992) *Risk Society: Towards a New Modernity*, London: Sage.

Belk, R. (1995) 'Studies in the new consumer behaviour', in Miller, D. (ed.) *Acknowledging Consumption*, London: Routledge.

Bell, D. (1976) *The Cultural Contradictions of Capitalism*, New York: Basic Books.

Bellenger, D.N., Robertson, D.H. and Hirschman, E.C. (1978) 'Impulse buying varies by product', *Journal of Advertising Research*, 18: 15–18.

Bennett, G., Platts, G. and Crossley, J. (2004) 'Inferring the inferred', in Thomas, L.C., Edelman, D.B. and Crook, J.N. (eds) *Readings in Credit Scoring: Foundations, Developments, and Aims*, Oxford: Oxford University Press, pp. 177–188.

Benson, A. (ed.) (2000) *I Shop Therefore I Am: Compulsive Shopping and the Search for Self*, Northvale, NJ: Jason Aronson.

Berlin, M. and Mester, L.J. (2004) 'Retail credit risk management and measurement: an introduction to the special issue', *Journal of Banking and Finance*, 28: 721–725.

Bernthal, M.J., Crockett, D. and Rose, R.L. (2005) 'Credit cards as lifestyle facilitators', *Journal of Consumer Research*, 32, 1: 130–145.

Bertola, G., Disney, R. and Grant, C. (2006) *The Economics of Consumer Credit*, Cambridge, MA: MIT Press.

Bertola, G., Hochguertel, S. and Winfred, K. (2005) 'Dealer pricing of consumer credit', *International Economic Review*, 46, 4: 1103–1142.

Blamire, J. (1984) *Dealing with Debt: The Complete Guide for Money Advisors*, Birmingham: Money Advice Centre.

Blum, K. and Noble, E.P. (1994) 'The sobering D2 story', *Science*, 265: 1346–1347.

Boatright, J.R. (1999) *Ethics in Finance*, Oxford: Blackwell.

Booker, J. (1991) *Temples of Mammon: The Architecture of Banking*, Edinburgh: Edinburgh University Press.

Borrie, G. and Diamond, A.L. (1964) *The Consumer, Society and the Law*, London: MacGibbon & Kee.

Boss, S. (2006) *Green with Envy: Why Keeping Up with the Joneses is Keeping Us in Debt*, New York: Warner Books.

Bourdieu, P. (1984) *Distinction: A Social Critique of the Judgement of Taste*, London: Routledge & Kegan Paul.

Braunsberger, K., Lucas, L.A. and Roach, D. (2004) 'The effectiveness of credit-card regulation for vulnerable consumers', *Journal of Services Marketing*, 18, 5: 358–370.

Braverman, H. (1974) *Labor and Monopoly Capital*, New York: Monthly Review Press.

Brewer, J. and Porter, R. (1993) *Consumption and the World of Goods*, London: Routledge.

Briggs, C. (2004) 'Empowered or marginalized? Rural women and credit in later thirteenth- and fourteenth-century England', *Continuity and Change*, 19, 1: 13–43.

Brown, S. (1995) *Postmodern Marketing*, London: International Thomson Business Press.

Brown, S. (1998) 'Romancing the market: sex shopping and subjective personal introspection', *Journal of Marketing Management*, 14: 783–798.

Brown, S., Taylor, K. and Wheatley Price, S. (2005) 'Debt and distress: evaluating the psychological cost of credit', *Journal of Economic Psychology*, 26, 5: 642–663.

Brown, S. and Turley, D. (1997) *Consumer Research: Postcards from the Edge*, London: Routledge.

Brunt, P.A. (1971) *Social Conflicts in the Roman Republic*, London: W.W. Norton.

Bucci, S. (2006) *Credit Repair Kit for Dummies*, Chichester, UK: Wiley.

Burton, D. (1990) 'Competition in UK retail financial services: some implications for the spatial distribution and function of bank branches', *Service Industries Journal*, 10, 3: 571–588.

Burton, D. (1994) *Financial Services and the Consumer*, London: Routledge.

Burton, D. (2001) 'Critical marketing theory: the blueprint?', *European Journal of Marketing*, 35 (5/6): 722–743.

Burton, D. (2002a) 'Consumer education and service quality: conceptual issues and practical implications', *Journal of Services Marketing*, 16, 2/3: 125–142.

Burton, D. (2002b) 'Postmodernism, social relations and remote shopping', *European Journal of Marketing*, 36, 7/8: 792–810.

Burton, D. (2002c) 'Towards a critical multicultural marketing theory', *Marketing Theory*, 2, 2: 207–236.

Burton, D., Knights, D., Leyshon, A., Alferoff, C. and Signoretta, P. (2004) 'Making a market: the UK retail financial services industry and the rise of the complex sub-prime credit market', *Competition and Change*, 8, 1: 3–26.

Burton, D., Knights, D., Leyshon, A., Alferoff, C. and Signoretta, P. (2005) 'Consumption denied? The decline of industrial branch insurance', *Journal of Consumer Culture*, 5, 2: 181–205.

Buswell, A. (2001) *Debt Counselling Handbook*, Birmingham: National Money Advice Training Unit.

Calder, L. (1999) *Financing the American Dream: A Cultural History of Consumer Credit*, Princeton, NJ: Princeton University Press.

Campbell, C. (1997) 'Shopping pleasure and the sex war', in Falk, P. and Campbell, C. (eds) *The Shopping Experience*, London: Sage.

Campbell, C. (2004) 'I shop therefore I know that I am: the metaphysical basis of modern consumerism', in Ekstrom, K.M. and Brembeck, H. (eds) *Elusive Consumption*, Oxford: Berg, pp. 27–44.

Chan, S. (2006) 'An outcry rises as debt collectors play rough', *New York Times*, 5 July.

Clapson, M. (1992) *A Bit of a Flutter: Popular Gambling and English Society, c. 1823–1961*, Manchester: Manchester University Press.

Clark, E. (1931) *Financing the Consumer*, New York: Harper.

Clarke, A.J. (1998) 'Window shopping at home: classifieds, catalogues and new consumer skills', in D. Miller (ed.) *Material Cultures*, London: Routledge, pp. 73–99.

Cochran, T.C. (1985) *Challenges to American Values: Society, Business, and Religion*, Oxford: Oxford University Press.

Cohen, L. (2004) *A Consumers' Republic*, New York: Vintage Books.

Cohen, M.J. (2007) 'Consumer credit, household financial management, and sustainable consumption', *International Journal of Consumer Studies*, 31, 1: 57–65.

Collier, D.A. (1991) 'A service quality process map for credit card processing', *Decision Sciences*, 22: 406–419.

Consumer Affairs (2004) 'Credit counseling riddled with fast-buck promoters, Congress finds', www.consumeraffairs.com, 25 March.

Copeland, E. (1995) *Women Writing about Money: Women's Fiction in England 1790–1820*, Cambridge: Cambridge University Press.

Coquery, N. (2004) 'The language of success', *Journal of Design History*, 17, 1: 71–89.

Corbridge, S. and Thrift, N. (1994) 'Money, power and space: introduction and overview', in Corbridge, S., Martin, R. and Thrift, N. (eds) *Money, Power and Space*, Oxford: Blackwell, pp. 1–26.

Cowan, A.M. and Cowan, C.D. (2004) 'Default correlation: an empirical investigation of a subprime lender', *Journal of Banking and Finance*, 28, 4: 753–771.

Credit Services Association, Debt Sellers and Buyers Group, www.dbsg-uk.com (accessed 2003).

Crockett, D. and Wallendorf, M. (2004) 'The role of normative political ideology in consumer behavior', *Journal of Consumer Research*, 31 (December): 511–528.

Crook, J. (1999) 'Who is discouraged from applying for credit?', *Economic Letters*, 65: 165–172.

Crook, J.N., Edelman, D.B. and Thomas, L.C. (2001) 'Special issue on credit scoring and data mining', *Journal of the Operational Research Society*, 52, 9: 971–1058.

Crook, J., Hamilton, R. and Thomas, L.C. (1992) 'The degradation of the scorecard over the business cycle', *IMA Journal of Mathematics Applied in Business and Industry*, 4: 111–123.

Cross, G. (1993) *Time and Money: The Making of Consumer Culture*, London: Routledge.

Crowston, C.H. (2002) 'The queen and her "minister of fashion": gender, credit and politics in pre-revolutionary France', *Gender and History*, 14, 1: 92–116.

Cunningham, J. and Roberts, P. (2006) *Inside Her Pretty Little Head*, London: Marshall Cavendish.

Current Opinion (1914) 'The democratization of credit', April: 313–314.

Curtis, S. (2004) 'Fun at the debtors' prison: undergraduates' university experience', *Education and Training*, 46, 2: 75–81.

Daunton, M. and Hilton, M. (2001) *The Politics of Consumption: Material Culture and Citizenship in Europe and America*, Oxford: Berg.

Davies, G. (1996) *A History of Money*, Cardiff: Cardiff University Press.

Desmond, J. (1998) 'Marketing and moral indifference', in M. Parker (ed.) *Ethics and Organizations*, London: Sage, pp. 173–196.

Dimnik, T. and Felton, S. (2006) 'Accountant stereotypes in movies distributed in North America in the twentieth century', *Accounting, Organizations and Society*, 31, 2: 129–155.

Dittmar, H., Beattie, J. and Friese, S. (1995) 'Gender identity and material symbols: objects and decision considerations in impulse purchase', *Journal of Economic Psychology*, 16: 491–511.

Dittmar, H. and Drury, J. (2000) 'Self-image: is it in the bag? A qualitative comparison between "ordinary" and "excessive" consumers', *Journal of Economic Psychology*, 21: 109–142.

Dodd, N. (1994) *The Sociology of Money*, Oxford: Polity Press.

Dominy, N. and Kempson, E. (2003) 'Can't pay or won't pay? A review of creditor and debtor approaches to the non-payment of bills', Lord Chancellor's Department, no. 4/03, London: LCD.

Domowitz, I. and Sartain, R.L. (1999) 'Determinants of the consumer bankruptcy decision', *Journal of Finance*, 54, 1: 403–420.

Donnelly, J.H., Berry, L.L. and Thompson, T.W. (1985) *Marketing Financial Services: A Strategic Vision*, Homewood, IL: Irwin.

Dossey, L. (2007) 'Debt and health', *Explore: The Journal of Science and Healing*, 3, 2: 83–90.

Douglas, M. (1997) 'In defence of shopping', in Falk, P. and Campbell, C. (eds) *The Shopping Experience*, London: Sage.

Drentea, P. and Lavrakas, P.J. (2000) '"Over the limit": the association among health, race and debt', *Social Science and Medicine*, 50, 4: 517–529.

Drucker, P. (1990) *Managing the Non-profit Organization*, London: Butterworths.

du Gay, P. and Salaman, G. (1992) 'The cult(ure) of the consumer', *Journal of Management Studies*, 29, 5: 615–633.

Durand, D. (1941) *Risk Elements in Consumer Instalment Financing*, New York: National Bureau of Economic Research.

Dvorkin, H.S. (2005) *Credit Hell: How to Dig Out of Debt*, Hoboken, NJ: John Wiley.

Dyer, G. (1992) *Advertising as Communication*, London: Routledge.

Dymski, G. (1994) 'The social construction of creditworthiness: asymmetric information and the trivialization of risk', unpublished mimeograph, Department of Economics, University of California, Riverside, CA.

Eagleton, T. (1991) *Ideology: An Introduction*, London: Verso.

Edwards, T. (2000) *Contradictions of Consumption*, Buckingham, UK: Open University Press.

Elgin, D. (1981) *Voluntary Simplicity: Toward a Way of Life that is Outwardly Simple, Inwardly Rich*, New York: Morrow.

Elliott, R. (1994) 'Addictive consumption: function and fragmentation in post-modernity', *Journal of Consumer Policy*, 17: 159–179.

Elliott, R. and Ritson, M. (1997) 'Post-structuralism and the dialectics of advertising', in Brown, S. and Turley, D. (eds) *Consumer Research: Postcards from the Edge*, London: Routledge, pp. 190–219.

Elliott, R., Eccles, S. and Gournay, K. (1996) 'Man management? Women and the use of debt to control personal relationships', *Journal of Marketing Management*, 12: 657–669.

Ennew, C., Watkins, T. and Wright, M. (1990) *Marketing Financial Services*, Oxford: Butterworth-Heinemann.

Ewen, S. (1976) *Captains of Consciousness: Advertising and the Social Roots of the Consumer Culture*, New York: McGraw-Hill.

Faber, R. and O'Guinn, T. (1988) 'Compulsive consumption and credit abuse', *Journal of Consumer Policy*, 11, 1: 97–109.

Faber, R.J., O'Guinn, T.C. and Krych, R. (1987) 'Compulsive consumption', *Advances in Consumer Research*, 14: 132–135.

Falk, P. (1997) 'The scopic regimes of shopping', in Falk, P. and Campbell, C. (eds) *The Shopping Experience*, London: Sage.

Farley, J.U., Hayes, A.F. and Kopalle, P.K. (2004) 'Choosing and upgrading financial service dealers in the US and UK', *International Journal of Research in Marketing*, 21, 4: 359–375.

Featherstone, M. (1990) 'Perspectives on consumer culture', *Sociology*, 24, 1: 5–22.

Featherstone, M. (1991) *Consumer Culture and Post-modernism*, London: Sage.

Fernie, J. (2004) *Principles of Retailing*, London: Routledge.

Fine, B. (2002) *The World of Consumption*, London: Routledge.

Finlay, S.M. (2006) 'Predictive models of consumer expenditure and over-indebtedness for assessing the affordability of new consumer credit applications', *Journal of the Operational Research Society*, 57, 6: 655–669.

Finn, M. (1996) 'Women, consumption and coverture in England, c.1760–1860', *Historical Journal*, 39, 3: 703–722.

Finn, M. (1998) 'Working-class women and the contest for consumer control in Victorian county courts', *Past and Present*, 161, November: 116–154.

Finn, M. (2001) 'Scotch drapers and the politics of modernity: gender, class and national identity in the Victorian tally trade', in Hilton, M. and Daunton, M. (eds) *The Politics of Consumption*, Oxford: Berg, pp. 89–107.

Finn, M. (2003) *The Character of Credit: Personal Debt in English Culture, 1740–1914*, Cambridge: Cambridge University Press.

Fisher, J.J. and Lyons, A.C. (2006) 'Till debt do us part: a model of divorce and personal bankruptcy', *Review of Economics of the Household*, 4, 1: 35–53.

Fisher, R.A. (1936) 'The use of multiple measures of taxonomic problems', *Annals of Eugenics*, 7: 179–188.

Fisk, R.P. and Tansuhaj, P.S. (1985) *Services Marketing: An Annotated Bibliography*, Stillwater: Oklahoma State University.

Fontaine, L. (2001) 'Antonio and Shylock: credit and trust in France, c.1680–c.1780', *Economic History Review*, 54, 1: 39–57.

Foucault, M. (1979) *Discipline and Punish*, Harmondsworth, UK: Penguin.

Friese, S. (2000) *Self-Concept and Identity in a Consumer Society: Aspects of Symbolic Product Meaning*, Marburg, Germany: Tectum.

Fuchs, D.A. and Lorek, S. (2005) 'Sustainable consumption governance: a history of promises and failures', *Journal of Consumer Policy*, 28: 261–288.

Fullerton, R.A. (1988) 'How modern is modern marketing? Marketing's evolution and the myth of the "Production Era"', *Journal of Marketing*, 52, January: 108–125.

Fullerton, R.A. and Punj, G. (1998) 'The unintended consequences of the culture of consumption: an historical-theoretical analysis of consumer misbehaviour', *Consumption, Markets and Culture*, 1, 4; 303–423.

Gabriel, C. and Lang, T. (1995) *The Unmanageable Consumer*, London: Sage.

Galbraith, J.K. (1969) *The Affluent Society*, Boston: Houghton Mifflin.

Galvin, M. (2002) 'Credit and parochial charity in fifteenth-century Bruges', *Journal of Medieval History*, 28, 2: 131–154.

Garcia, G. (1980) 'Credit cards: an interdisciplinary survey', *Journal of Consumer Research*, 6, March: 327–337.

Gelpi, R. and Julien-Labruyere, F. (1999) *A History of Consumer Credit: Doctrines and Practices*, New York: St Martin's Press.

Germain, R.N. (1996) *Dollars through the Doors: A Pre-1930 History of Bank Marketing in America*, Westport, CT: Greenwood Press.

Getter, D.E. (2006) 'Consumer credit risk and pricing', *Journal of Consumer Affairs*, 40, 1: 41–64.

Gibbons, D. (2001) *Debt and Benefits for Ex-offenders: An Advisor's Handbook*, London: Legal Action Group.

Giddens, A. (1991) *Modernity and Self-identity*, Cambridge: Polity Press.

Gilchrist, J.T. (1969) *The Church and Economic Activity in the Middle Ages*, London: Macmillan.

Gordon, A. (2006) 'From Singer to Shinpan: consumer credit in modern Japan', in Garon, S. and Maclachlan, P.L. (eds) *The Ambivalent Consumer: Questioning Consumption in East Asia and the West*, Ithaca, NY: Cornell University Press.

Gould, S.J. (1997) 'An introspective study of purposeful, mood self-regulation consumption: the consumption and mood framework', *Psychology and Marketing*, 14, 4: 395–426.

Grable, J.E. and Yoo, S. (2006) 'Student racial differences in credit card debt and financial behaviors and stress', *College Student Journal*, 40, 2: 400–408.

Gramlich, E.M. (2000) 'Subprime lending, predatory lending', www.federalreserve. gov/boarddocs/speeches/2000.

Graves, S.M. (2003) 'Landscapes of predation, landscapes of neglect: a location analysis of payday lenders and banks', *Professional Geographer*, 55, 3: 303–317.

Griffiths, M. (1995) *Adolescent Gambling*, London: Routledge.

Griffiths, M. (2000) 'The sustainability of consumer credit growth in late twentieth century Australia', *Journal of Consumer Studies and Home Economics*, 24, 1: 23–33.

Gronow, J. and Warde, A. (2001) *Ordinary Consumption*, London: Routledge.

Grove-White, R. (1998) 'Environmental knowledge and public policy needs', in Lash, S., Szerszynski, B. and Wynne, B. (eds) *Risk, Environment and Modernity: Towards a New Ecology*, London: Sage, pp. 269–286.

Haggerty, K.D. and Ericson, R.V. (2000) 'The surveillant assemblage', *British Journal of Sociology*, 51, 4: 650–655.

Hanch, C.C. (1927) 'The Case for Installment Buying', *Forum*, 77, May: 660.

Hand, D.J. and Henley, W.E. (2004) 'Can reject inference ever work?', in Thomas, L.C., Edelman, D.B. and Crook, J.N. (2004) *Readings in Credit Scoring: Foundations, Developments, and Aims*, Oxford: Oxford University Press, pp. 133–145.

Hanley, A. and Wilhelm, M.S. (1992) 'Compulsive buying: an exploration into self-esteem and money attitudes', *Journal of Economic Psychology*, 13: 5–18.

Heller, C.F. and Houdek, J.T. (2004) 'Women lenders as sources of land credit in nineteenth-century Michigan', *Journal of Interdisciplinary History*, 35, 1: 37–67.

Henry, P.C. (2005) 'Social class, market situation, and consumers' metaphors of (dis)empowerment', *Journal of Consumer Research*, 31, March: 766–882.

Hickman, M. (2007) 'Banks get 10,000 claims a day for illegal charges', *Independent*, 23 February: 5.

Hilton, M. (2003) *Consumerism in 20th-century Britain*, Cambridge: Cambridge University Press.

Hilton, M. and Daunton, M. (2001) *The Politics of Consumption*, Oxford: Berg.

Hinton, T. and Berthoud, R. (1988) *Money Advice Services*, Oxford: Policy Studies Institute.

Hirschman, E.C. (1979) 'Difference in consumer behavior by credit card payment', *Journal of Consumer Research*, 6, June: 58–66.

Hirschman, E.C. (1992) 'The consciousness of addiction: toward a general theory of compulsive consumption', *Journal of Consumer Research*, 19, September: 155–179.

Hirschman, E.C. (1993) 'Ideology in consumer research, 1980 and 1990: a Marxist and feminist critique', *Journal of Consumer Research*, 20, March: 537–555.

Hirschman, E.C. and Holbrook, M.B. (1992) *Postmodern Consumer Research*, London: Sage.

Hirschman, E.C. and Stern, B.B. (2001) 'Do consumers' genes influence their behavior? Findings on Novelty Seeking and Compulsive Consumption', *Advances in Consumer Research*, 28: 403–410.

Howcroft, B. (1985) 'Competitive features in the provision of consumer credit', *Service Industries Journal*, 5, 2: 153–168.

Hudson, M. (1996) 'The poverty industry', in M. Hudson (ed.) *Merchants of Misery: How Corporate America Profits from Poverty*, Monroe, ME: Common Courage, pp. 1–16.

Hugel, P. and Kelly, J. (2002) 'Internet gambling, credit cards and money laundering', *Journal of Money Laundering Control*, 6, 1: 57–65.

Ingham, G. (1996) 'Money is a social relation', *Review of Social Economy*, 54, 4: 507–529.

Ingham, G. (2001) 'Fundamentals of a theory of money: untangling Fine, Lapavitsas and Zelizer', *Economy and Society*, 30, 3: 304–323.

Ison, T.G. (1979) *Credit Marketing and Consumer Protection*, London: Croom Helm.

Jackson, T. (2007) 'The repricing of risk has finally got under way', *Financial Times*, 5 March: 22.

Jeacle, I. and Walsh, E.J. (2002) 'From moral evaluation to rationalization: accounting and the shifting technologies of credit', *Accounting, Organizations and Society*, 27: 737–761.

Johnson, A. (2007) 'HSBC bad debts rocket to £5.5bn', *Daily Express*, 6 March: 49.

Johnson, P. (1985) *Saving and Spending: The Working-Class Economy in Britain 1870–1939*, Oxford: Clarendon Press.

Johnson, R.W. (2004) 'Legal, social and economic issues in implementing scoring in the United States', in Thomas, L.C., Edelman, D.B. and Crook, J.N. (eds) *Readings in Credit Scoring: Foundations, Developments, and Aims*, Oxford: Oxford University Press, pp. 5–15.

Jones, J. (1996) '*Coquettes* and *grisettes*: women buying and selling in ancien régime Paris', in de Grazia, V. and Furlough, E. (eds) *The Sex of Things*, Berkeley: University of California.

Jones, N. (1989) *God and the Moneylenders*, Oxford: Basil Blackwell.

Jowett, J. (2003) 'Middleton and debt in *Timon of Athens*', in Woodbridge, L. (ed.) *Money in the Age of Shakespeare*, New York: Palgrave Macmillan, pp. 220–235.

Karpatkin, R.H. (1999) 'Towards a fair and just marketplace for all consumers: the responsibilities of marketing professionals', *Journal of Public Policy and Marketing*, 18, 2: 118–122.

Kasser, T. (2002) *The High Price of Materialism*, Cambridge, MA: MIT Press.

Keat, R. (1994) 'Scepticism, authority and the market', in Keat, R., Whiteley, N. and Abercrombie, N. (eds) *The Authority of the Consumer*, London: Routledge, pp. 23–42.

Keith, R.J. (1960) 'The marketing revolution', *Journal of Marketing*, 24 (January): 35–38.

Kempson, E. and Whyley, C. (1996) *Kept Out or Opted Out? Understanding and Combating Financial Exclusion*, York: Joseph Rowntree Foundation.

Kempson, E. and Whyley, C. (1999) 'Extortionate credit in the UK: a report to the Department of Trade and Industry', School of Geographical Sciences, University of Bristol, Bristol.

Kennedy, P. (2004) 'Selling virtue: the political and economic contradiction of the green/ethical marketing in the United Kingdom', in Micheletti, M., Follesdal, A. and Stolle, D. (eds) *Politics, products and markets*, London: Transaction Publishers.

Kim, J., Sorhaindo, B. and Garman, E.T. (2006) 'Relationship between financial stress and workplace absenteeism of credit counselling clients', *Journal of Family and Economic Issues*, 27, 3: 458–478.

Kingma, S. (1997) 'Gaming is play, it should remain fun! The gaming complex, pleasure and addiction', in Sulkunen, P., Holmwood, J., Radner, H. and Schulze, G. (eds) *Constructing the New Consumer*, Basingstoke, UK: Macmillan, pp. 173–193.

Klein, L. (1999) *It's in the cards: Consumer Credit and the American Experience*, Westport, CT: Praeger.

Klein, N. (2000) *No Logo: Taking Aim at Brand Bullies*, London: Flamingo.

Kniffen, W.H. (1914) 'The theory and practice of credit', *Banker's Magazine*, 89, December: 2211.

Knights, D. and Odih, P. (1999) 'What's in a name? The dynamics of branding personal financial services', *Financial Services Marketing*, 4, 3: 42–45.

Knights, D. and Vurdubakis, T. (1993) 'Calculations of risk: towards an understanding of insurance as a moral and political technology', *Accounting, Organizations and Society*, 18, 7/8: 729–764.

Knights, D., Sturdy, A. and Morgan, G. (1994) 'The consumer rules: an examination of the rhetoric and "reality" of marketing in financial services'. *European Journal of Marketing*, 28, 3: 42–54.

Knights, D., Noble, F., Vurdubakis, T. and Willmott, H. (2001) 'Chasing shadows: control, virtuality and the production of trust'. *Organization Studies*, 22, 2: 311–336.

Kolodinsky, J., Murphy, M., Baehr, A. and Lesser, S. (2005) 'Time price differentials in the rent-to-own industry: implications for empowering vulnerable consumers', *International Journal of Consumer Studies*, 29, 2: 119–124.

Koran, L.M., Faber, R.J., Aboujaoude, E., Large, M.D. and Serpe, R.T. (2006) 'Estimated prevalence of compulsive buying behaviour in the United States', *American Journal of Psychiatry*, 163: 1806–1812.

Lancet (1997) 'The body in question', *Lancet*, 349, 9059, 19th April: 1111.

Langenderfer, J. and Shrimp, T.A. (2001) 'Consumer vulnerability to scams, swindles, and fraud: a new theory of visceral influences on persuasion', *Psychology and Marketing*, 18, 7: 763–783.

Lasch, C. (1978) *The Culture of Narcissism: American Life in an Age of Diminishing Expectation*, New York: Norton.

Lash, S., Szerszynski, B. and Wynne, B. (1998) *Risk, Environment and Modernity: Towards a new Ecology*, Sage: London.

Lash, S. and Urry, J. (1994) *Economies of Signs and Spaces*, London: Sage.

Lasn, K. (1999) *Culture Jam: The Uncooling of America*, New York: Eagle Brook.

Lee, J. (2003) 'The poor in the financial market: changes in the use of financial products, institutions, and services from 1995 to 1998', *Journal of Consumer Policy*, 26: 203–231.

Lee, M. (2004) *Predatory Bender: America in the Aughts / Predatory Lending: Toxic Credit in the Global Inner City*, Bronx, NY: Inner City Press.

Leidner, R. (1993) *Fast Food, Fast Talk*, Berkeley: University of California Press.

Leland, J. (2007) 'Survey on identity fraud finds a steady decline since 2003', *New York Times*, 4th February.

Leonard, K.J. (1995) 'The development of a rule-based expert system model for fraud alert in consumer credit', *European Journal of Operational Research*, 80: 350–356.

Lester, V.M. (1999) *Victorian Insolvency*, Oxford: Clarendon Press.

Leung, W.K. and Lai, K.K. (2001) 'Improving the quality of the credit authorization process', *International Journal of Service Industry Management*, 12, 4: 328–341.

Lewis, D. and Weigert, A. (1985) 'Trust as a social reality', *Social Forces*, 63, 4: 967–985.

Lewis, E. (1992) *An Introduction to Credit Scoring*, San Rafael, CA: Fair Isaac.

Leyshon, A. and Pollard, J. (2000) 'Geographies of industrial convergence: the case of retail banking', *Transactions of the Institute of British Geographers*, NS 25: 203–220.

Leyshon, A. and Thrift, N. (1999) 'Lists come alive: electronic systems of knowledge and the rise of credit-scoring in retail banking', *Economy and Society*. 28, 4: 434–466.

Leyshon, A. and Thrift, N. (1997) 'Geographies of financial exclusion: financial abandonment in Britain and the United States', in Leyshon, A. and Thrift, N. *MoneySpace: Geographies of Monetary Transformation*, London: Routledge.

Leyshon, A., Thrift, N. and Pratt, J. (1998) 'Reading financial services: text, consumers, and financial literacy', *Environment and Planning D: Society and Space*, 16, 29–55.

Leyshon, A., Burton, D., Knights, D., Alferoff, C. and Signoretta, P. (2004) 'Towards an ecology of retail financial services: understanding the persistence of door-to-door credit and insurance providers', *Environment and Planning A*, 36: 625–645.

Leyshon, A., Signoretta, P., Knights, D., Alferoff, C. and Burton, D. (2006) 'Walking with moneylenders: the ecology of the UK home-collection credit industry', *Urban Studies*, 43, 1: 161–186.

Livesey, R. (2004) 'Reading for character: women social reformers and narratives of the urban poor in late Victorian and Edwardian London', *Journal of Victorian Culture*, 9, 1: 43–67.

Lord, R. (2005) *American Nightmare: Predatory Lending and the Foreclosure of the American Dream*, Monroe, ME: Common Courage.

Lown, J.M. (2005) 'Educating and empowering consumers to avoid bankruptcy', *International Journal of Consumer Studies*, 29, 5: 401–408.

Lucas, A. (2004) 'Updating scorecards: removing the mystique', in Thomas, L.C., Edelman, D.B. and Crook, J.N. (2004) *Readings in Credit Scoring: Foundations, Developments, and Aims*, Oxford, Oxford University Press: pp. 93–109.

Luhmann, N. (1979) *Trust and Power*, Chichester, UK: Wiley.

Lury, C. (1996) *Consumer Culture*, Cambridge: Polity Press.

Lyons, A.C. (2003) 'How credit access has changed over time for U.S. households', *Journal of Consumer Affairs*, 37 (2): 231–255.

Lyons, A.C. and Fisher, J. (2006) 'Gender differences in debt repayment problems after divorce', *Journal of Consumer Affairs*, 40, 2: 324–346.

McCorkhell, G. (2000) *Direct and Database Marketing*, London: Kogan Page.

McCracken, G. (1987) 'The history of consumption: a literature review and consumer guide', *Journal of Consumer Policy*, 10: 139–166.

McGee, A. (1992) *The Financial Services Ombudsmen*, London: Fourmat Publishing.

McGoldrick, P.J. and Greenland, S.J. (1994) *Retailing of Financial Services*, London: McGraw-Hill.

McGowen, R. (2005) 'The Bank of England and the policing of forgery 1797–1821', *Past and Present*, 186, February: 81–96.

McGregor, S.L.T. and Berry, R.E. (1997) 'Mandatory financial counselling for Canadian bankrupts', *Journal of Financial Counselling and Planning*, 7: 1–11.

McGregor, S.L.T. and Berry, R.E. (2001) 'Analysis of Canadian, American and Swedish bankruptcy policy', *International Journal of Consumer Studies*, 25, 3: 208–227.

McIntosh, M.K. (2005) 'Women, credit, and family relationships in England, 1300–1620', *Journal of Family History*, 30, 2: 143–163.

McIver, C. (1980) *Marketing Financial Services*, London: Institute of Bankers.

McKendrick, N., Brewer, J. and Plumb, J.H. (1982) *The Birth of a Consumer Society: The Commercialization of Eighteenth-Century England*, London: Europa.

McMillen, J. (1996) 'Understanding gambling: history, concepts and theories', in McMillen, J. (ed.) *Gambling Cultures: Studies in History and Interpretation*, London: Routledge.

Mandel, R. and Humphrey, C. (2002) *Markets and Moralities: Ethnographies of Postsocialism*, Oxford: Berg.

Mann, B.H. (2002) *Republic of Debtors: Bankruptcy in the Age of American Independence*, Cambridge, MA: Harvard University Press.

Manning, R.D. (2000) *Credit Card Nation: The Consequences of America's Addiction to Credit*, New York: Basic Books.

Marcuse, H. (1964) *One-Dimensional Man: Structures in the Ideology of Advanced Industrial Society*, London: Routledge & Kegan Paul.

Marlatt, G.A., Baer, J.S., Donovan, D.M. and Kivlahan, D.R. (1988) 'Addictive behaviors: etiology and treatment', *Annual Review of Psychology*, 39: 223–252.

Marron, D. (2007) '"Lending by numbers": credit scoring and the constitution of risk within American consumer credit', *Economy and Society*, 36, 1: 103–133.

Marshall, J.N. (2004) 'Financial institutions in disadvantaged areas: a comparative analysis of policies encouraging financial inclusion in Britain and the United States, *Environment and Planning A*, 36, 2: 241–262.

Martin, R. (2002) *Financialization of Daily Life*, Philadelphia: Temple University Press.

Mate, M.E. (1998) *Daughters, Wives and Widows after the Black Death*, Woodbridge, UK: Boydell.

Mate, M.E. (1999) *Women in Medieval English Society*, Cambridge: Cambridge University Press.

Mendelson, S. and Crawford, P. (1998) *Women in Early Modern England*, Oxford: Clarendon Press.

Michael, J. (2004) *Repair Your Credit and Knock Out Your Debt*, London: McGraw-Hill.

Miers, D. (2004) *Regulating Commercial Gambling: Past, Present, and Future*, Oxford: Oxford University Press.

Miller, A. (1968) *The Price: A Play*, New York: Penguin.

Miller, D. (1987) *Material Culture and Mass Consumption*, Oxford: Basil Blackwell.

Miller, D. (1997) 'Could shopping ever really matter?', in Falk, P. and Campbell, C. (eds) *The Shopping Experience*, London: Sage.

Miller, D. (2001) 'Behind closed doors', in Miller, D. (ed.) *Home Possessions: Material Culture Behind Closed Doors*, Oxford: Berg.

Mitchell, J. (1991) *Banker's Racket or Consumer Benefit?*, London: Policy Studies Institute.

Mitchell, R. (2004) 'Gambling on a payments win', *Credit Card Management*, 16, 13: 16–21.

Monbiot, G. (2000) *The Captive State: The Corporate Takeover of Britain*, London: Macmillan.

Montanino, F. (1977) 'Directions in the study of deviance: a bibliographic essay, 1960–1977', in Sagarin, E. (ed.) *Deviance and Social Change*, Beverly Hills, CA: Sage, pp. 277–304.

Morgan, G. and Knights, D. (eds) (1997) *Deregulation and European Financial Services*, London: Macmillan.

Mukerji, C. (1983) *From Graven Images: Patterns of Modern Materialism*, New York: Columbia University Press.

Muldrew, C. (1998) *The Economy of Obligation: The Culture of Credit and Social Relations in Early Modern England*, Basingstoke, UK: Palgrave Macmillan.

Nader, R. (1973) *The Consumer and Corporate Accountability*, New York: Harcourt Brace Jovanovich.

Narayan, D., Chambers, R., Shah, M.K. and Petesch, P. (2000) *Voices of the Poor: Crying Out for Change*, Oxford: Oxford University Press on behalf of the World Bank.

Neri, A. (2001) 'The planning of marketing strategies in consumer credit: an approach based on graphical chain models for ordinal variables', *Journal of the Operational Research Society*, 52, 9: 1034–1044.

Nevett, T.R. (1985) 'Media planning criteria in nineteenth century Britain', in Hollander, S.C. and Nevett, T.R. (eds) *Marketing in the Long Run*, East Lansing: Michigan State University, pp. 18–29.

Newman, K. (1984) *Financial Marketing and Communication*, Eastbourne, UK: Holt, Rinehart & Winston.

Nightingale, P. (2002) 'The English parochial clergy as investors and creditors in the first half of the fourteenth century', in Schofield, P.R. and Mayhew, N.J. (eds) *Credit and Debt in Medieval England c.1180–c.1350*, Oxford: Oxbow Books, pp. 89–105.

Nugent, T.L. (2003) 'Usury and counterfeiting in Wilson's *The Three Ladies of London* and *The Three Lords and Three Ladies of London*, and in Shakespeare's *Measure for Measure*', in Woodbridge, L. (ed.) *Money in the Age of Shakespeare*, New York: Palgrave Macmillan, pp. 201–218.

Nystrom, P.H. (1928) *Bibliography of Retailing*, New York: Columbia University Press.

O'Connell, S. and Reid, C. (2005) 'Working-class consumer credit in the UK, 1925–60: the role of the check trader', *Economic History Review*, 58, 2: 378–405.

O'Donovan, P. and McCarthy, M. (2002) 'Irish consumer preference for organic meat', *British Food Journal*, 104: 353–370.

Office of Fair Trading (2006) *Consumer Education: Establishing an Evidence Base*, London: Office of Fair Trading (www.oft.gov.uk).

O'Guinn, T.C. and Faber, R.J. (1989) 'Compulsive buying: a phenomenological exploration', *Journal of Consumer Research*, 16: 147–157.

Olney, M.L. (1991) *Buy Now, Pay Later*, Chapel Hill: University of North Carolina Press.

O'Malley, L., Patterson, M. and Evans, M. (1999) *Exploring Direct Marketing*, London: International Thomson Business Press.

Otnes, C.C. and Lowrey, T.M. (2004) *Contemporary Consumption Rituals*, Mahwah, NJ: Lawrence Erlbaum.

Owens, A., Green, D.R., Bailey, C. and Kay, A.C. (2006) 'A measure of worth: probate valuations, personal wealth and indebtedness in England, 1810–1840', *Historical Research*, 79, 205: 383–403.

Packard, V. (1957) *The Hidden Persuaders*, London: Longmans Green.

Palmer, T.S., Pinto, M.B. and Parente, D.H. (2001) 'College students' credit card debt and the role of parental involvement: implications for public policy', *Journal of Public Policy and Marketing*, 20, 1: 105–113.

Pahl, J. (1989) *Money and Marriage*, London: Macmillan.

Park, H. and Burns, L.D. (2005) 'Fashion orientation, credit card use, and compulsive buying', *Journal of Consumer Marketing*, 22, 3: 135–141.

Parker, G. (1990) *Getting and Spending: Credit and Debt in Britain*, Aldershot, UK: Avebury.

Perkin, J. (1989) *Women and Marriage in Nineteenth-Century England*, London: Routledge.

Peterson, C.L. (2004) *Taming the Sharks: Towards a Cure for the High-Cost Credit Market*, Akron, OH: University of Akron Press.

Phillips, H. (2006) 'Just can't get enough: can gambling, shopping, sex and gaming really be as addictive as the hardest drugs?', *New Scientist*, 26 August: 30–35.

Phillips, S., Alexander, A. and Shaw, G. (2005) 'Consumer misbehavior: the rise of self-service grocery retailing and shoplifting in the United Kingdom c. 1950–1970', *Journal of Macromarketing*, 25, 1: 66–75.

Platts, G. and Howe, I. (2004) 'A single European scorecard? Does data predict differently across Europe: an Experian Scorex investigation', in Thomas, L.C., Edelman, D.B. and Crook, J.N. (eds) *Readings in Credit Scoring: Foundations, Developments, and Aims*, Oxford: Oxford University Press, pp. 195–204.

Posner, R.A. (1998) *Law and Literature*, Cambridge, MA: Harvard University Press.

Postan, M.M. (1924) 'Credit in medieval trade', *Economic History Review* 1, reprinted in Postan, M.M. (1973) *Medieval Trade and Finance*, Cambridge: Cambridge University Press.

Poster, M. (1995) 'Postmodern virtualities', in Featherstone, M. and Burrows, R. (eds) *Cyberspace/Cyberbodies/Cyberpunk*, London: Sage.

Poster, M. (1996) 'Databases as discourses: or electronic interpellations', in Lyon, D. and Zureik, E. (eds) *Computing, Surveillance and Privacy*, Minneapolis: Minnesota University Press.

Ramsay, I. (1997) 'Models of consumer bankruptcy: implications for research and policy', *Journal of Consumer Policy*, 20: 269–287.

Rappaport, E. (1996) '"A husband and his wife's dresses": consumer credit and the debtor family in England, 1864–1914', in de Grazia, V. and Furlough, E. (eds) *The Sex of Things*, Berkeley: University of California Press.

Rathmell, J.M. (1974) *Services Marketing*, New York: John Wiley.

Redlich, F. (1935) *Reklame. Bergriff-Geschichte-Theorie*, Stuttgart: Enke.

Reith, G. (1999) *The Age of Chance: Gambling in Western Culture*, London: Routledge.

Rindfleisch, A., Burroughs, J.E. and Denton, F. (1997) 'Family structure, materialism, and compulsive consumption', *Journal of Consumer Research*, 23: 312–325.

Ritchel, M. (2002) 'Credit card theft is thriving online as a global market', *New York Times*, 13 May: A1, A14.

Ritzer, G. (1995) *Expressing America: A Critique of the Global Credit Card Society*, Thousand Oaks, CA: Pine Forge Press.

Ritzer, G. (2001) *Explorations in the Sociology of Consumption*, London: Sage.

Roberts, R. (1973) *The Classic Slum*, Harmondsworth, UK: Penguin.

Rock, P. (1973) *Making People Pay*, London: Routledge & Kegan Paul.

Rook, D.W. (1987) 'The buying impulse', *Journal of Consumer Research*, 14: 189–199.

Rose, I. (1998) *The DIY Credit Repair Manual: The Easy and Inexpensive Way to Re-establish Your Credit Rating*, Totton, UK: Rosey Publications.

Rowlingson, K. (1994) *Moneylenders and their Customers*, London: Policy Studies Institute.

Rutherford, J.W. (2003) *Selling Mrs. Consumer: Christine Frederick and the Rise of Household Efficiency*, Athens, GA: University of Georgia.

Ryan, M. (1996) *Social Work and Debt Problems*, Aldershot, UK: Avebury.

Salehi, B. (1997) 'Rising student debt and higher education costs in a restructured economy', unpublished manuscript, American University.

Sargeant, A. and West, D.C. (2001) *Direct and Interactive Marketing*, Oxford: Oxford University Press.

Saunders, P. (1986) *Social Theory and the Urban Question*, London: Hutchinson Education.

Savage, M., Barlow, J., Dickens, P. and Fielding, A. (1992) *Property, Bureaucracy and Culture*, London: Routledge.

Sayer, A. (1999) 'Valuing culture and economy', in Ray, L. and Sayer, A. (eds) *Culture and Economy after the Cultural Turn*, London: Sage.

Scherhorn, G., Reisch, L.A. and Raab, L.A. (1990) 'Addictive buying in West Germany: an empirical investigation', *Journal of Consumer Policy*, 13: 155–189.

Scheuermann, M. (1993) *Her Bread to Earn: Women, Money and Society from Defoe to Austen*, Lexington: University of Kentucky Press.

Schofield, P.R. (2002) 'Access to credit in the early fourteenth-century English countryside', in Schofield, P.R. and Mayhew, N.J. (eds) *Credit and Debt in Medieval England c.1180–c.1350*, Oxford: Oxbow Books, pp. 106–121.

Schor, J. (1998) *The Overspent American: Upscaling, Downshifting and the New Consumer*, New York: Basic Books.

Scott, R. (1976) *The Female Consumer*, London: Associated Business Programmes.

Seligman, R.A. (1927) *Economics of Installment Buying: A Study in Consumer's Credit*, New York: Harper.

Simpson, B. (2001) 'The shadowy world of web gambling', *Credit Card Management*, 14, 5: 16–22.

Skeel, D.A. (2001) *Debt's Dominion: A History of Bankruptcy Law in America*, Princeton, NJ: Princeton University Press.

Skeggs, B. (2003) *Class, Self, Culture*, London: Routledge.

Smalley, O.A. and Sturdivant, F.D. (1973) *The Credit Merchants: A History of Spiegel Inc.*, Carbondale: Southern Illinois University Press.

Smith, J. and McCalla, S. (2006) *Consumer Credit Act 2006*, London: Law Society.

Smith, R. (2004) 'Casino society', *Credit Management*, April: 27–32.

Soman, D. and Cheema, A. (2002) 'The effect of credit on spending decisions: the role of the credit limit and credibility', *Marketing Science*, 21, 1: 32–53.

Spring, J. (2003) *Educating the Consumer-Citizen: A History of the Marriage of Schools, Advertising, and Media*, Mahwah, NJ: Lawrence Erlbaum.

Steevens, G.W. (1897) *The Land of the Dollar*, New York: Dodd, Mead.

Stern, B.B. (1990) 'Literary criticism and the history of marketing thought: a new perspective on "reading" marketing theory', *Journal of the Academy of Marketing Science*, 18, 4: 329–336.

Stern, B.B. (1993) 'Feminist literary criticism and the deconstruction of ads: a postmodern view of advertising and consumer response', *Journal of Consumer Research*, 19, March: 556–566.

Stern, B.B. (1998) 'Deconstructing consumption text: a strategy for reading the (re)constructed consumer', *Consumption, Markets and Culture*, 1, 4: 361–392.

Stiglitz, J. (1985) 'Credit markets and the control of capital', *Journal of Money, Credit and Banking*, 17: 133–152.

Stiglitz, J.E. (2000) 'The contribution of the economics of information to twentieth century economics', *Quarterly Journal of Economics*, 115: 1441–1478.

Strange, J. (2003) 'Only a pauper whom nobody owns: reassessing the pauper grave c. 1880–1914', *Past and Present*, 178, February: 148–175.

Strasser, S. (2003) 'The alien past: consumer culture in historical perspective', *Journal of Consumer Policy*, 26: 375–393.

Strauss, S.D. and Jaffe, A. (2000) *The Complete Idiot's Guide to Beating Debt*, Indianapolis: Alpha Books.

Sullivan, T.A., Warren, E. and Westbrook, J.L. (1989) *As We Forgive Our Debtors: Bankruptcy and Consumer Credit in America*, Oxford: Oxford University Press.

Sullivan, T.A., Warren, E. and Westbrook, J.L. (2000) *The Fragile Middle Class: Americans in Debt*, New Haven, CT: Yale University Press.

Szerszynski, B. (1998) 'On knowing what to do: environmentalism and the modern problematic', in Lash, S., Szerszynski, B. and Wynne, B. (eds) *Risk, Environment and Modernity: Towards a New Ecology*, London: Sage, pp. 104–137.

Tanner, C. and Wolfing Kast, S. (2003) 'Promoting sustainable consumption: determinants of green purchases of Swiss consumers', *Psychology and Marketing*, 20: 883–902.

Tapp, A. (2005) *Principles of Direct and Database Marketing*, Harlow, UK: Pearson Education.

Tawney, R.H. (1926) *Religion and the Rise of Capitalism*, Harmondsworth, UK: Penguin.

Taylor, A. (2002) *Working Class Credit and Community since 1918*, Basingstoke, UK: Palgrave Macmillan.

Tebbutt, M. (1984) *Making Ends Meet: Pawnbroking and the Working Class*, London: Methuen.

Thogersen, J. (2005) 'How may consumer policy empower consumers for sustainable lifestyles?', *Journal of Consumer Policy*, 28: 143–178.

Thomas, L.C. (2000) 'A survey of credit and behavioural scoring: forecasting financial risk of lending to consumers', *International Journal of Forecasting*, 16, 2: 149–172.

Thomas, L.C., Edelman, D.B. and Crook, J.N. (2002) *Credit Scoring and its Applications*, Philadelphia: Society for Industrial and Applied Mathematics.

Thomas, L.C., Edelman, D.B. and Crook, J.N. (2004) *Readings in Credit Scoring: Foundations, Developments, and Aims*, Oxford: Oxford University Press.

Thompson, E.P. (1971) 'The moral economy of the English crowd in the eighteenth century', *Past and Present*, 50, February: 76–136.

Truesdale, J.R. (1927) *Credit Bureau Management*, Englewood Cliffs, NJ: Prentice-Hall.

Valence, G., d'Astous, A. and Fortier, L. (1988) 'Compulsive buying: concept and measurement', *Journal of Consumer Policy*, 11: 419–433.

Van Deventer, D.R. and Imai, K. (2003) *Credit Risk Models and the Basel Accords*, Singapore: John Wiley.

Veblen, T. (1912) *The Theory of the Leisure Class: An Economic Study of Institutions*, New York: Macmillan.

Ventura, J. (1998) *The Credit Repair Kit*, Chicago: Dearborn Financial Publishing.

Vold, G.B. and Bernard, T.J. (1986) *Theoretical Criminology*, Oxford: Oxford University Press.

Vukowich, W.T. (2002) *Consumer Protection in the 21st Century: A Global Perspective*, New York: Transnational Publishers.

Walker, C.M. (1996) 'Financial management, coping and debt in households under financial strain', *Journal of Economic Psychology*, 17: 789–807.

Walker, M. (1996) 'The medicalisation of gambling as an "addiction"', in McMillen, J. (ed.) *Gambling Cultures: Studies in History and Interpretation*, London: Routledge.

Wallendorf, M. (2001) 'Literally literacy', *Journal of Consumer Research*, 27, 4: 505–512.

Warde, A. (1997) *Consumption, Food and Taste*, London: Sage.

Weber, M. (1999) *The Protestant Ethic and the Spirit of Capitalism*, London: HarperCollins.

Weiss, B. (1986) *The Hell of the English: Bankruptcy and the Victorian Novel*, Lewisburg, PA: Bucknell University Press.

Wernick, B. (1991) *Promotional Culture: Advertising, Ideology, and Expression*, London: Sage.

Weston, C. (2007) 'Immigrants must pay extra for home loans', *Irish Independent*, 21 February: 8.

Weston, L.P. (2006) *Deal with Your Debt: The Right Way to Manage Your Bills and Pay Off What You Owe*, London: Prentice-Hall.

Wilkinson, G. and Tingay, J. (2004) 'The use of affordability data: does it add real value?', in Thomas, L.C., Edelman, D.B. and Crook, J.N. (eds) *Readings in Credit Scoring: Foundations, Developments, and Aims*, Oxford: Oxford University Press, pp. 63–71.

Williams, B. (2004) *Debt for Sale: A Social History of the Credit Trap*, Philadelphia: University of Pennsylvania Press.

Williams, R. (1982) *Dream Worlds: Mass Consumption in Late Nineteenth Century France*, Berkeley: University of California Press.

Woodruffe, H.R. (1996) 'Compensatory consumption (or why do women go shopping when they're fed up? And other stories)', *Proceedings of the Twenty-fifth Annual Conference of the European Marketing Academy*, Budapest.

Wolfe, K.A. (2006) 'House-passed bill targets web gambling', *Congressional Quarterly Weekly*, 64, 28: 1975.

Wolfe, M., Madge, P., Kruse, J., Smith, C., Harris, F. and Wilson, J. (1998) *Debt Advice Handbook*, London: Child Poverty Action Group.

Wolvendge, J. (1976) *Ain't It Grand*, Harmondsworth, UK: Penguin.

Wood, M. (1998) 'Socio-economic status, delay of gratification, and impulse buying', *Journal of Economic Psychology*, 19: 295–320.

Woodbridge, L. (2003) *Money in the Age of Shakespeare*, New York: Palgrave Macmillan.

World Commission on Environment and Development (1987) *Our Common Future*, Oxford: Oxford University Press.

Worthington, A.C. (2006) 'Debt as a source of stress in Australian households', *International Journal of Consumer Studies*, 30, 1: 2–15.

Wynne, B. (1998) 'May the sheep safely graze? A reflexive view of the expert–lay knowledge divide', in Lash, S., Szerszynski, B. and Wynne, B. (eds) *Risk, Environment and Modernity: Towards a New Ecology*, London: Sage.

Xiao, J.J., Sorhaindo, B. and Garman, E.T. (2006) 'Financial behaviours of consumers in credit counselling', *International Journal of Consumer Studies*, 30, 2: 108–121.

Zelizer, V. (1994) *The Social Meaning of Money*, New York: Basic Books.

Zucker, L. (1986) 'Production of trust: institutional sources of economic structure 1840–1920', *Research in Organizational Behavior*, 8: 53–111.

Zukin, S. (2005) *Point of Purchase*, London: Routledge.

Index